BUILDING THINKING SKILLS®
Book 1

SERIES TITLES
BUILDING THINKING SKILLS®—PRIMARY
BUILDING THINKING SKILLS®—BOOK 1
BUILDING THINKING SKILLS®—BOOK 2
BUILDING THINKING SKILLS®—BOOK 3 FIGURAL
BUILDING THINKING SKILLS®—BOOK 3 VERBAL

SANDRA PARKS AND HOWARD BLACK

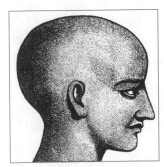

© 1984, 1997
THE CRITICAL THINKING COMPANY
www.CriticalThinking.com
P.O. Box 448 • Pacific Grove • CA 93950-0448
Phone 800-458-4849 • FAX 831-393-3277
ISBN 0-89455-250-3
Printed in the United States of America

Table of Contents

CHAPTER FOUR—FIGURAL CLASSIFICATIONS

CHAPTER FIVE—FIGURAL ANALOGIES

CHAPTER SIX—DESCRIBING THINGS

CHAPTER SEVEN—VERBAL SIMILARITIES AND DIFFERENCES

CHAPTER EIGHT—VERBAL SEQUENCES

NOTE TO TEACHER:
For students who are not ready for the written activities in Chapter One, this chapter may be done at the end of the Figural unit.

CHAPTER ONE

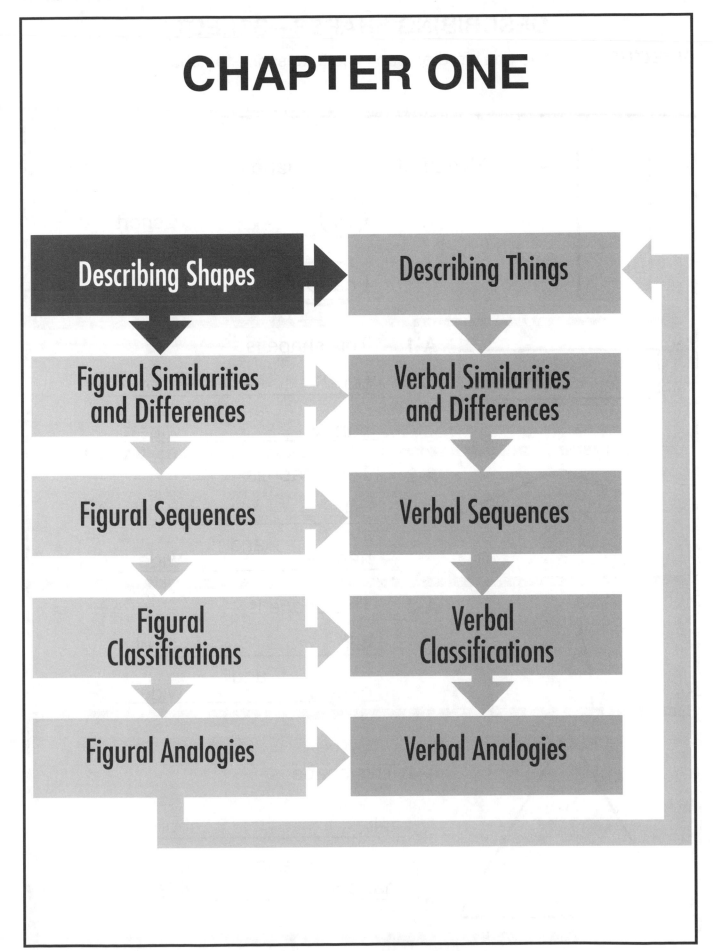

DESCRIBING SHAPES—SELECT

DIRECTIONS: Circle one word on each line to describe the shape.

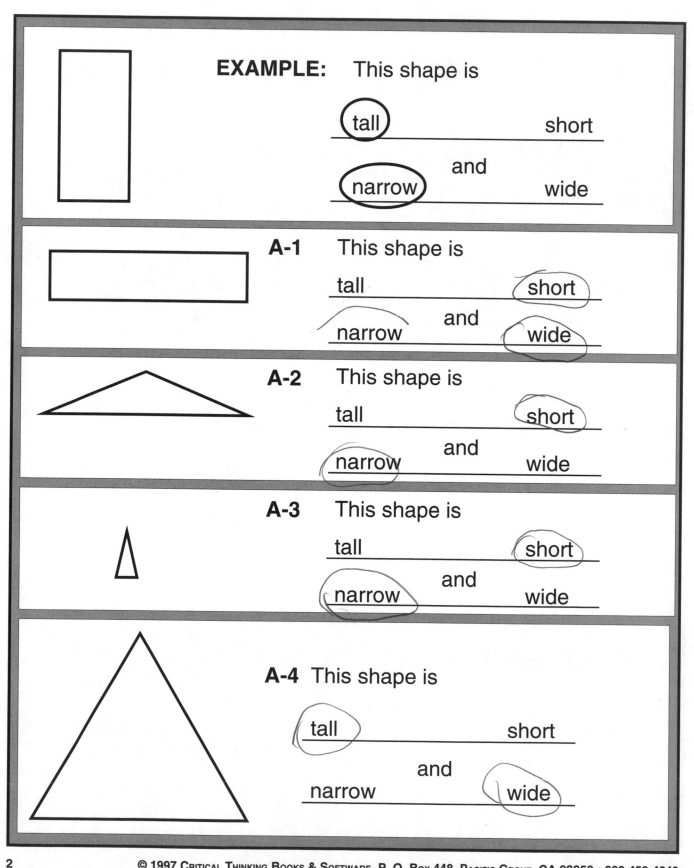

EXAMPLE: This shape is

(tall)   short

(narrow)   and   wide

A-1 This shape is

tall   (short)

narrow   and   (wide)

A-2 This shape is

tall   (short)

(narrow)   and   wide

A-3 This shape is

tall   (short)

(narrow)   and   wide

A-4 This shape is

(tall)   short

narrow   and   (wide)

DESCRIBING SHAPES—SELECT

DIRECTIONS: Look at each shape. Say or write the number of square corners each shape has. Use the numbers in the choice box.

CHOICE BOX: 0,1, 2, 3, 4, 5, 6

EXAMPLE: This is a square corner. ⌐

A-5

This shape has __4__ square corners.

A-6

This shape has __B__ square corner.

A-7

This shape has __0__ square corners.

A-8

This shape has __2__ square corners.

A-9

This shape has __3__ square corners.

DESCRIBING SHAPES—SELECT

DIRECTIONS: Say or write the number of corners each shape has. Say or write how many are square corners. Use the words in the choice box.

CHOICE BOX: all, none, one, two, three, four, five, six

EXAMPLE: This shape has ___three___ corners, and ___one___ is a square corner.

A-10

This shape has ___5___ corners, and ___2___ are square corners.

A-11

This shape has ___4___ corners, and ___4___ are square corners.

A-12

This shape has ___5___ corners, and ___2___ are square corners.

A-13

This shape has ___6___ corners, and ___4___ are square corners.

DESCRIBING SHAPES—SELECT

DIRECTIONS: Count how many sides each shape has. Circle the correct number. Say or write how many sides are the same length. Use the words and numbers in the choice box.

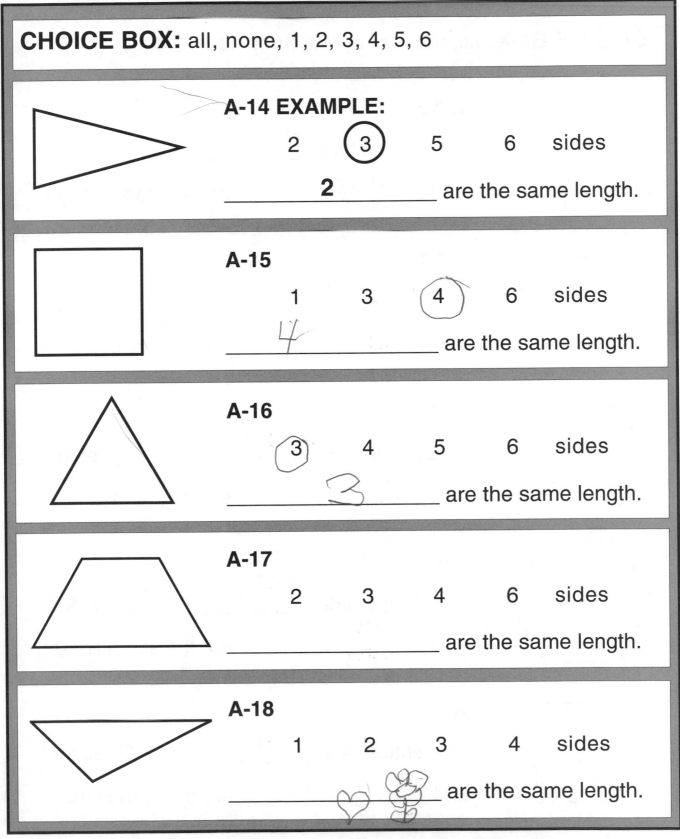

CHOICE BOX: all, none, 1, 2, 3, 4, 5, 6

A-14 EXAMPLE:

2   ③   5   6   sides

_____**2**_____ are the same length.

A-15

1   3   ④   6   sides

_____4_____ are the same length.

A-16

③   4   5   6   sides

_____3_____ are the same length.

A-17

2   3   4   6   sides

_____ are the same length.

A-18

1   2   3   4   sides

_____ are the same length.

DESCRIBING SHAPES—SELECT

DIRECTIONS: Say or write how many sides each shape has. Then say or write how many sides are the same length. Use the words in the choice box.

CHOICE BOX: all, none, one, two, three, four, five, six

A-19

This shape has ___3___ sides

and ___~~2~~ none___ are the same length.

A-20

This shape has ___5___ sides

and ___2___ are the same length.

A-21

This shape has ___4___ sides

and ___2___ are the same length.

A-22

This shape has ___6___ sides

and ___6___ are the same length.

A-23

This shape has ___5___ sides

and ___0___ are the same length.

DESCRIBING SHAPES—SELECT

DIRECTIONS: Say or write how many sides and corners each shape has. Say or write the name of each shape. Use the words in the choice box.

CHOICE BOX: hexagon, octagon, pentagon, rectangle, triangle, trapezoid

A-24

4 sides   4 corners

This shape is named _rectangle_.

A-25

5 sides   5 corners

This shape is named ~~hexagon~~ pentagon.

A-26

3 sides   3 corners

This shape is named _triangle_.

A-27

6 sides   6 corners

This shape is named _octagon_.

DESCRIBING SHAPES—EXPLAIN

DIRECTIONS: Describe each shape. Use complete sentences to say or write the description.

EXAMPLE

2 in.

2 in.

DESCRIPTION

This shape is a triangle. It has three sides. Two sides are the same length. It has no square corners. It is two inches wide and two inches high.

A-28

3 in.

2 in.

DESCRIPTION

This is a rectangle. It has 4 sides. 2 sides are the same. I has two sgaure coners. It is 3 in. high and 2 in. wide.

DESCRIBING SHAPES—EXPLAIN

DIRECTIONS: Describe each shape. Use complete sentences to say or write the description.

A-29

3 in.

2 in.

DESCRIPTION

This is a triangle. It has three sides. No sides are the same. I has no square corners. It is 3 in. high a 2 in. wide.

A-30

3 in.

2 in.

DESCRIPTION

This is a pentagon. It has five sides and five corners. Four sides are the same. It has two square corners. It is three in. high and two in. wide.

DESCRIBING SHAPES—EXPLAIN

DIRECTIONS: Say or write a description of the shape in the picture at the left. Use complete sentences.

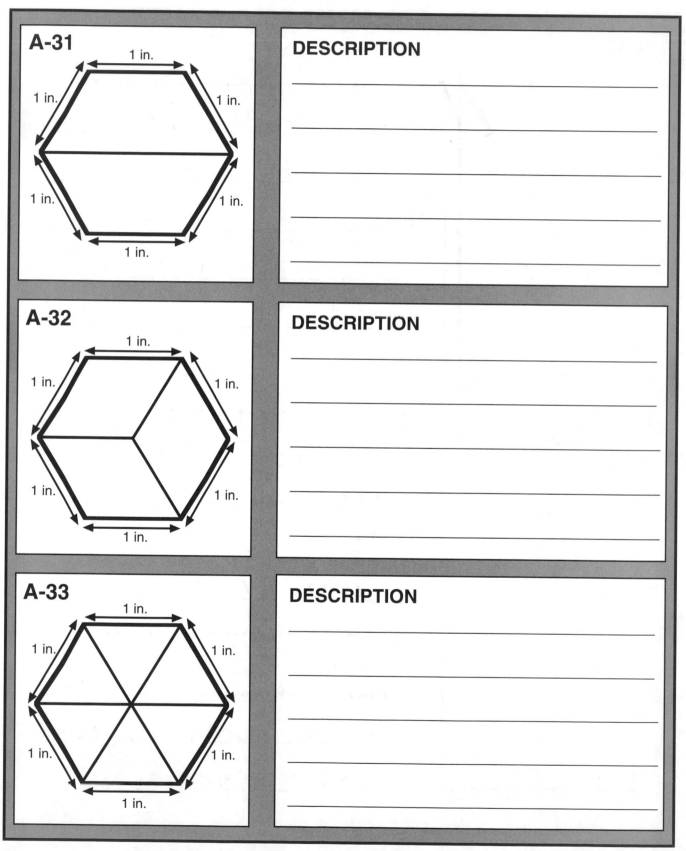

A-31

1 in.
1 in.   1 in.
1 in.   1 in.
1 in.

DESCRIPTION

A-32

1 in.
1 in.   1 in.
1 in.   1 in.
1 in.

DESCRIPTION

A-33

1 in.
1 in.   1 in.
1 in.   1 in.
1 in.

DESCRIPTION

© 1997 CRITICAL THINKING BOOKS & SOFTWARE, P. O. BOX 448, PACIFIC GROVE, CA 93950 • 800-458-4849

FOLLOWING DIRECTIONS

DIRECTIONS: Mark the shapes according to the directions.

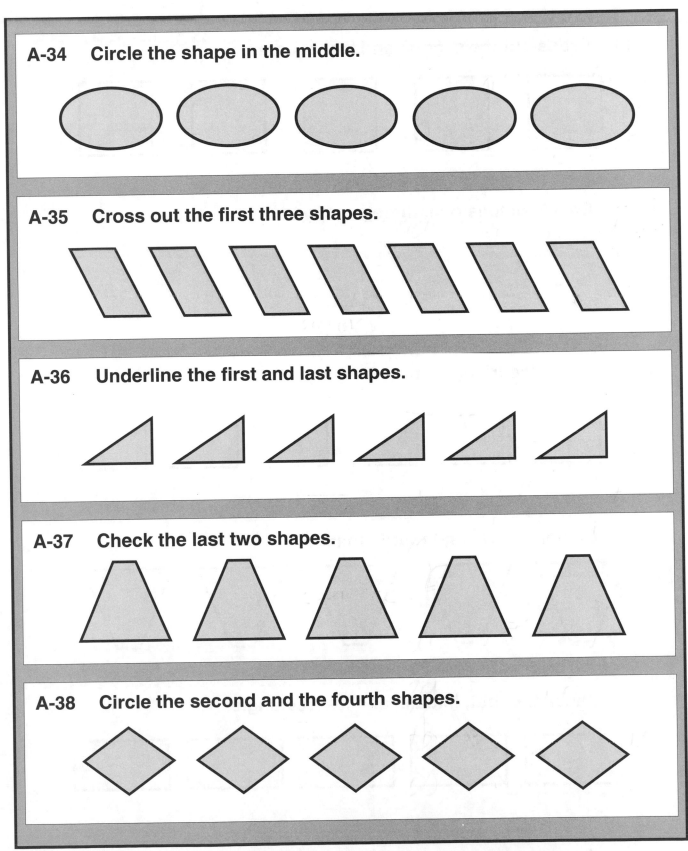

A-34   Circle the shape in the middle.

A-35   Cross out the first three shapes.

A-36   Underline the first and last shapes.

A-37   Check the last two shapes.

A-38   Circle the second and the fourth shapes.

FOLLOWING DIRECTIONS

DIRECTIONS: Mark the shapes according to the directions.

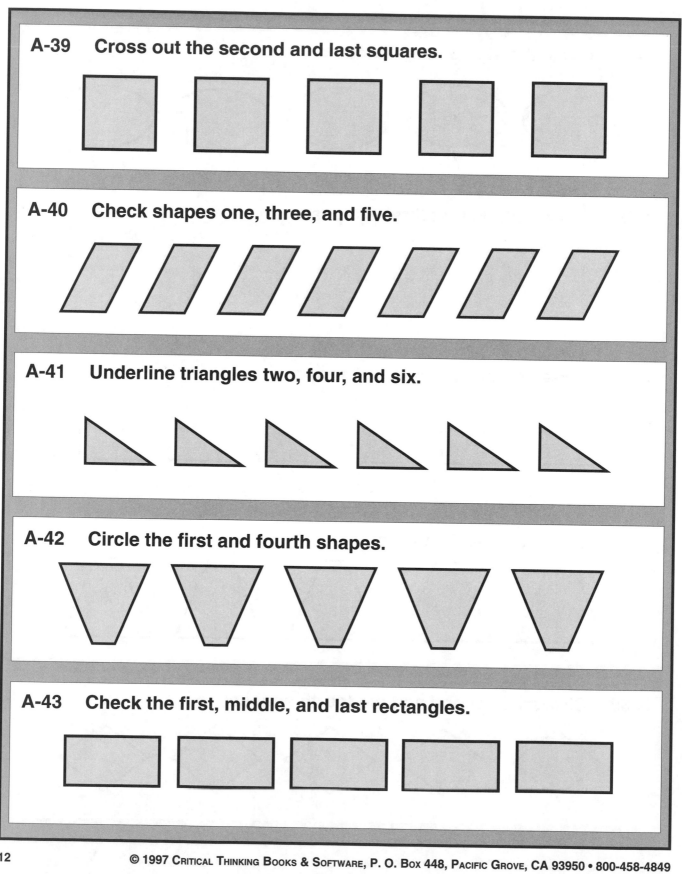

A-39   Cross out the second and last squares.

A-40   Check shapes one, three, and five.

A-41   Underline triangles two, four, and six.

A-42   Circle the first and fourth shapes.

A-43   Check the first, middle, and last rectangles.

© 1997 Critical Thinking Books & Software, P. O. Box 448, Pacific Grove, CA 93950 • 800-458-4849

GIVING DIRECTIONS

DIRECTIONS: Look at the shapes that are marked. Ask yourself, "How would I tell someone to mark the shapes this way?" Say or write the directions you would give.

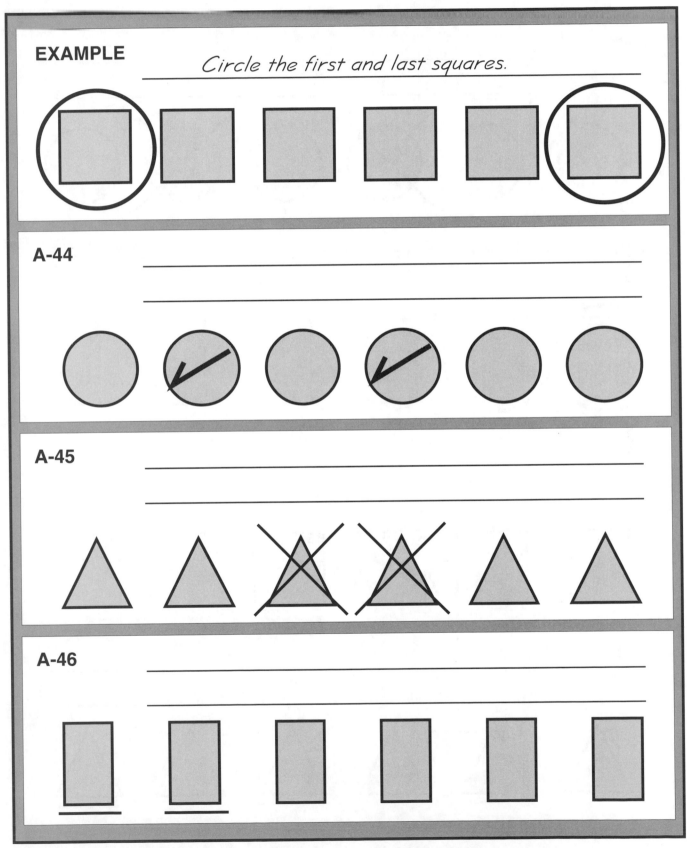

EXAMPLE   *Circle the first and last squares.*

A-44

A-45

A-46

GIVING DIRECTIONS

DIRECTIONS: Look at the shapes that are marked. Ask yourself, "How would I tell someone to mark the shapes this way?" Say or write the directions you would give.

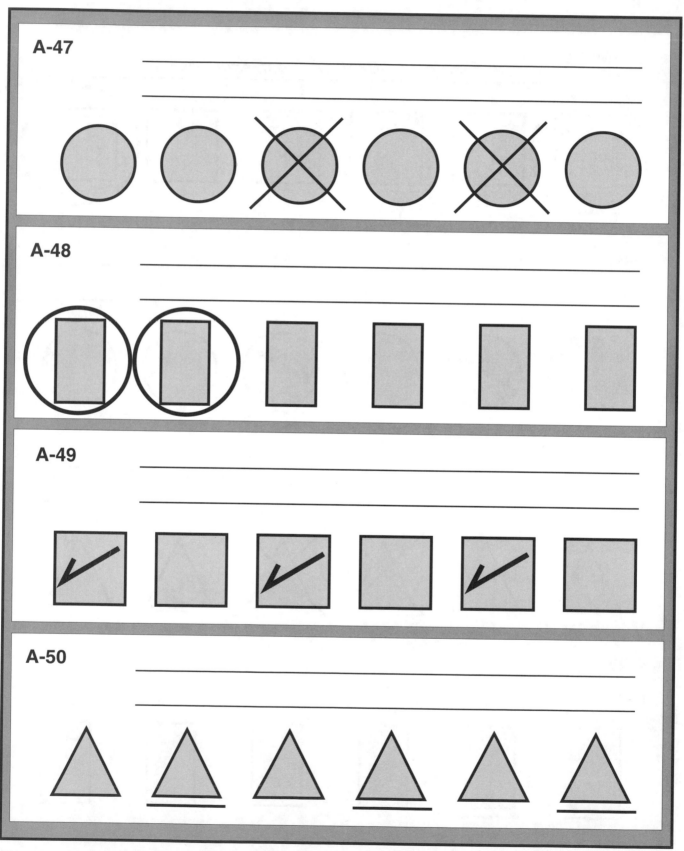

A-47 _____

A-48 _____

A-49 _____

A-50 _____

GIVING DIRECTIONS

DIRECTIONS: Decide how you want to mark the shapes. Say or write directions for marking them. (Exchange papers with a classmate and see if you can follow each other's directions.)

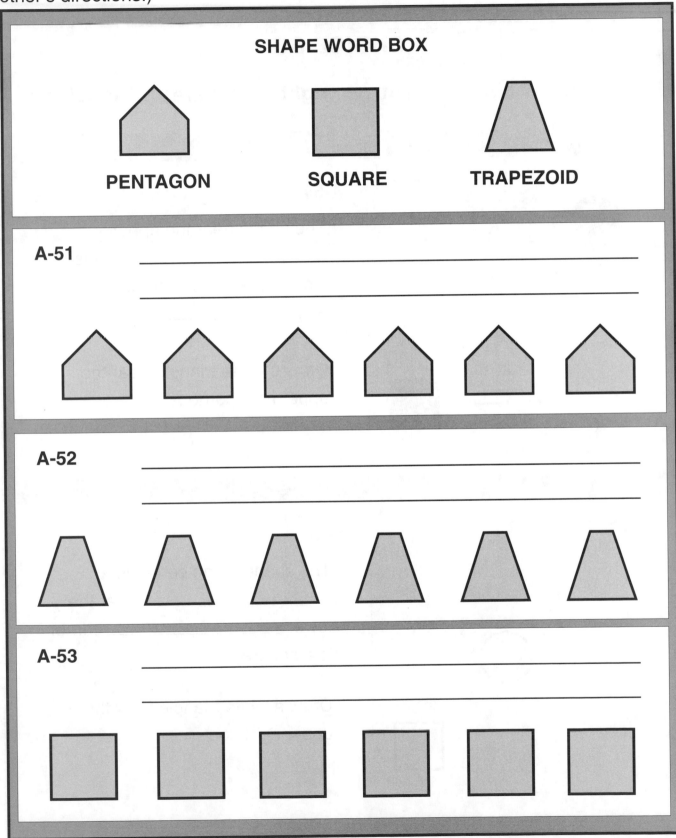

SHAPE WORD BOX

PENTAGON   SQUARE   TRAPEZOID

A-51 _____

A-52 _____

A-53 _____

DESCRIBING POSITION—A

INSTRUCTIONS: Complete the sentences with the correct words from the choice box. Say or write your answers. Draw a figure as directed.

CHOICE BOX

center   circle   left   right   square   triangle

A-54

The shape near the upper _____ corner is a circle. Near the lower right corner is a _____ .

Draw a white triangle near the upper right corner.

A-55

The shape in the center is a _____ . Near the lower _____ corner is a square.

Draw a white triangle near the upper right corner.

DESCRIBING POSITION—A

INSTRUCTIONS: Complete the sentences with the correct words from the choice box. Say or write your answers. Draw a figure as directed.

CHOICE BOX

center   circle   left   right   square   triangle

A-56

The shape near the upper

_____ corner is a

black square. Near the lower

_____ corner is a

white _____ .

Draw a black circle near the lower left corner.

A-57

The black rectangle is near the

upper _____ corner.

The white _____ is

near the lower _____

corner.

Draw a black triangle near the upper left corner.

DESCRIBING POSITION—B

DIRECTIONS: Using interlocking cubes, build the patterns shown below. Say or write a description of your pattern.

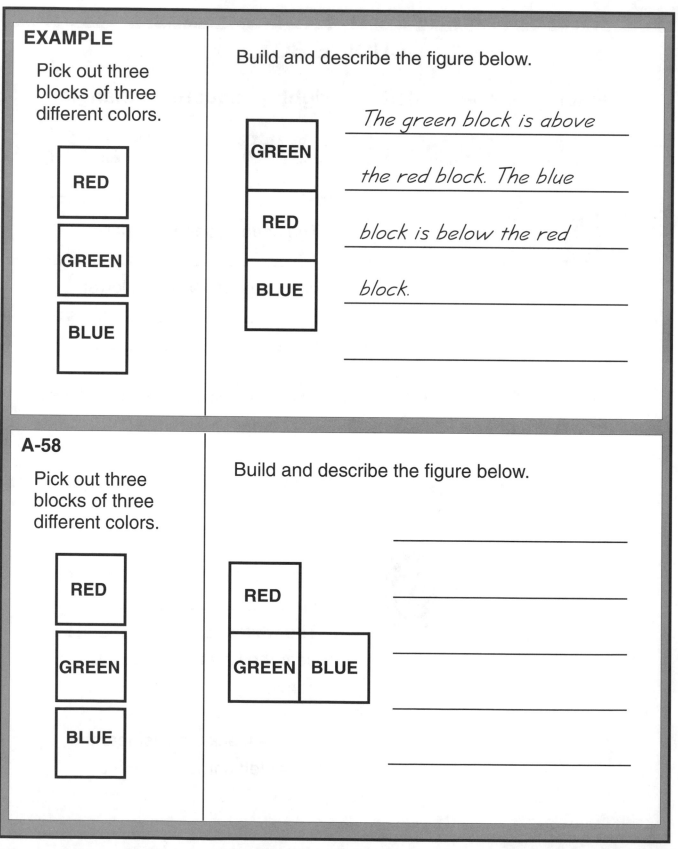

EXAMPLE

Pick out three blocks of three different colors.

RED

GREEN

BLUE

Build and describe the figure below.

GREEN

RED

BLUE

The green block is above

the red block. The blue

block is below the red

block.

A-58

Pick out three blocks of three different colors.

RED

GREEN

BLUE

Build and describe the figure below.

RED

GREEN | BLUE

DESCRIBING POSITION—B

DIRECTIONS: Using interlocking cubes, build the patterns shown below. Say or write a description of your pattern.

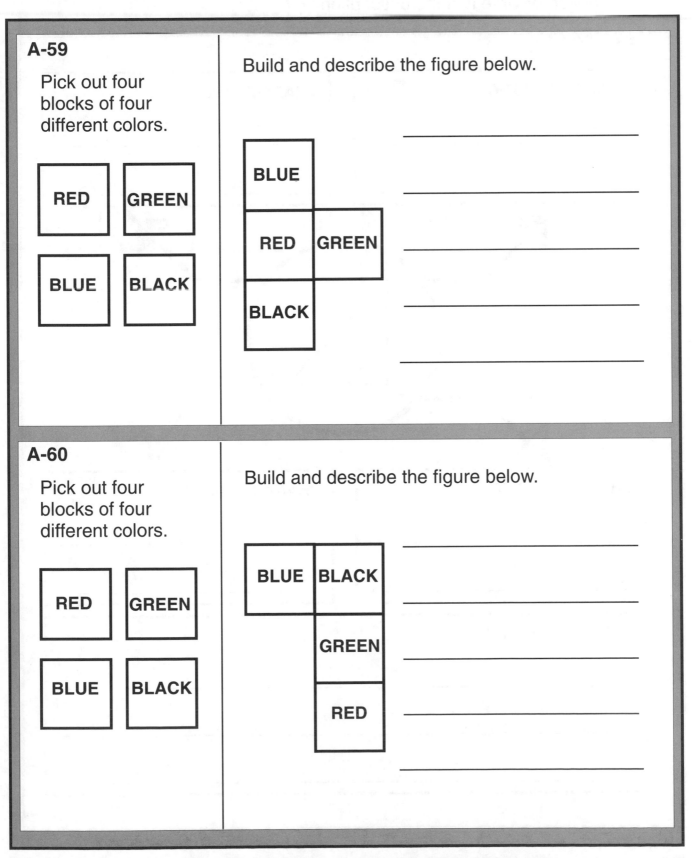

A-59

Pick out four blocks of four different colors.

RED   GREEN

BLUE   BLACK

Build and describe the figure below.

BLUE
RED GREEN
BLACK

_____

_____

_____

_____

_____

A-60

Pick out four blocks of four different colors.

RED   GREEN

BLUE   BLACK

Build and describe the figure below.

BLUE BLACK
      GREEN
      RED

_____

_____

_____

_____

_____

CHARACTERISTICS OF A SHAPE

DIRECTIONS: Look at the triangle in the center of the diagram. Say or write four characteristics of the triangle. Use these characteristics to describe the triangle. Say your description or write it in the description box.

A-61

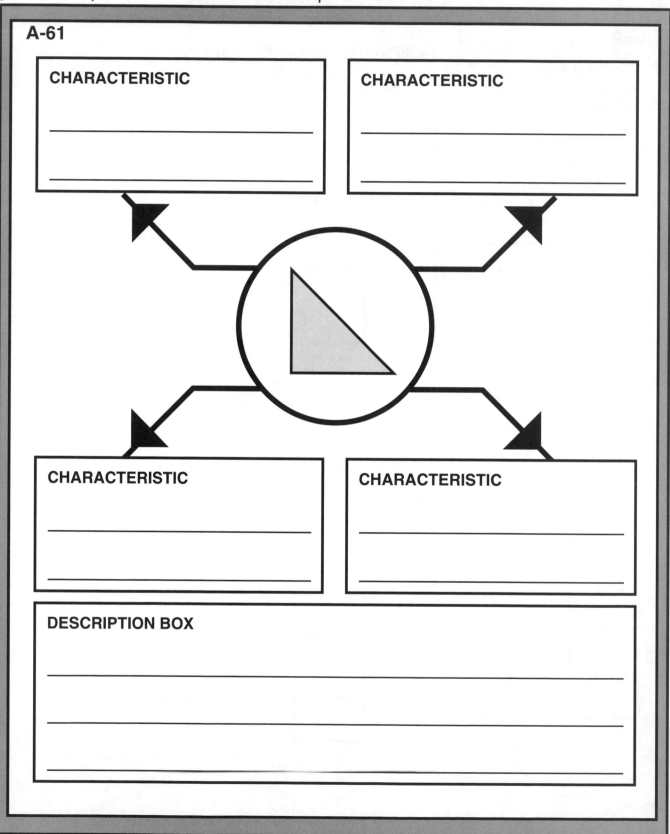

CHARACTERISTIC

_____

_____

CHARACTERISTIC

_____

_____

CHARACTERISTIC

_____

_____

CHARACTERISTIC

_____

_____

DESCRIPTION BOX

_____

_____

_____

CHARACTERISTICS OF A SHAPE

DIRECTIONS: Look at the trapezoid in the center of the diagram. Say or write four characteristics of the trapezoid. Use these characteristics to describe the trapezoid. Say your description or write it in the description box.

A-62

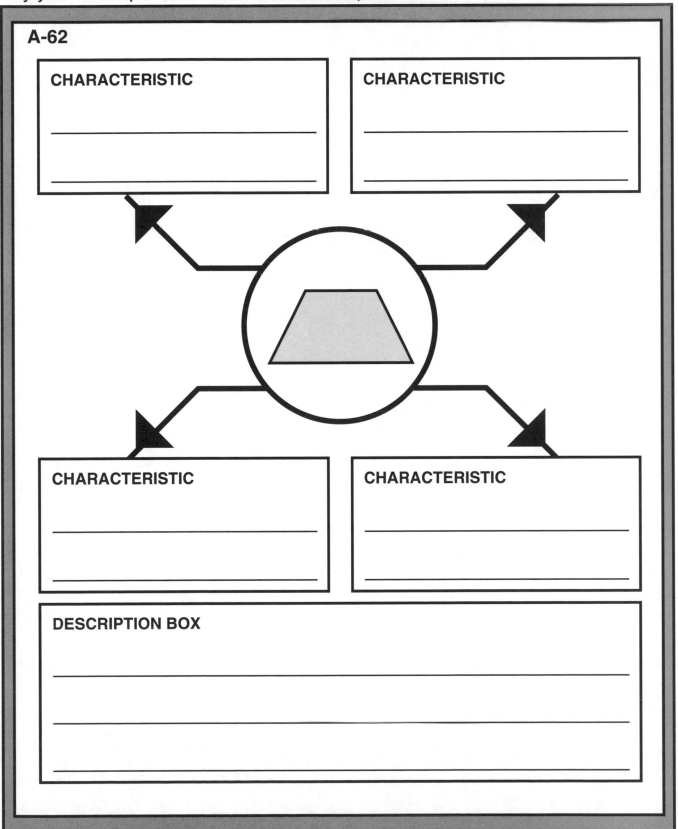

CHARACTERISTIC

CHARACTERISTIC

CHARACTERISTIC

CHARACTERISTIC

DESCRIPTION BOX

CHAPTER TWO

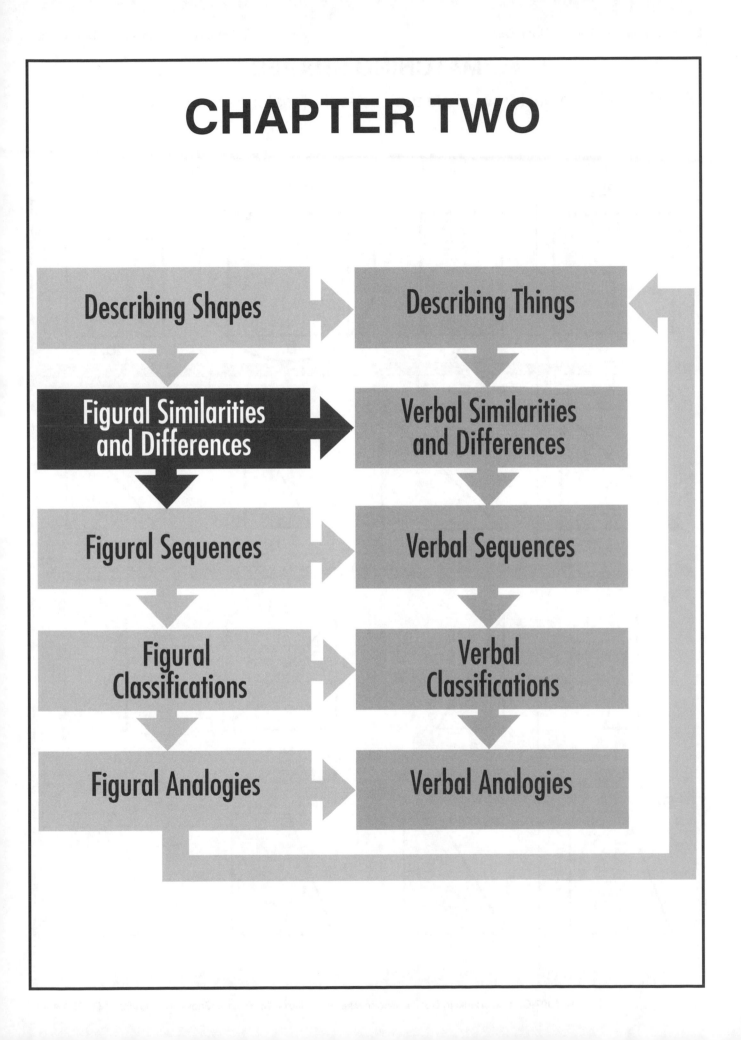

MATCHING SHAPES

DIRECTIONS: In each row, circle the shape that matches the one at the left.

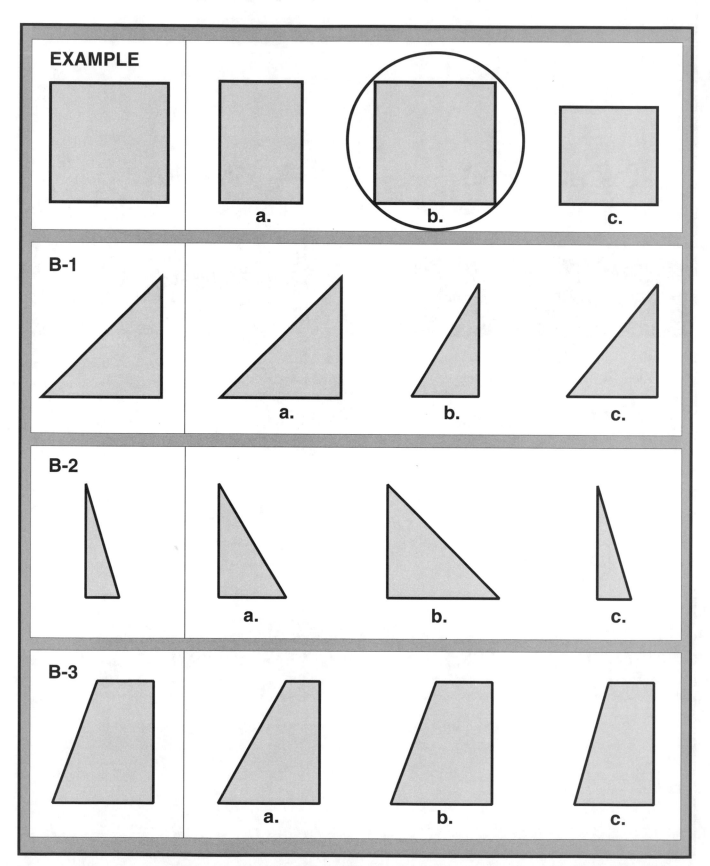

EXAMPLE

a.   b.   c.

B-1

a.   b.   c.

B-2

a.   b.   c.

B-3

a.   b.   c.

MATCHING SHAPES

DIRECTIONS: In each row, circle the shape that matches the one at the left.

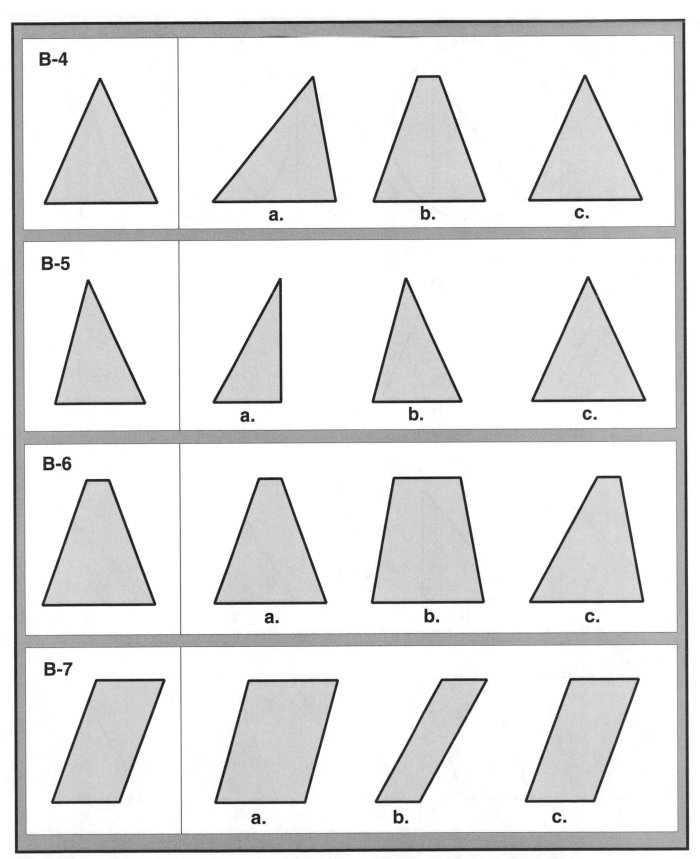

MATCHING SHAPES

DIRECTIONS: In each row, circle the shapes that are the same.

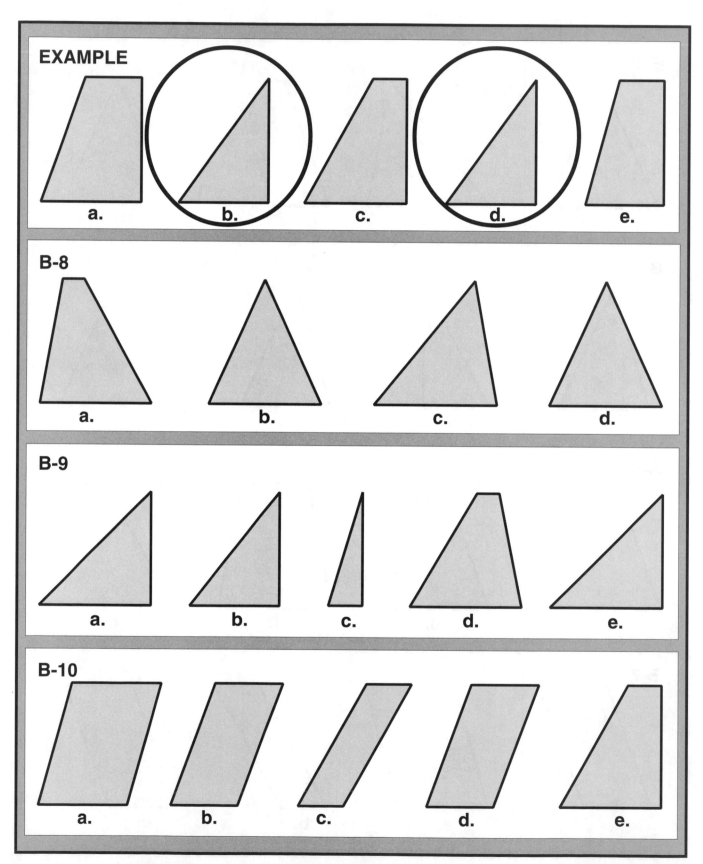

EXAMPLE

a.   b.   c.   d.   e.

B-8

a.   b.   c.   d.

B-9

a.   b.   c.   d.   e.

B-10

a.   b.   c.   d.   e.

MATCHING SHAPES

DIRECTIONS: In each row, circle the shapes that are the same.

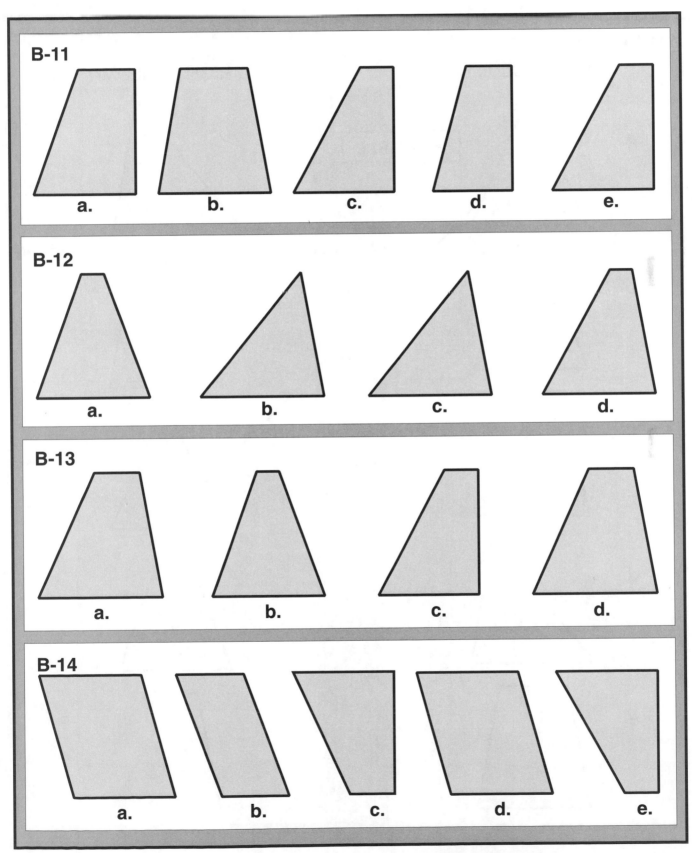

MATCHING SHAPES

DIRECTIONS: Draw a line from each shape in the left column to its twin in the right column. (A twin is the same shape and size as the original.)

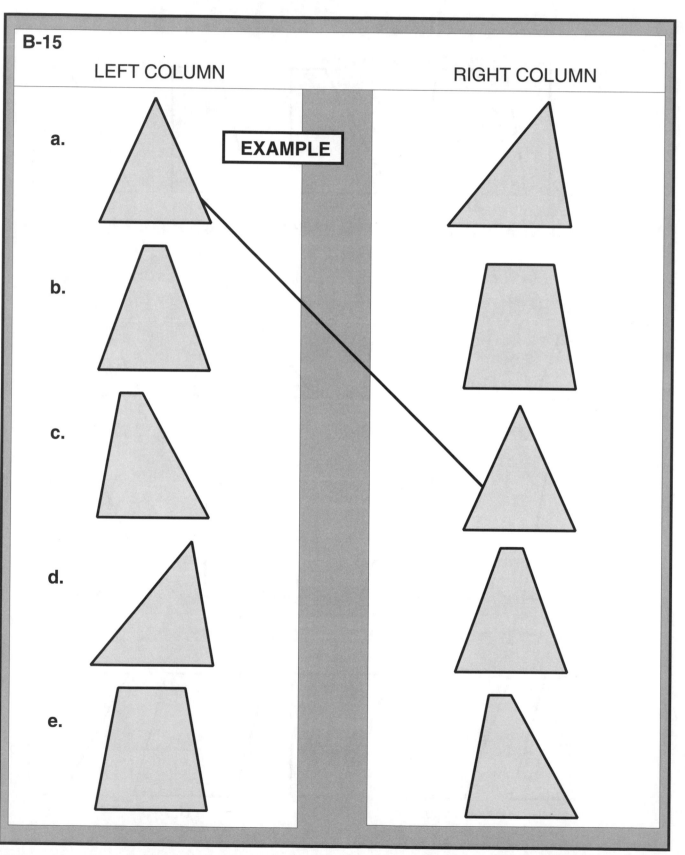

MATCHING SHAPES

DIRECTIONS: Draw a line from the shape in the left column to its twin in the right column.

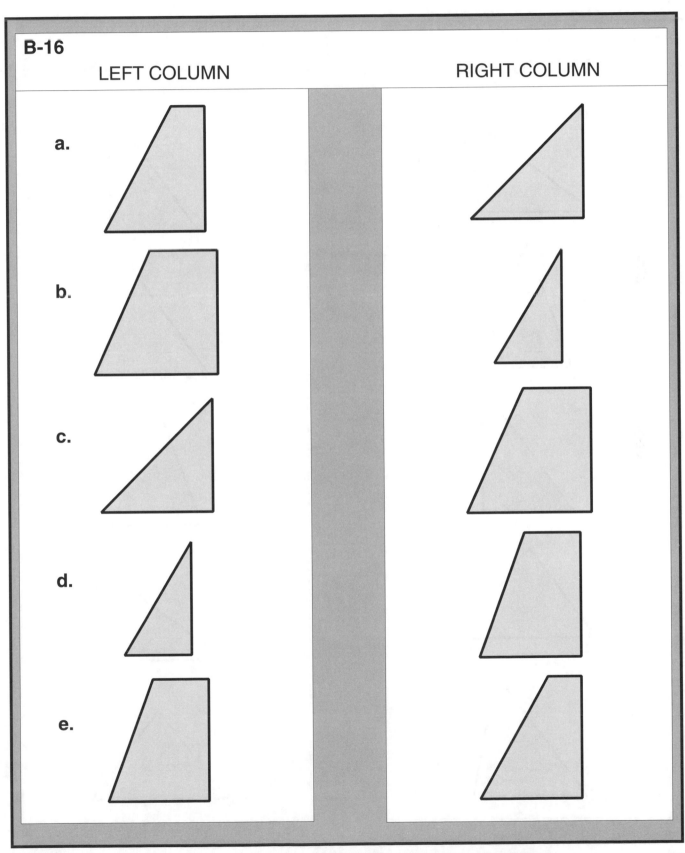

MATCHING SHAPES

DIRECTIONS: Draw a line from the figure in the left column to its twin in the right column.

B-17

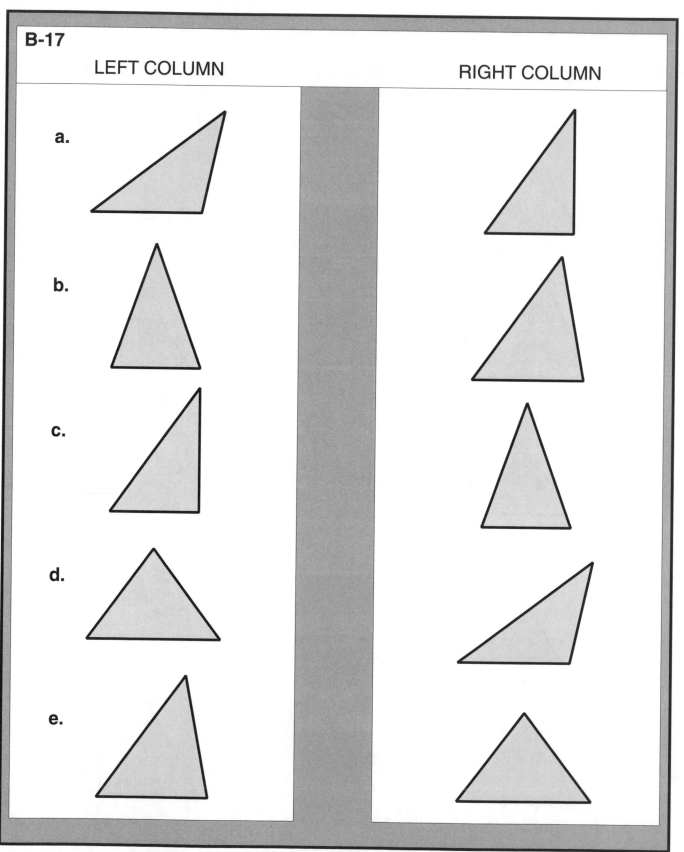

LEFT COLUMN

RIGHT COLUMN

a.

b.

c.

d.

e.

WHICH SHAPE DOES NOT MATCH?

DIRECTONS: Cross out the shape in each row that does *not* match the one at the left. The matching shapes must all face the same direction.

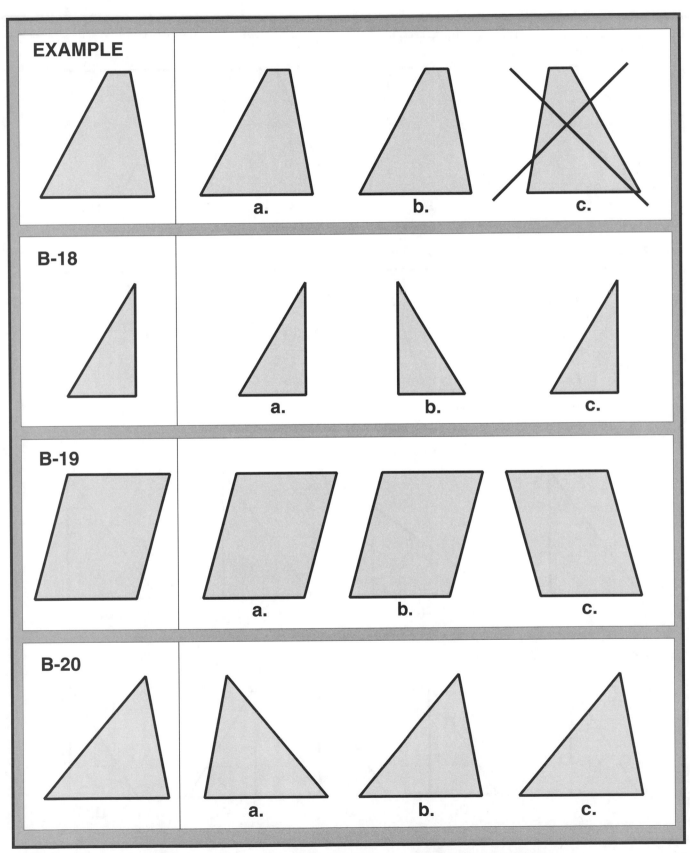

WHICH SHAPE DOES NOT MATCH?

DIRECTONS: Cross out the shape in each row that does *not* match the one at the left. The matching shapes must all face the same direction.

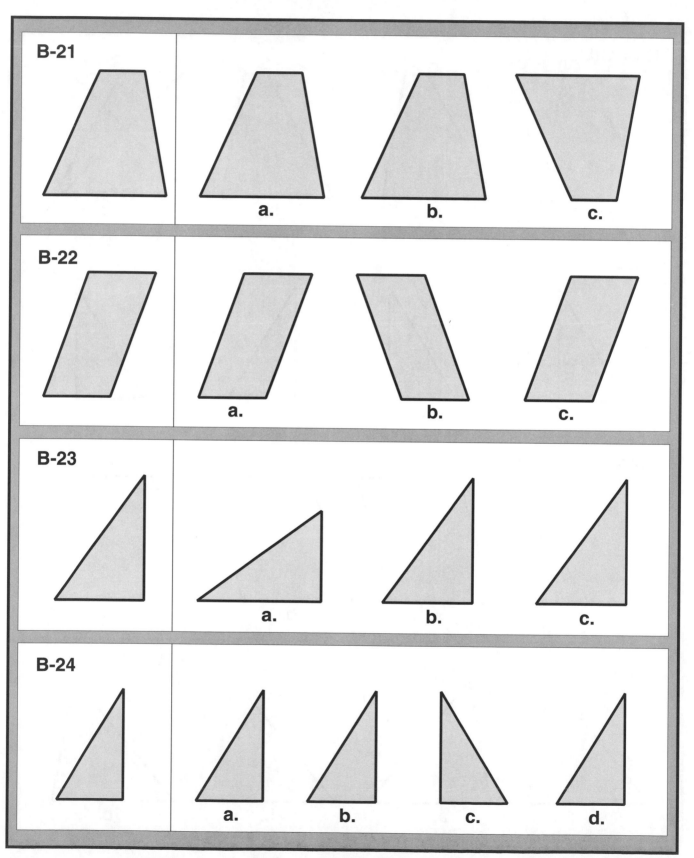

B-21

a.   b.   c.

B-22

a.   b.   c.

B-23

a.   b.   c.

B-24

a.   b.   c.   d.

MATCHING SHAPES THAT HAVE BEEN TURNED

DIRECTIONS: "Twins" are figures having the same shape and size even if they face a different direction. Draw a line from the figure in the left column to its twin in the right column. BE CAREFUL—THE SHAPES HAVE BEEN TURNED!

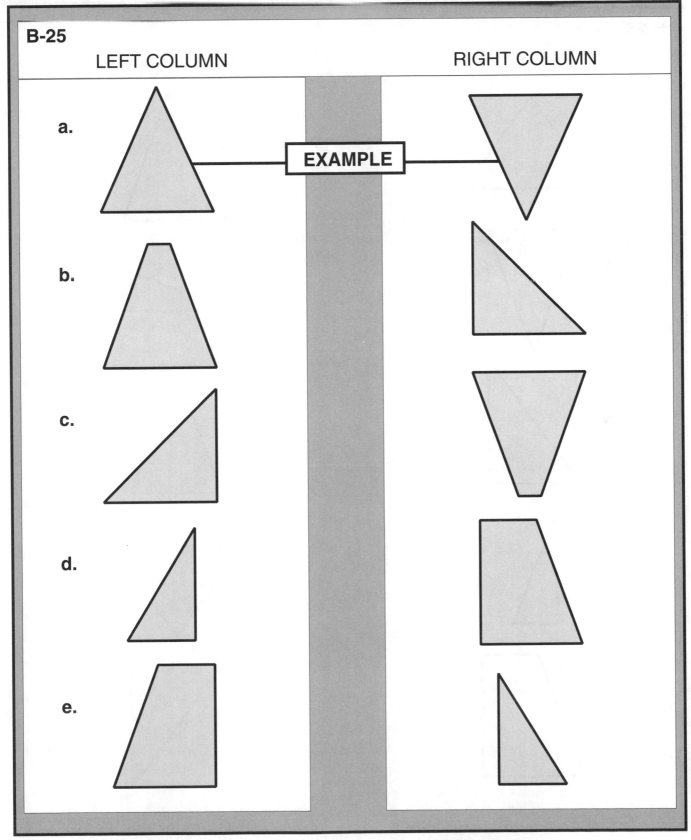

MATCHING SHAPES THAT HAVE BEEN TURNED

DIRECTIONS: Figures having the same shape and size are "twins" even if they face a different direction. Draw a line from the figure in the left column to its twin in the right column. BE CAREFUL—THE SHAPES HAVE BEEN TURNED!

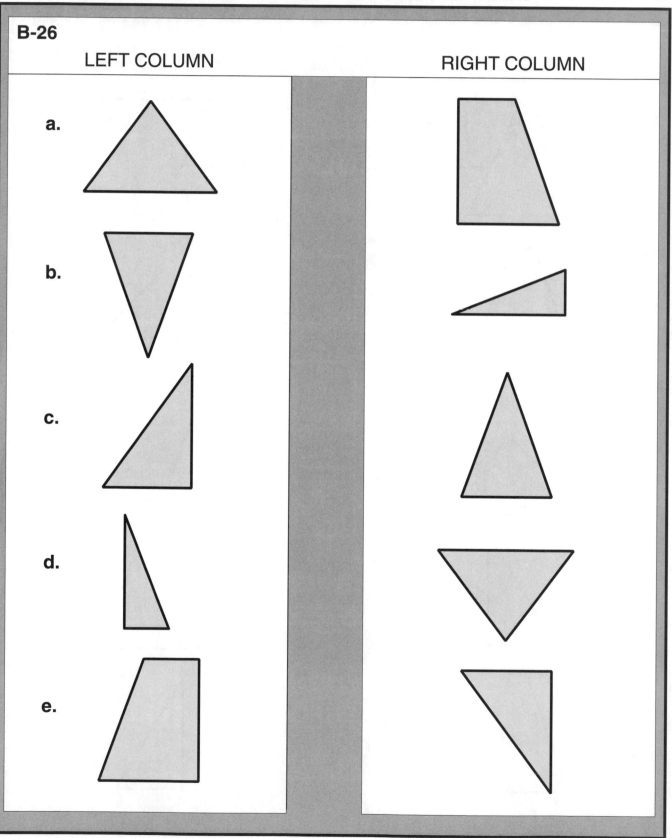

B-26

LEFT COLUMN   RIGHT COLUMN

a.

b.

c.

d.

e.

FINDING SHAPES

DIRECTIONS: In the box at the right, circle any shape that matches exactly one of the shapes in the box at the left.

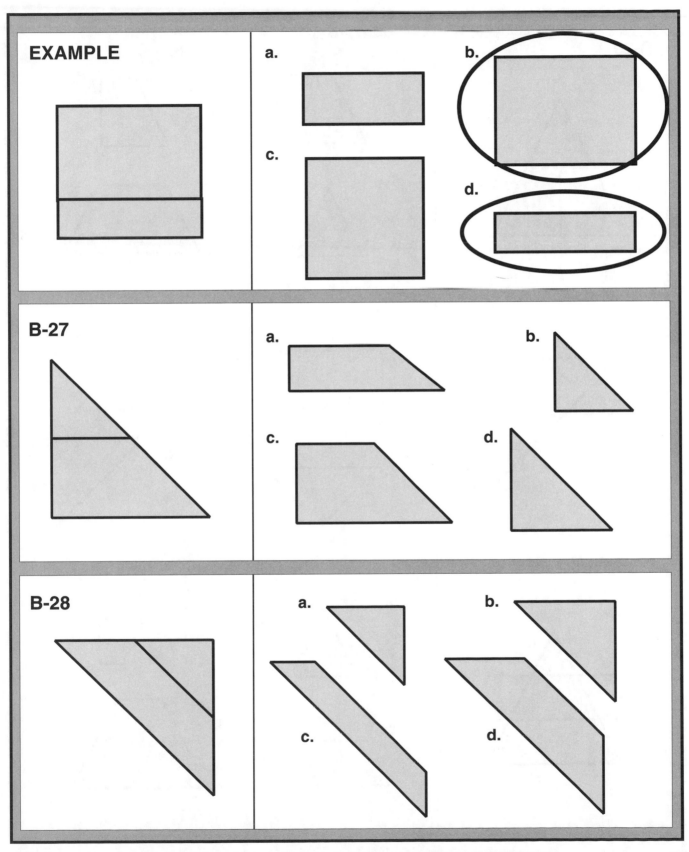

FINDING SHAPES

DIRECTIONS: In the box at the right, circle any shape that matches exactly one of the shapes in the box at the left.

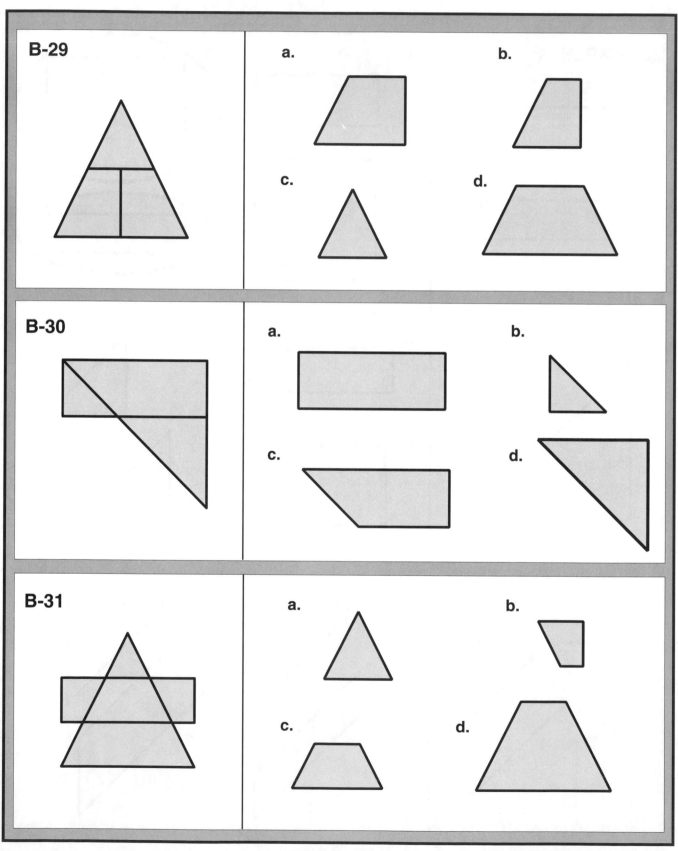

FINDING SHAPES

DIRECTIONS: In the box at the right, circle any shape that matches exactly one of the shapes in the box at the left.

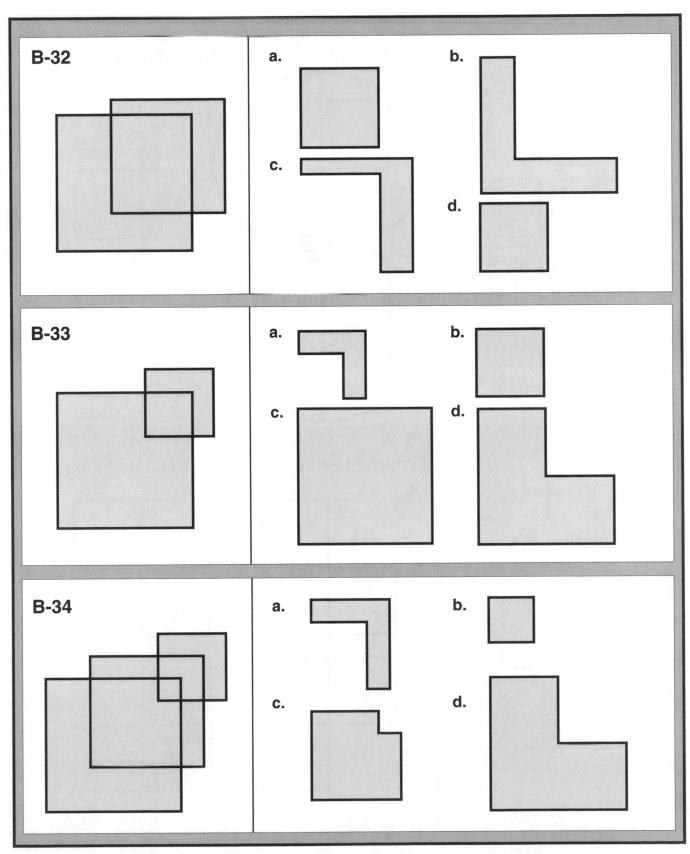

COMBINING INTERLOCKING CUBES

DIRECTIONS: In the box at the right, circle the shapes that can be formed by joining the collection of interlocking cubes shown at the left.

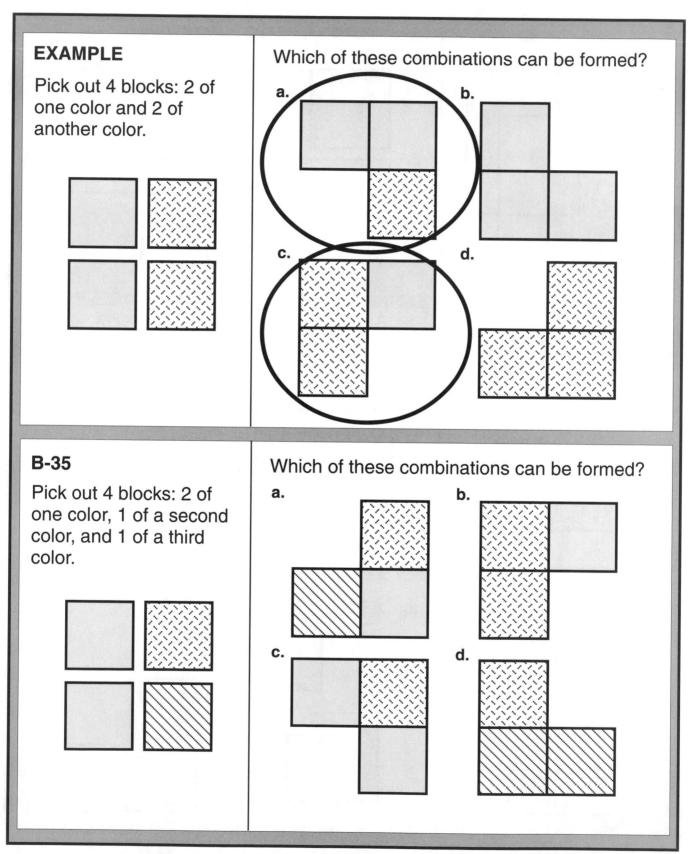

EXAMPLE

Pick out 4 blocks: 2 of one color and 2 of another color.

Which of these combinations can be formed?

a.

b.

c.

d.

B-35

Pick out 4 blocks: 2 of one color, 1 of a second color, and 1 of a third color.

Which of these combinations can be formed?

a.

b.

c.

d.

COMBINING INTERLOCKING CUBES

DIRECTIONS: Circle the patterns that can be formed by joining the collection of interlocking cubes shown.

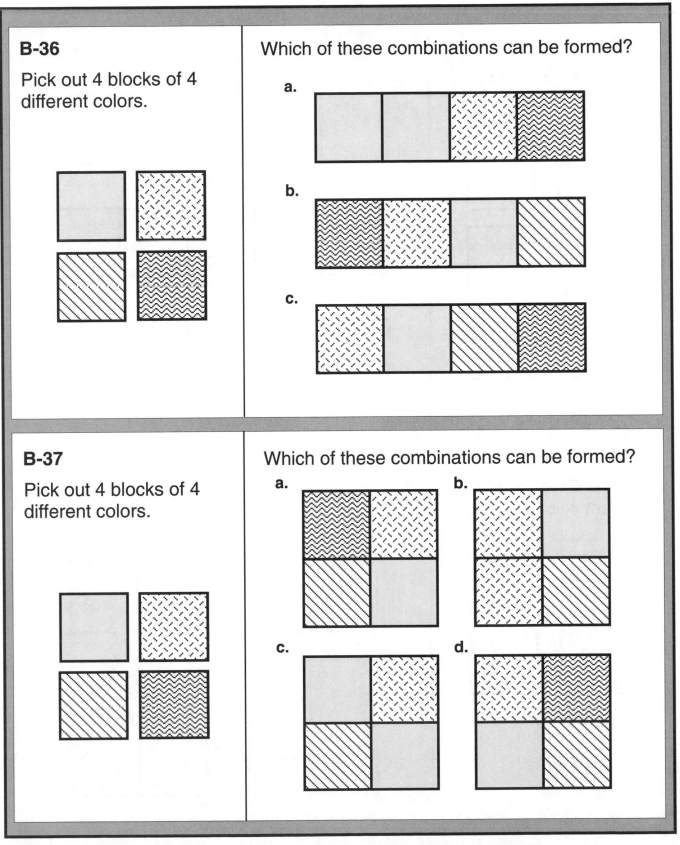

B-36

Pick out 4 blocks of 4 different colors.

Which of these combinations can be formed?

a.

b.

c.

B-37

Pick out 4 blocks of 4 different colors.

Which of these combinations can be formed?

a.

b.

c.

d.

COMBINING INTERLOCKING CUBES

DIRECTIONS: Circle the patterns that can be formed by joining the collection of interlocking cubes shown.

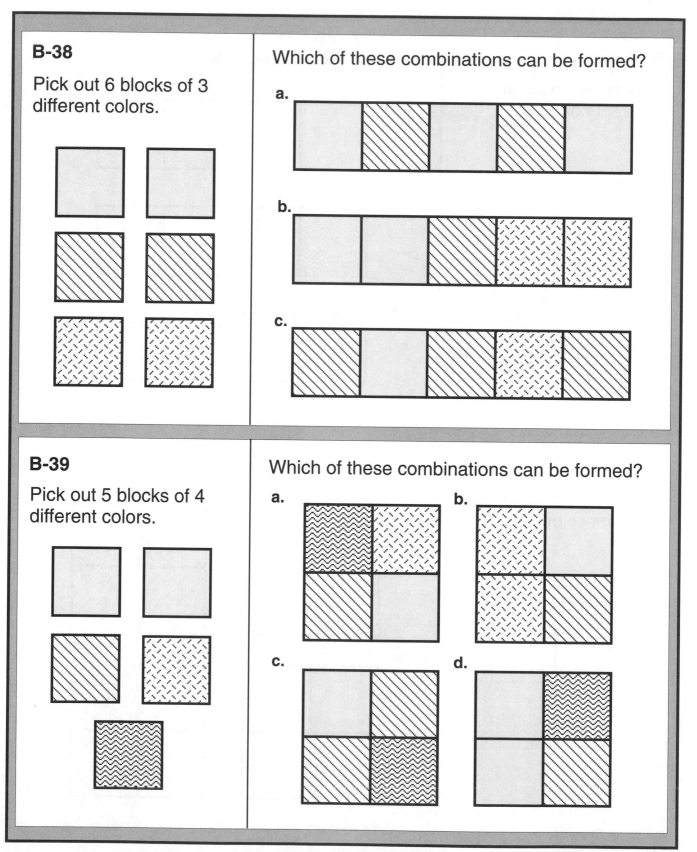

B-38

Pick out 6 blocks of 3 different colors.

Which of these combinations can be formed?

a.

b.

c.

B-39

Pick out 5 blocks of 4 different colors.

Which of these combinations can be formed?

a.   b.

c.   d.

COMBINING SHAPES

DIRECTIONS: Circle the figures that can be formed by joining the two shapes in the box.

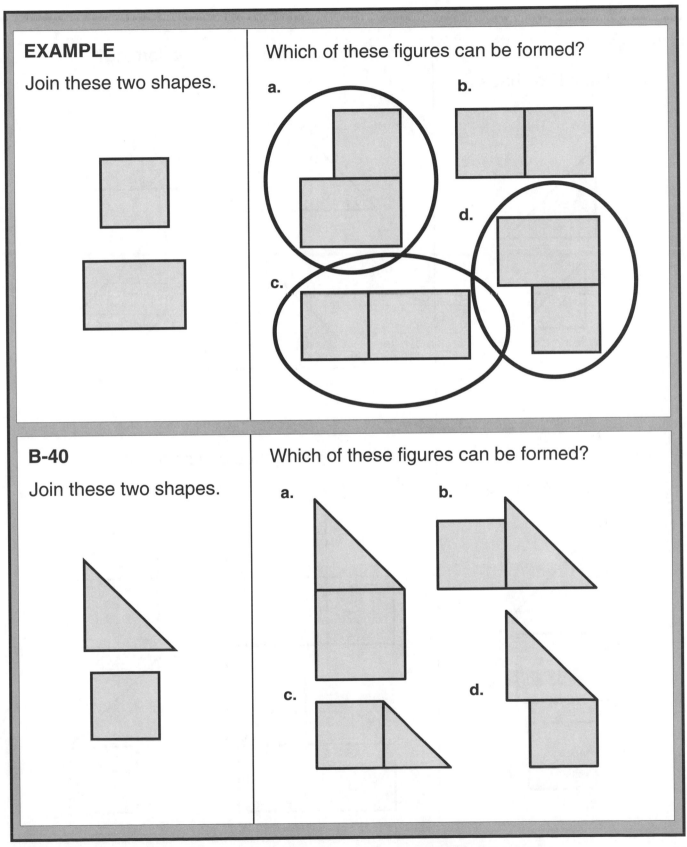

EXAMPLE

Join these two shapes.

Which of these figures can be formed?

a.

b.

c.

d.

B-40

Join these two shapes.

Which of these figures can be formed?

a.

b.

c.

d.

COMBINING SHAPES

DIRECTIONS: Circle the shapes that can be formed by joining the shapes in the box.

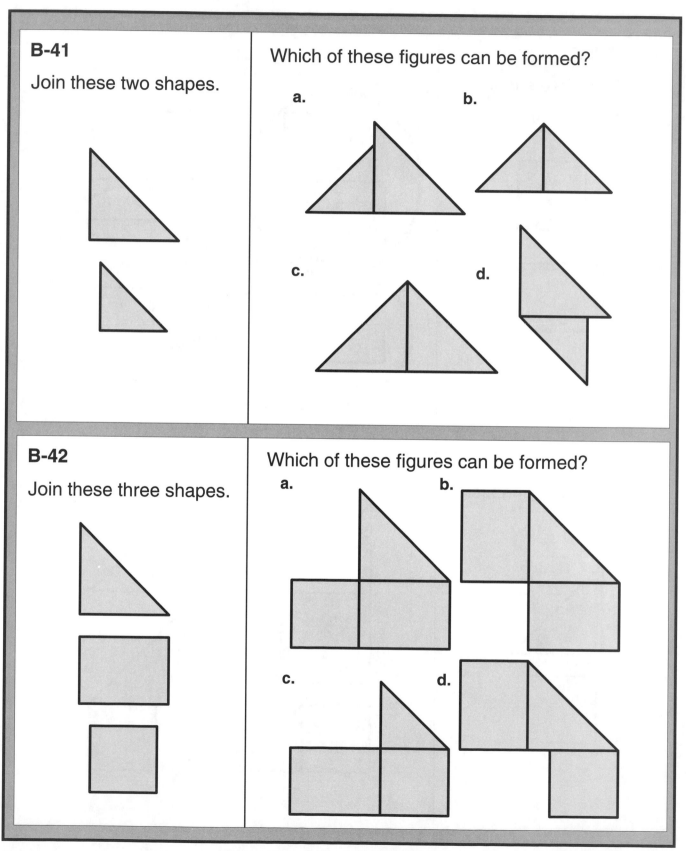

B-41

Join these two shapes.

Which of these figures can be formed?

a.   b.

c.   d.

B-42

Join these three shapes.

Which of these figures can be formed?

a.   b.

c.   d.

FINDING AND TRACING PATTERNS

DIRECTIONS: Circle any figure that contains the shape on the left. The shape must be in the same position but may have extra lines. Trace over the matching shape to make sure you are right.

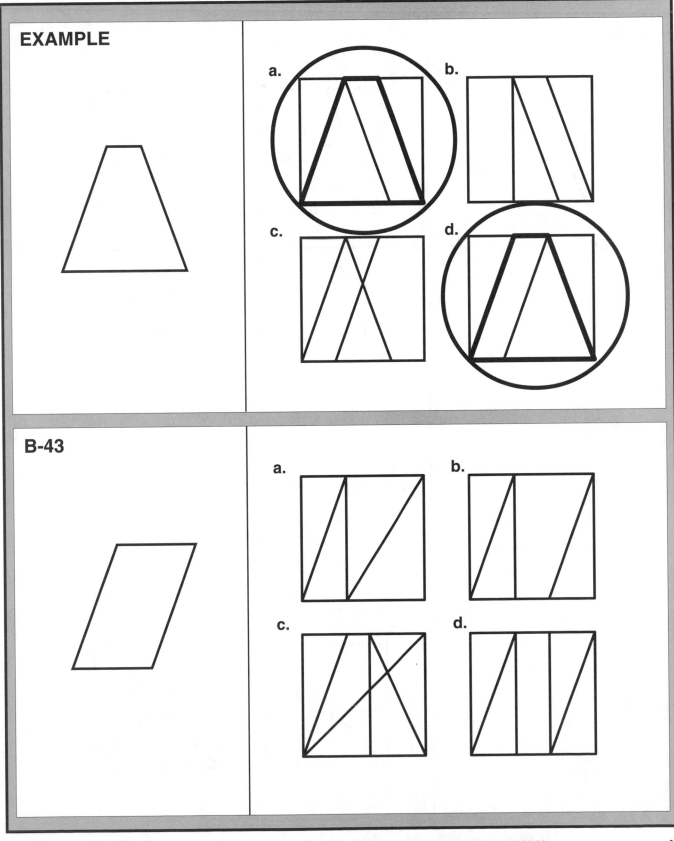

FINDING AND TRACING PATTERNS

DIRECTIONS: Circle any figure that contains the shape on the left. The shape must be in the same position but may have extra lines. Trace over the matching shape to make sure you are right.

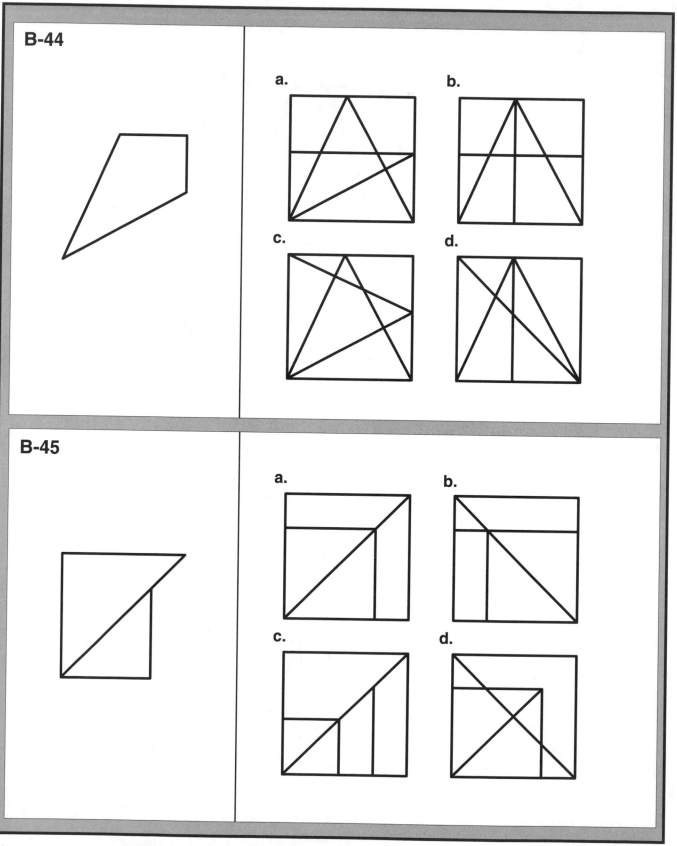

FINDING AND TRACING PATTERNS

DIRECTIONS: Circle any figure that contains the shape on the left. The shape must be in the same position but may have extra lines. Trace over the matching shape to make sure you are right.

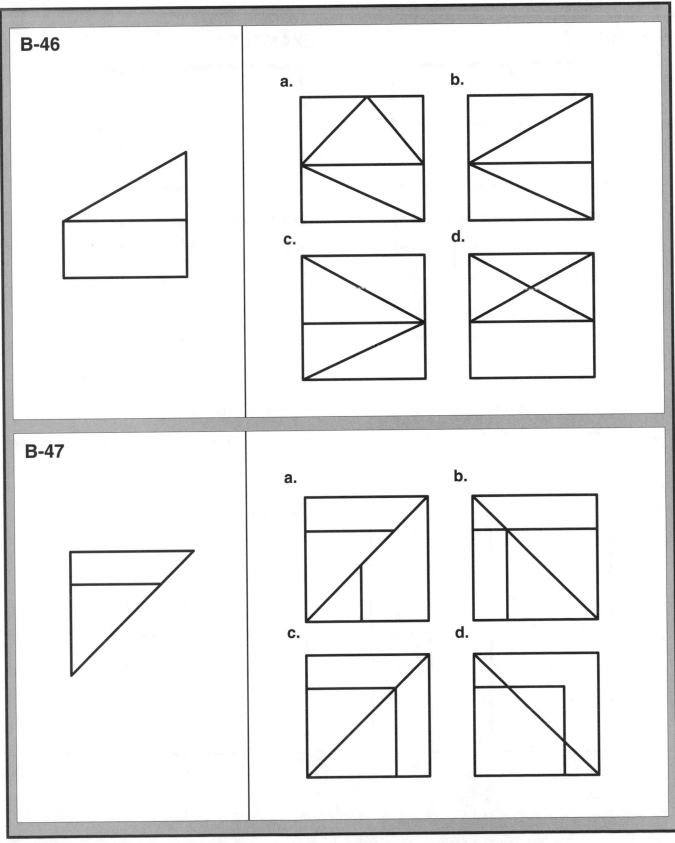

DIVIDING SHAPES INTO EQUAL PARTS—A

DIRECTIONS: Divide each of the shapes below into equal parts. Build each shape with interlocking cubes. Use two colors (one for each part).

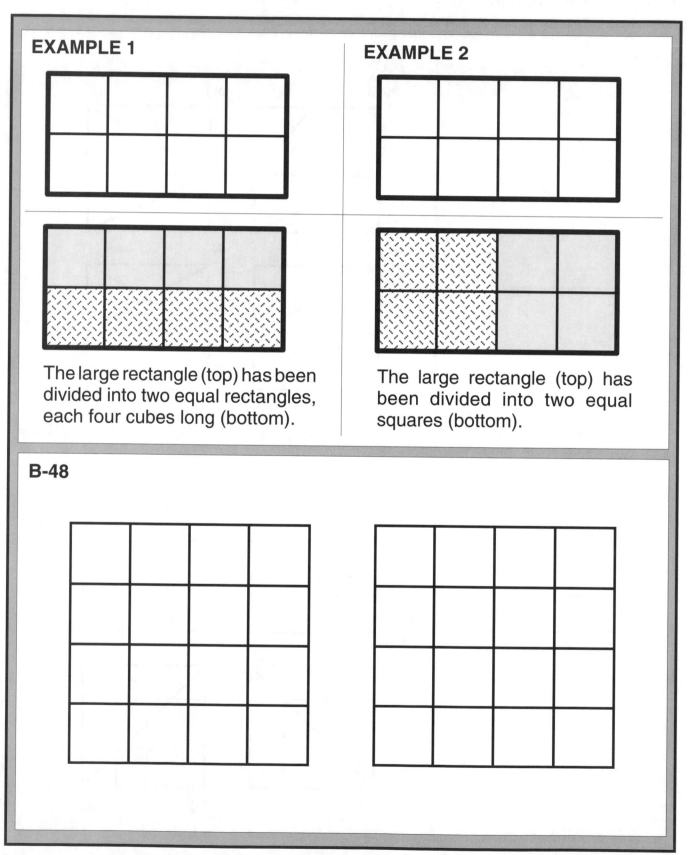

EXAMPLE 1

The large rectangle (top) has been divided into two equal rectangles, each four cubes long (bottom).

EXAMPLE 2

The large rectangle (top) has been divided into two equal squares (bottom).

B-48

DIVIDING SHAPES INTO EQUAL PARTS—A

DIRECTIONS: Divide each of the shapes below into equal parts. Build each shape with interlocking cubes. Use two colors (one for each part).

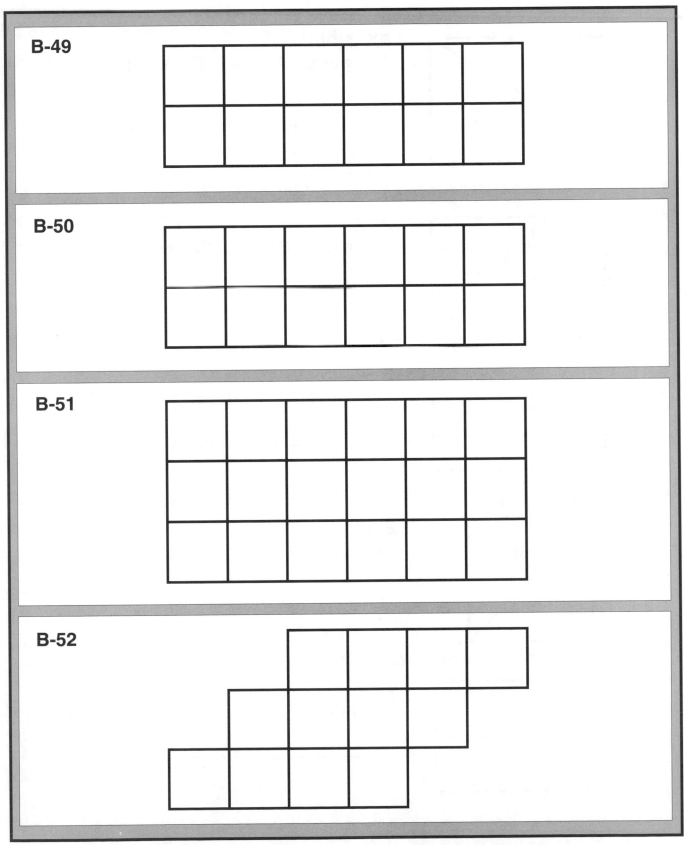

B-49

B-50

B-51

B-52

DIVIDING SHAPES INTO EQUAL PARTS—B

DIRECTIONS: Look at the two parts of the shape. Answer the question, "Are the parts exactly alike?" Write *yes* or *no* in the blank below each question.

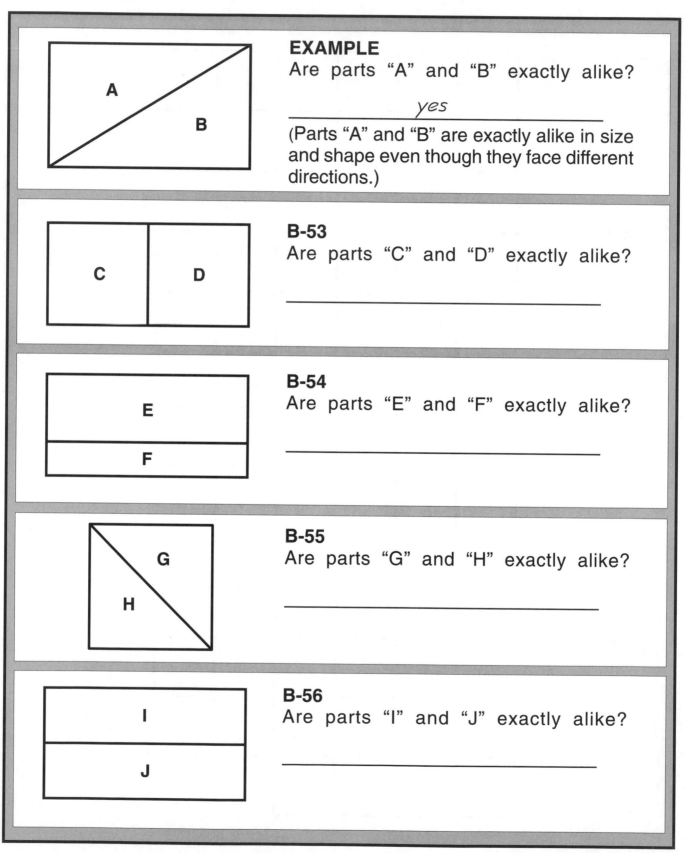

EXAMPLE
Are parts "A" and "B" exactly alike?

_____ *yes* _____

(Parts "A" and "B" are exactly alike in size and shape even though they face different directions.)

B-53
Are parts "C" and "D" exactly alike?

_____

B-54
Are parts "E" and "F" exactly alike?

_____

B-55
Are parts "G" and "H" exactly alike?

_____

B-56
Are parts "I" and "J" exactly alike?

_____

DIVIDING SHAPES INTO EQUAL PARTS—B

DIRECTIONS: Look at the two parts of the shape. Answer the question, "Are the parts exactly alike?" Write *yes* or *no* in the blank below each question.

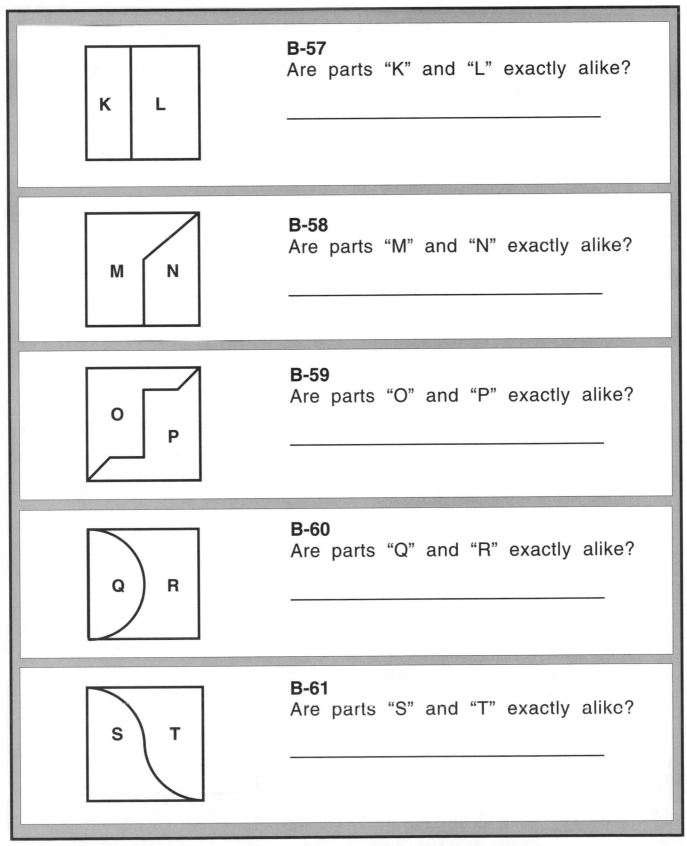

B-57
Are parts "K" and "L" exactly alike?

_____

B-58
Are parts "M" and "N" exactly alike?

_____

B-59
Are parts "O" and "P" exactly alike?

_____

B-60
Are parts "Q" and "R" exactly alike?

_____

B-61
Are parts "S" and "T" exactly alike?

_____

DIVIDING SHAPES INTO EQUAL PARTS—C

DIRECTIONS: Here are four rectangles. Divide each into two shapes that are exactly alike. Use one straight line each time. The divided shapes do not have to face in the same direction.

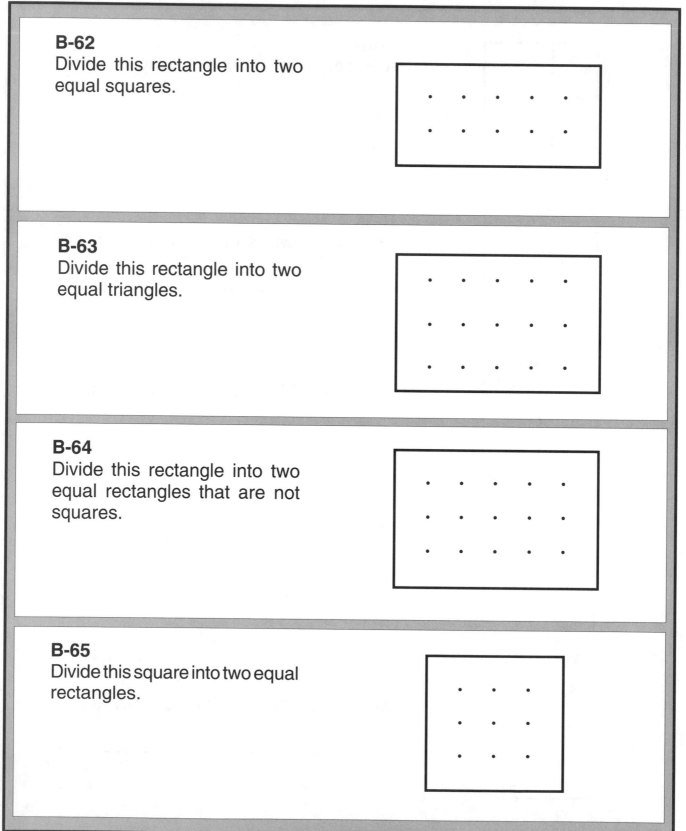

B-62
Divide this rectangle into two equal squares.

B-63
Divide this rectangle into two equal triangles.

B-64
Divide this rectangle into two equal rectangles that are not squares.

B-65
Divide this square into two equal rectangles.

DIVIDING SHAPES INTO EQUAL PARTS—C

DIRECTIONS: Here are five triangles. Divide each of them into two equal triangles that are exactly alike. The divided shapes do not have to face in the same direction.

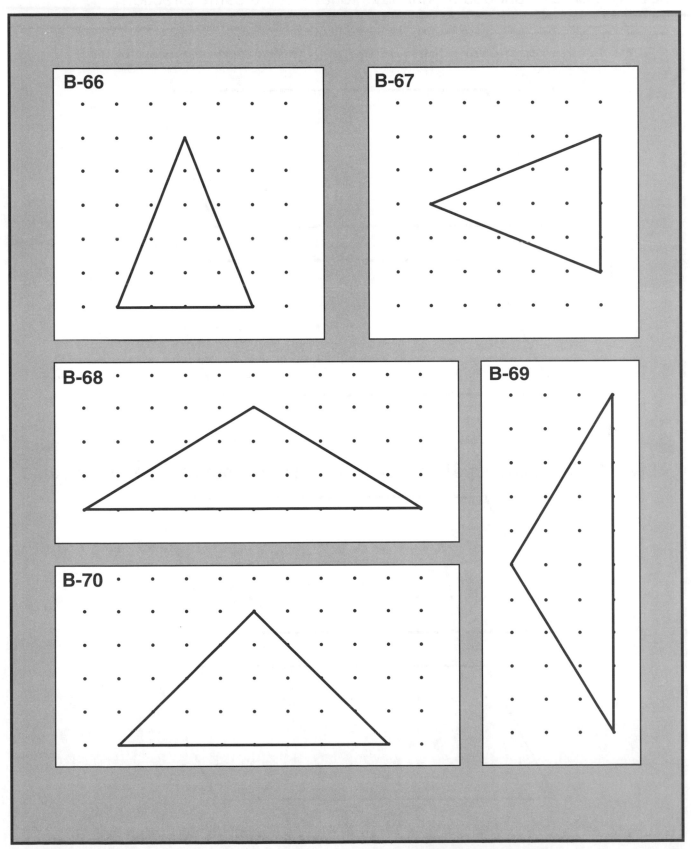

B-66

B-67

B-68

B-69

B-70

DIVIDING SHAPES INTO EQUAL PARTS—C

DIRECTIONS: Here are several four-sided shapes called parallelograms (opposite sides are parallel). Divide each parallelogram into two equal shapes, as directed below. The divided shapes do not have to face in the same direction.

B-71 Divide each shape into two equal triangles that are exactly alike.

B-72 Divide each shape into two equal parallelograms that are exactly alike.

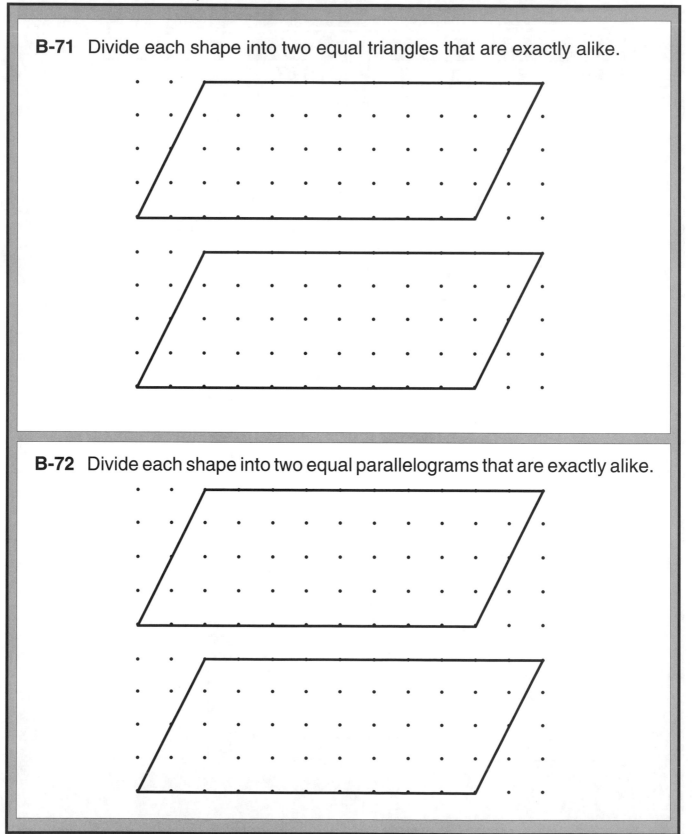

WHICH SHAPE COMPLETES THE SQUARE?

DIRECTIONS: Circle the shape that completes the big square.

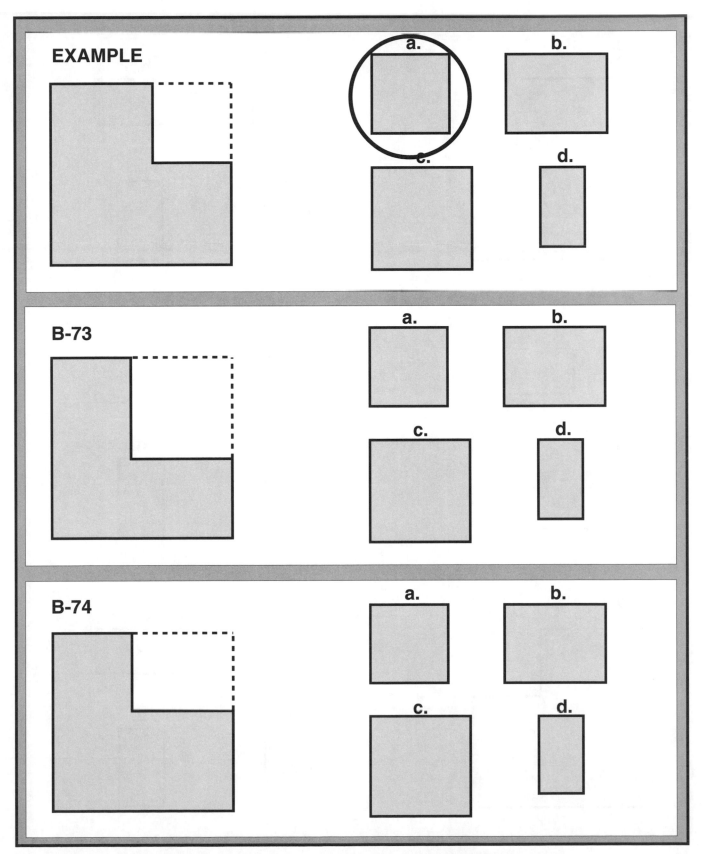

WHICH SHAPE COMPLETES THE SQUARE?

DIRECTIONS: Circle the shape that completes the big square.

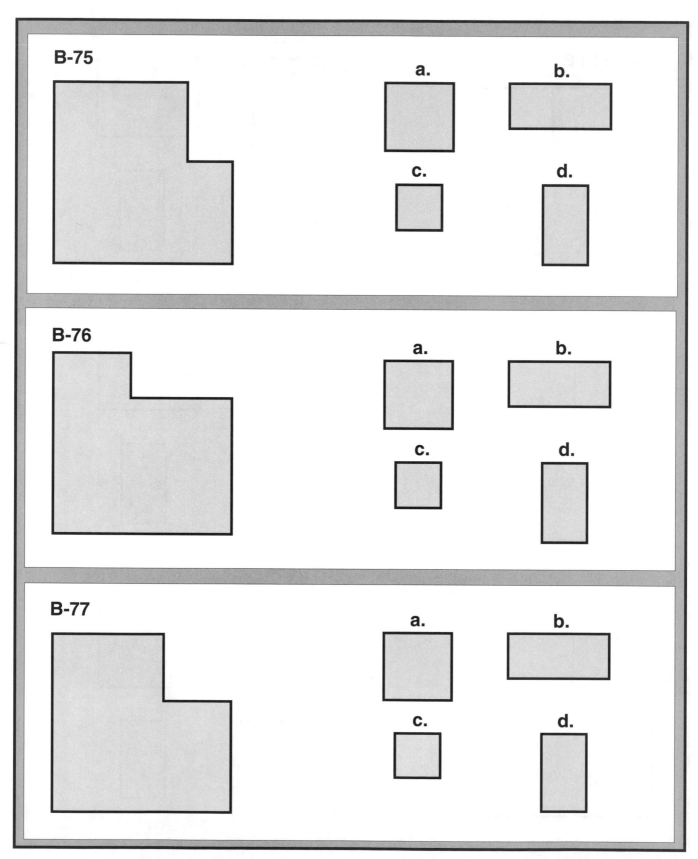

B-75

a.

b.

c.

d.

B-76

a.

b.

c.

d.

B-77

a.

b.

c.

d.

WHICH SHAPE COMPLETES THE SQUARE?

DIRECTIONS: Circle the shape that completes the big square.

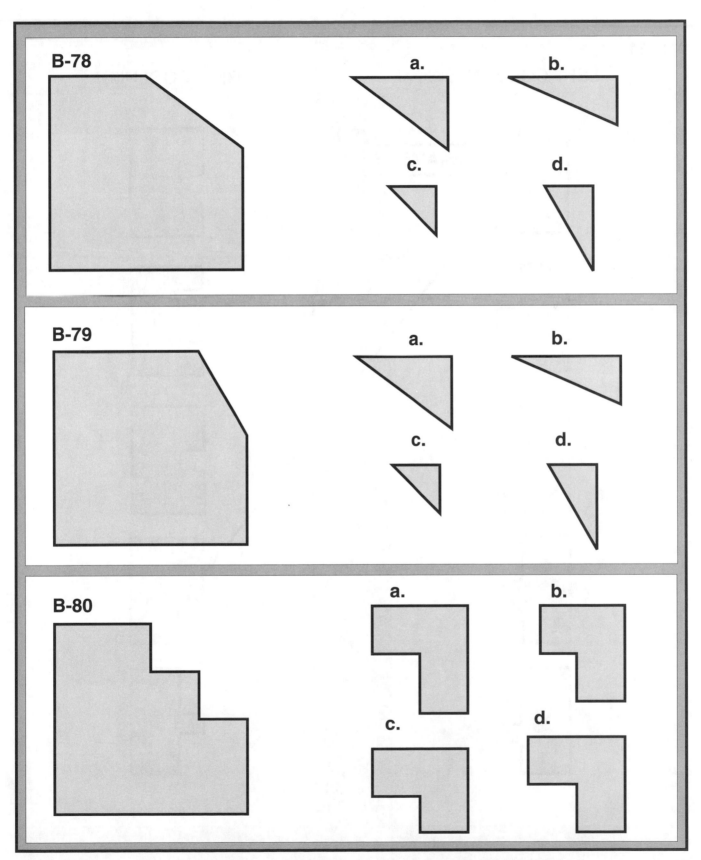

WHICH SHAPES MAKE SQUARES?

DIRECTIONS: Draw a line from a shape in the left column to the shape in the right column that completes the square.

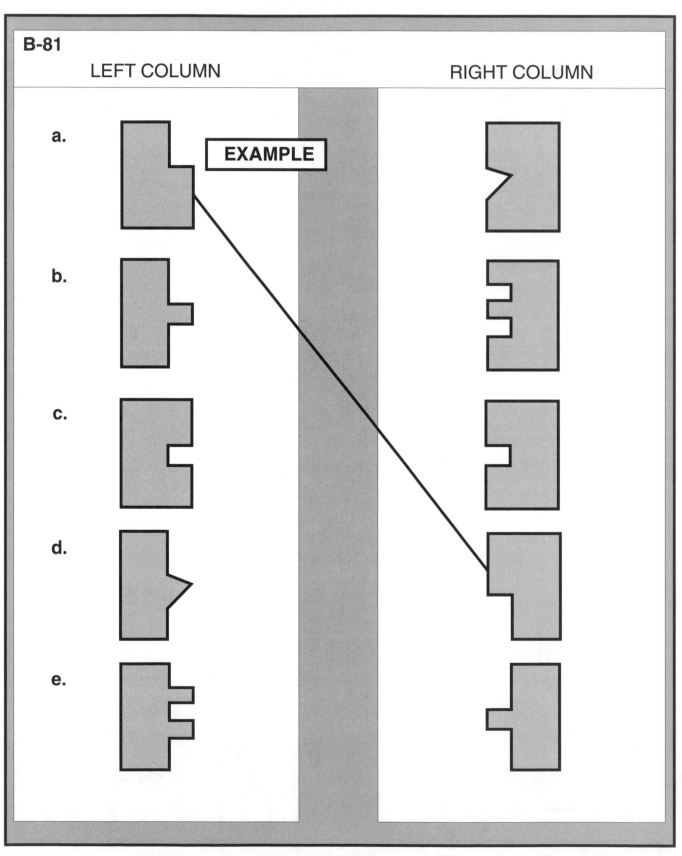

WHICH SHAPES MAKE SQUARES?

DIRECTIONS: Draw a line from a shape in the left column to the shape in the right column that completes the square.

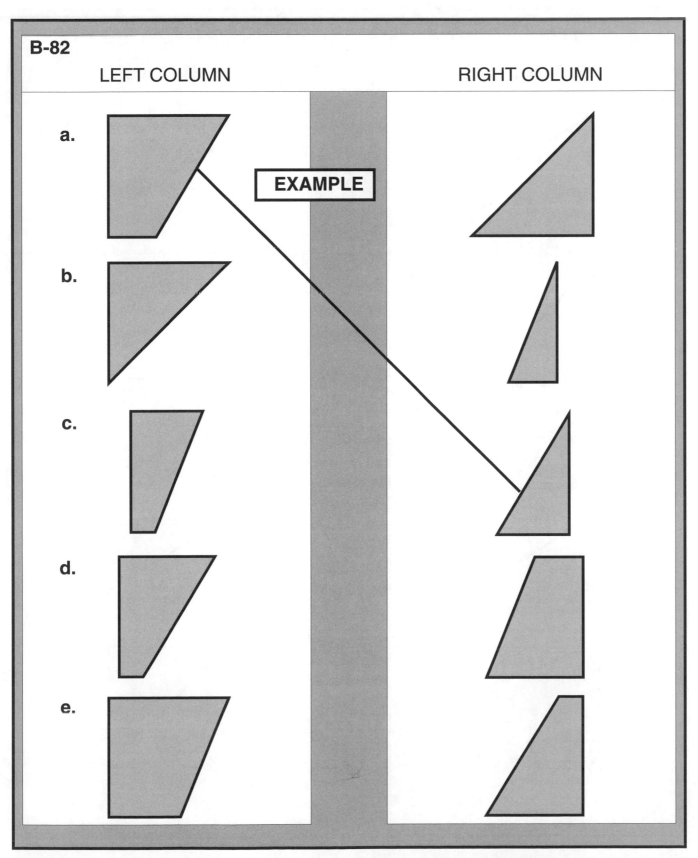

WHICH SHAPES MAKE SQUARES?

DIRECTIONS: Draw a line from a shape in the left column to the shape in the right column that completes the square.

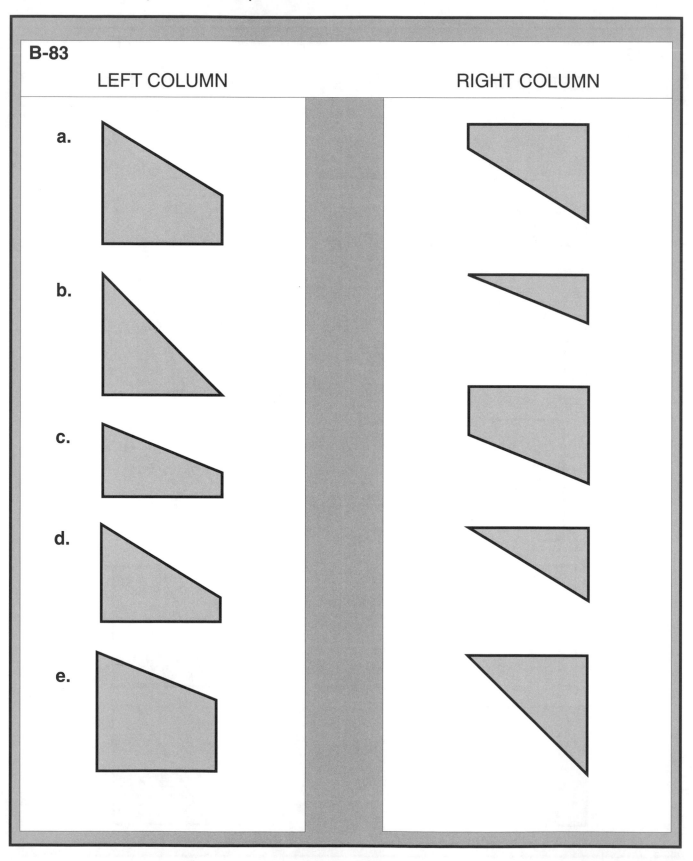

B-83

LEFT COLUMN   RIGHT COLUMN

a.

b.

c.

d.

e.

COPYING A FIGURE

DIRECTIONS: Copy each of the figures below by building them with interlocking cubes.

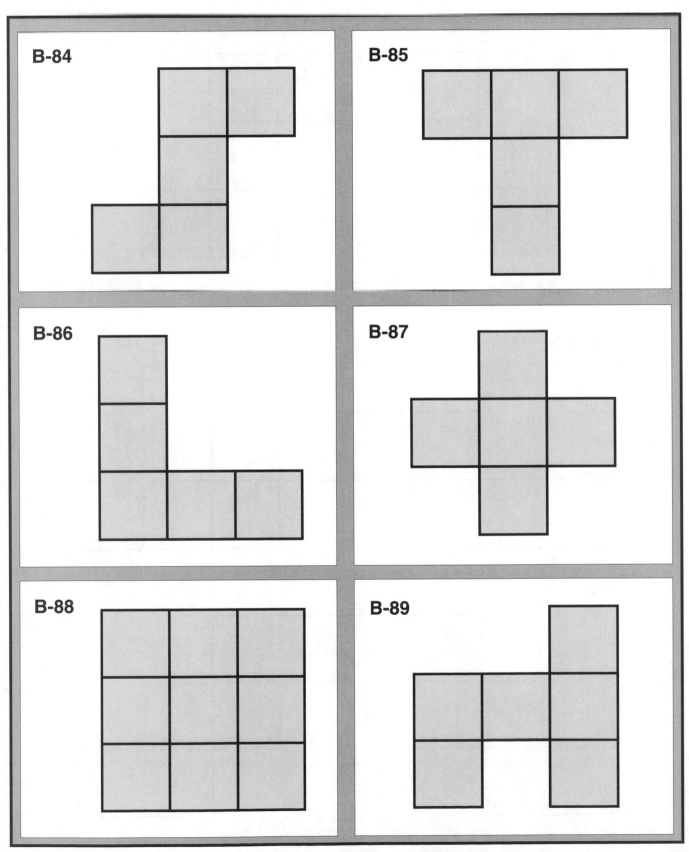

COPYING A FIGURE

DIRECTIONS: Copy each of the figures below by building them with interlocking cubes.

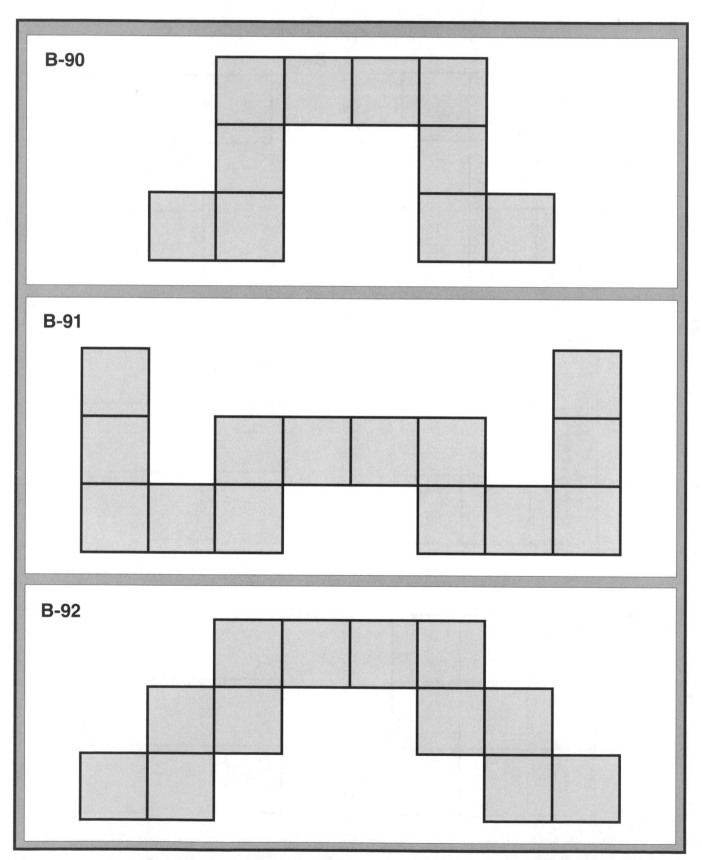

B-90

B-91

B-92

DRAWING IDENTICAL SHAPES

DIRECTIONS: Use the grid to draw a shape identical to the shape on the left. Note that identical means exactly the same size and shape. Color your drawing.

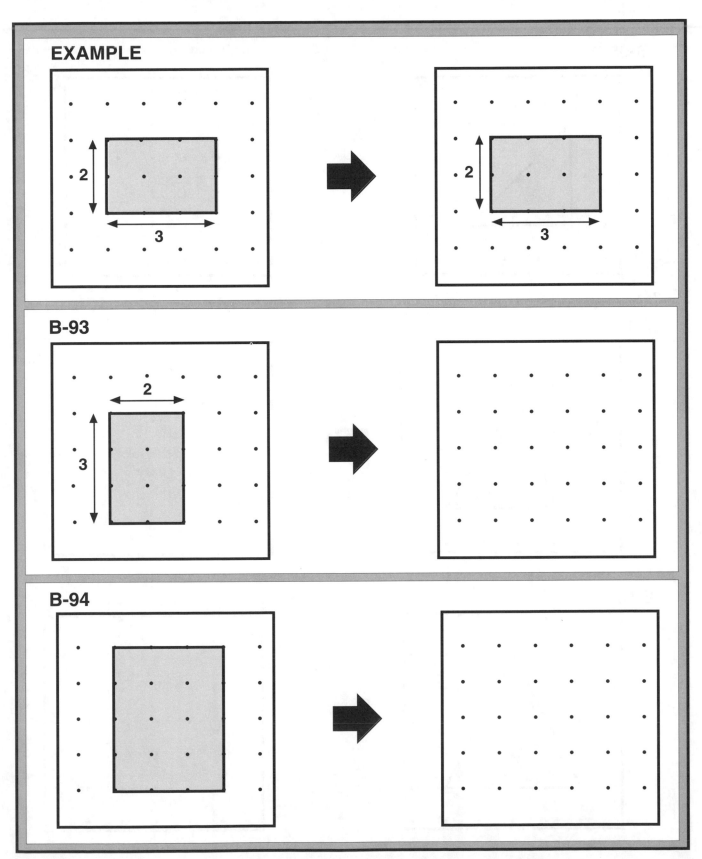

DRAWING IDENTICAL SHAPES

DIRECTIONS: Use the grid on the right to draw a shape identical to the shape on the left. Note that identical means exactly the same size and shape. Color your drawing.

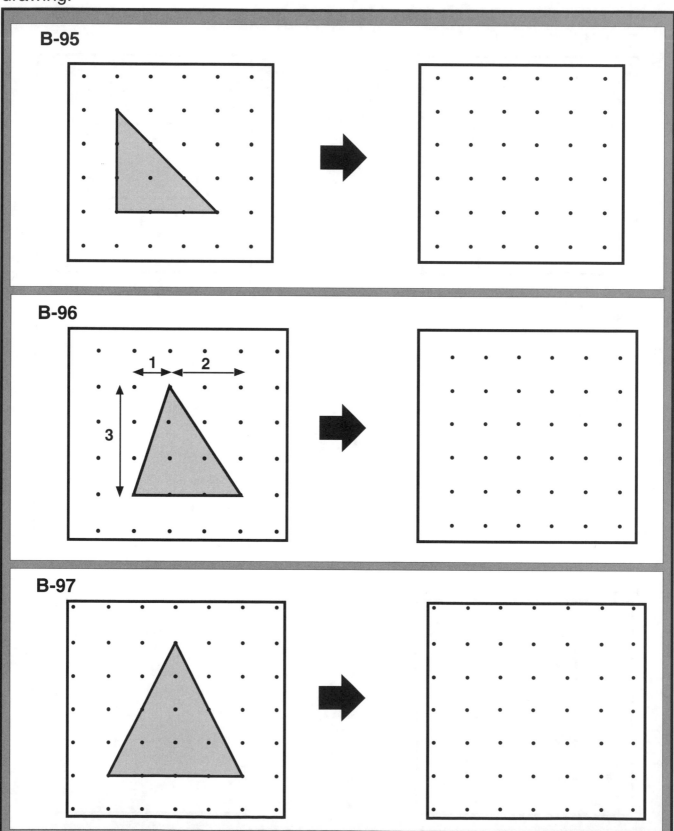

DRAWING IDENTICAL SHAPES

DIRECTIONS: Use the grid on the right to draw a shape identical to the shape on the left. Note that identical means exactly the same size and shape. Color your drawing.

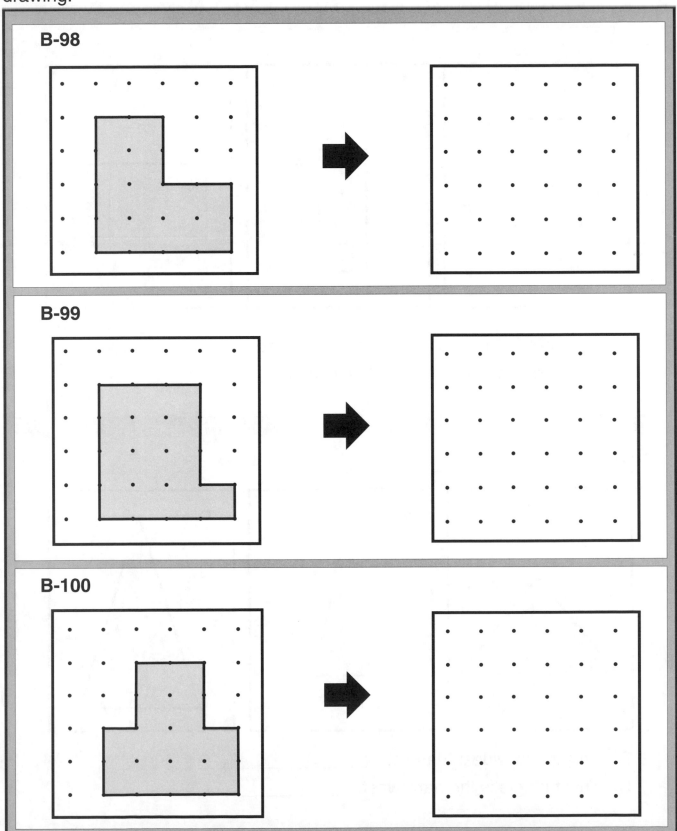

COMPARING SHAPES—SELECT

DIRECTIONS: Under the three pictures, two shapes are described. Read each description and decide which of the pictures it describes. Write the letter of the correct picture on the line.

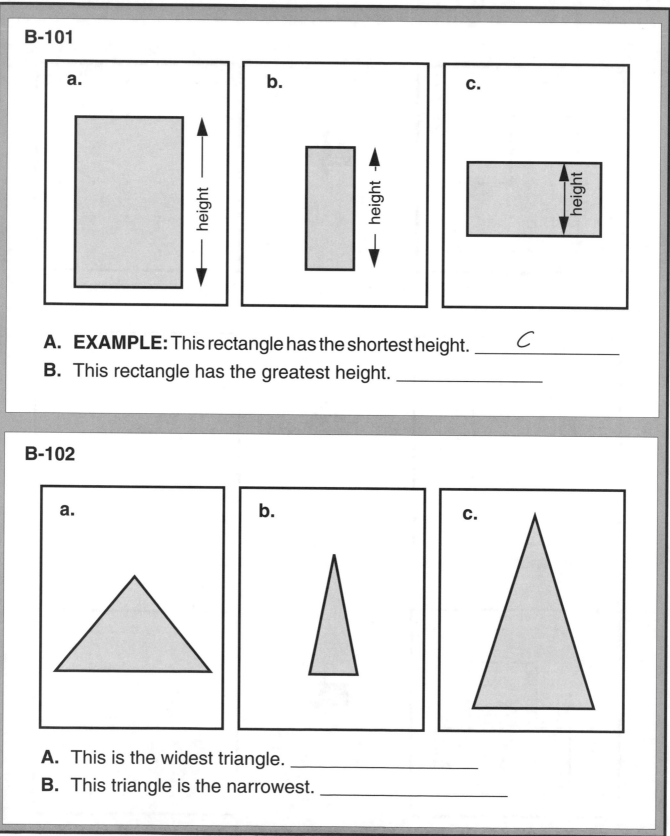

B-101

a.

height

b.

height

c.

height

A. EXAMPLE: This rectangle has the shortest height. _____*C*_____

B. This rectangle has the greatest height. _____

B-102

a.

b.

c.

A. This is the widest triangle. _____

B. This triangle is the narrowest. _____

COMPARING SHAPES—SELECT

DIRECTIONS: Under the three pictures, two shapes are described. Read each description and decide which of the pictures it describes. Write the letter of the correct picture on the line.

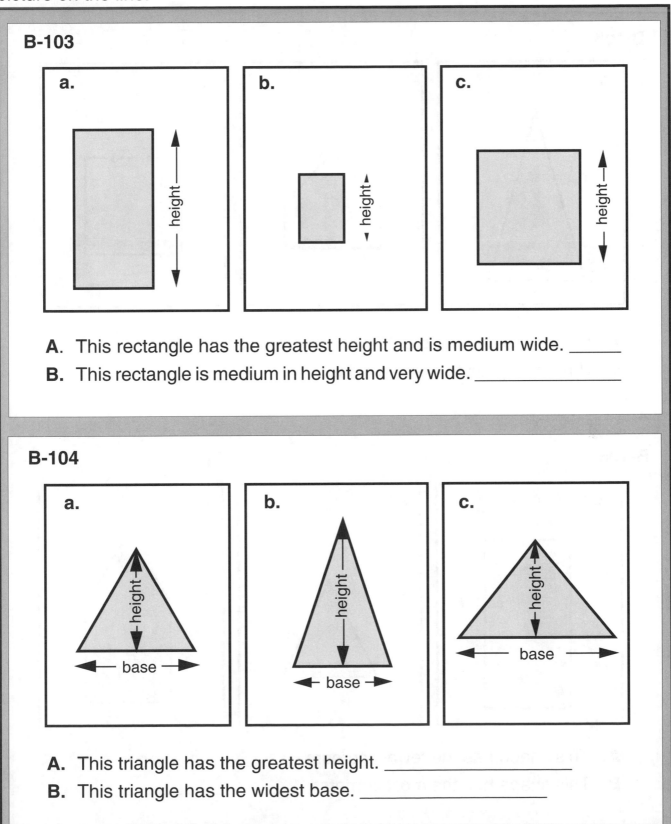

B-103

a.

b.

c.

A. This rectangle has the greatest height and is medium wide. _____

B. This rectangle is medium in height and very wide. _____

B-104

a.

b.

c.

A. This triangle has the greatest height. _____

B. This triangle has the widest base. _____

COMPARING SHAPES—SELECT

DIRECTIONS: Under the three pictures, two shapes are described. Read each description and decide which of the pictures it describes. Write the letter of the correct picture on the line.

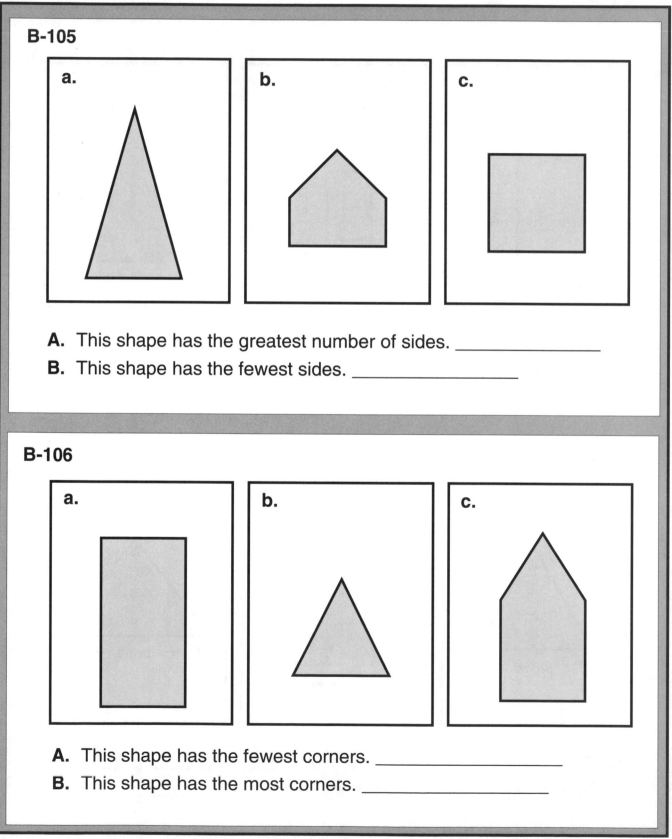

B-105

a.

b.

c.

A. This shape has the greatest number of sides. _____

B. This shape has the fewest sides. _____

B-106

a.

b.

c.

A. This shape has the fewest corners. _____

B. This shape has the most corners. _____

COMPARING SHAPES—EXPLAIN

DIRECTIONS: Compare the shapes in each box. Describe them, using complete sentences.

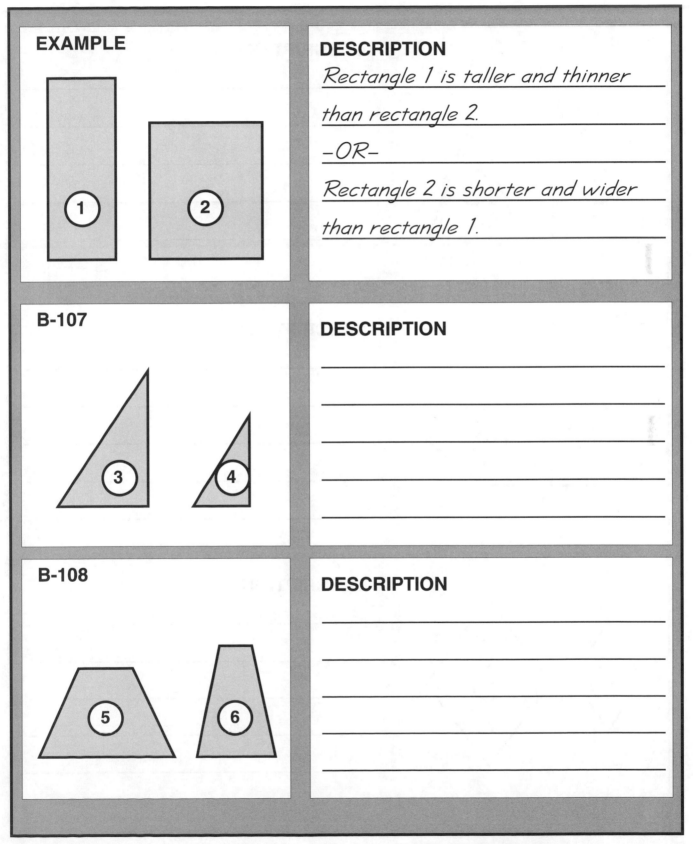

EXAMPLE

1
2

DESCRIPTION

Rectangle 1 is taller and thinner than rectangle 2.

–OR–

Rectangle 2 is shorter and wider than rectangle 1.

B-107

3
4

DESCRIPTION

_____

_____

_____

_____

_____

B-108

5
6

DESCRIPTION

_____

_____

_____

_____

_____

COMPARING SHAPES—EXPLAIN

DIRECTIONS: Compare the shapes in each box. Describe them, using complete sentences.

B-109

7   8

DESCRIPTION

_____

_____

_____

_____

B-110

9   10

DESCRIPTION

_____

_____

_____

_____

B-111

11   12

DESCRIPTION

_____

_____

_____

_____

COMPARING SHAPES—EXPLAIN

DIRECTIONS: Use this diagram to organize your thinking about how the triangle and rectangle are alike and how they are different.

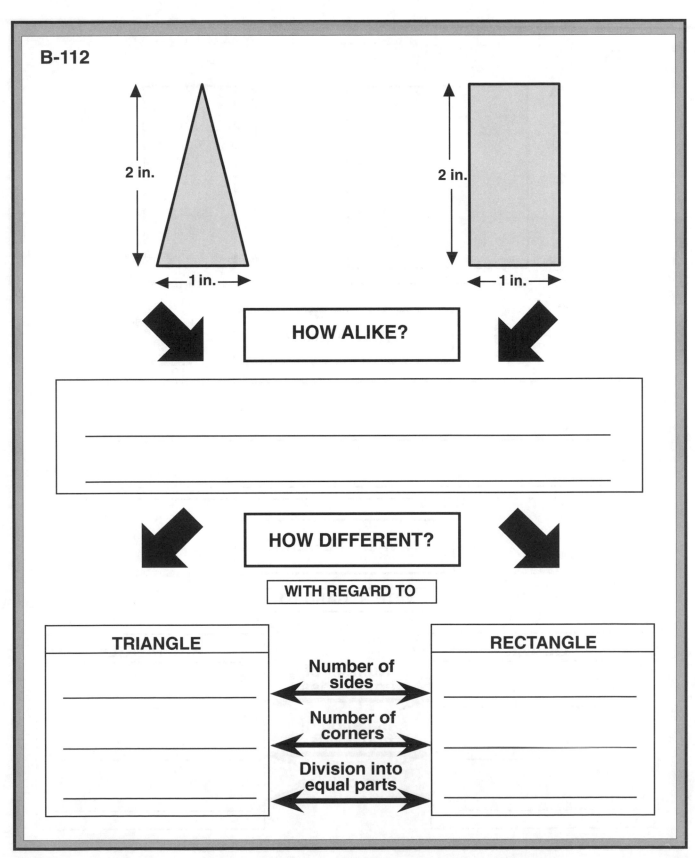

B-112

2 in.

1 in.

2 in.

1 in.

HOW ALIKE?

HOW DIFFERENT?

WITH REGARD TO

TRIANGLE

RECTANGLE

Number of sides

Number of corners

Division into equal parts

COMPARING SHAPES—EXPLAIN

DIRECTIONS: Use this diagram to organize your thinking about how the triangle and rectangle are alike and how they are different.

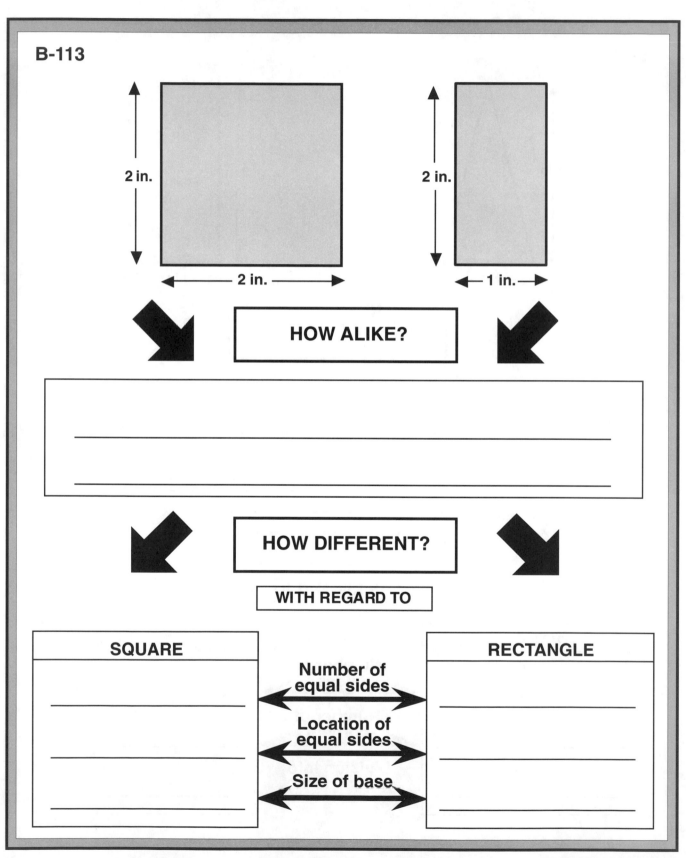

B-113

2 in.

2 in.

2 in.

1 in.

HOW ALIKE?

HOW DIFFERENT?

WITH REGARD TO

SQUARE

RECTANGLE

Number of equal sides

Location of equal sides

Size of base

CHAPTER THREE

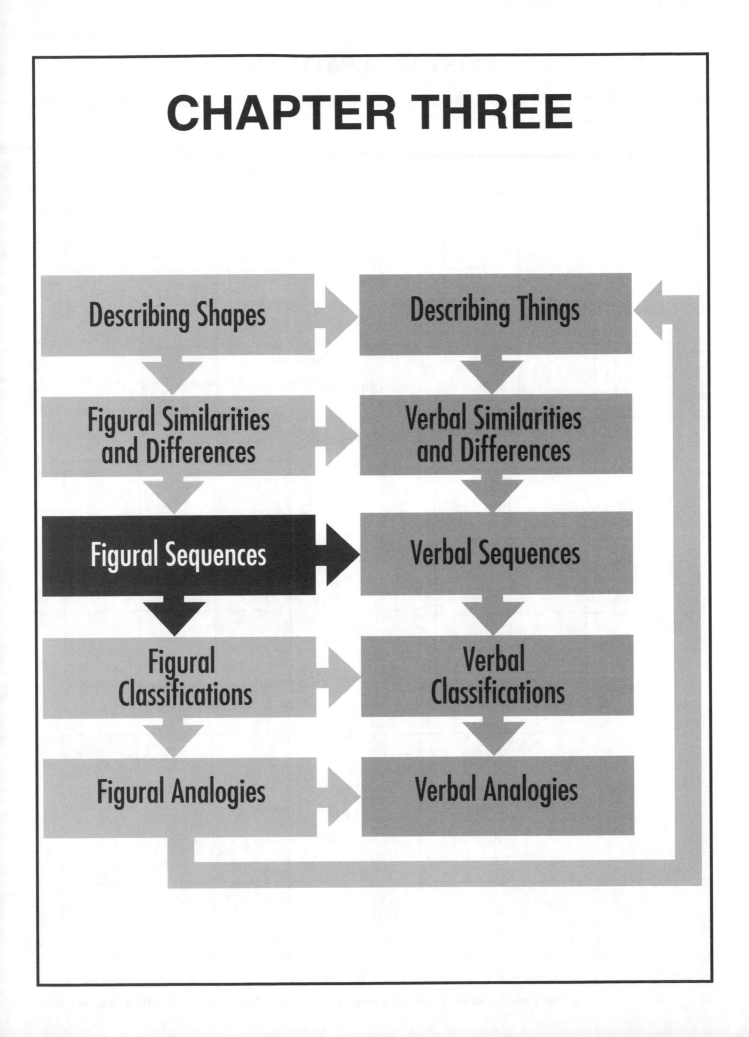

Describing Shapes → Describing Things

Figural Similarities and Differences → Verbal Similarities and Differences

Figural Sequences → Verbal Sequences

Figural Classifications → Verbal Classifications

Figural Analogies → Verbal Analogies

COPYING A PATTERN

DIRECTIONS: Place a colored interlocking cube on each square, following the instructions in each box.

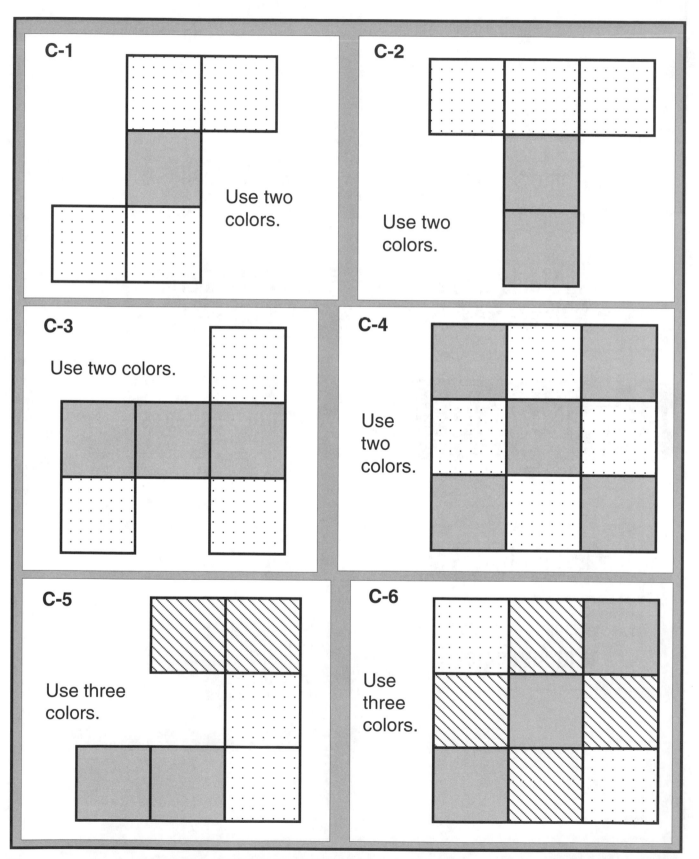

C-1

Use two colors.

C-2

Use two colors.

C-3

Use two colors.

C-4

Use two colors.

C-5

Use three colors.

C-6

Use three colors.

COPYING A PATTERN

DIRECTIONS: Place a colored interlocking cube on each square, following the instructions in the color key.

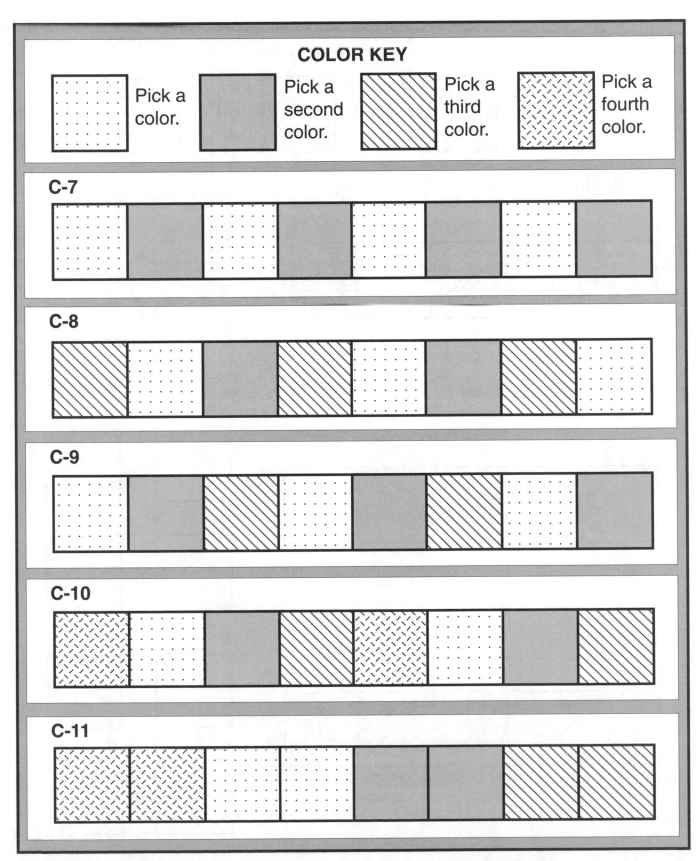

WHICH COLOR COMES NEXT?—SELECT

DIRECTIONS: Place a colored interlocking cube on each square, following the given pattern. Circle the cube that comes next. Color your pattern.

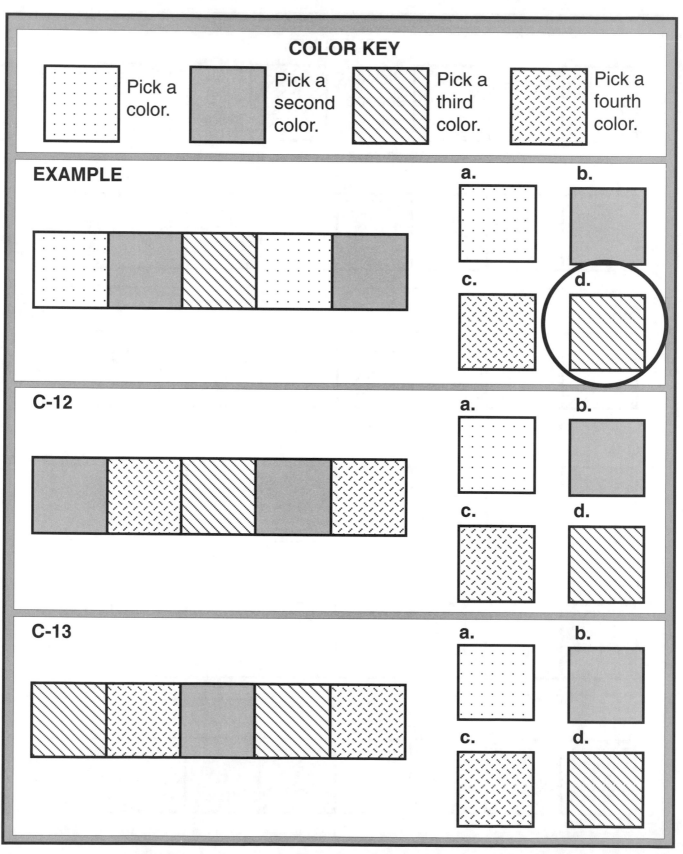

WHICH COLOR COMES NEXT?—SELECT

DIRECTIONS: Place a colored interlocking cube on each square. Select the cube that comes next. Color your pattern.

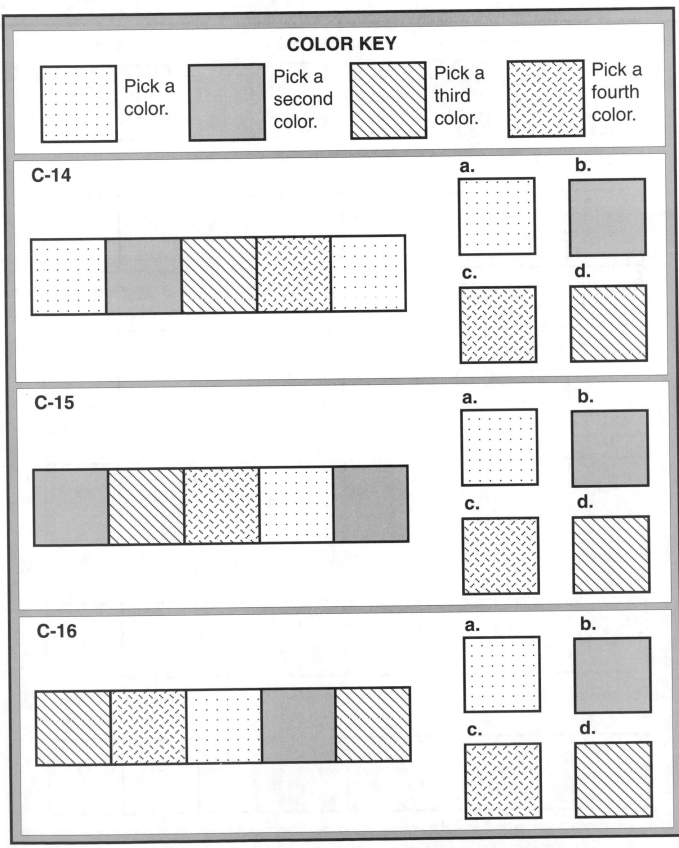

WHICH COLOR COMES NEXT?—SELECT

DIRECTIONS: Place a colored interlocking cube on each shaded square. In each unshaded square, add a cube that comes next in the pattern. Color the pictures to match the cubes.

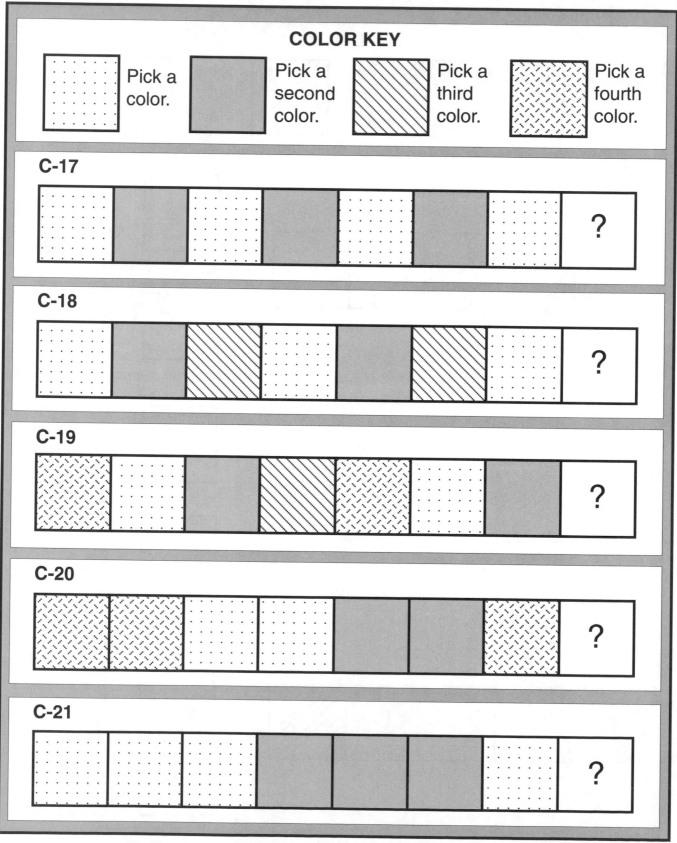

WHICH COLORS COME NEXT?—SELECT

DIRECTIONS: Place a colored interlocking cube on each shaded square. In each unshaded pair of squares, add the two cubes that come next in the pattern. Color the pictures to match the cubes.

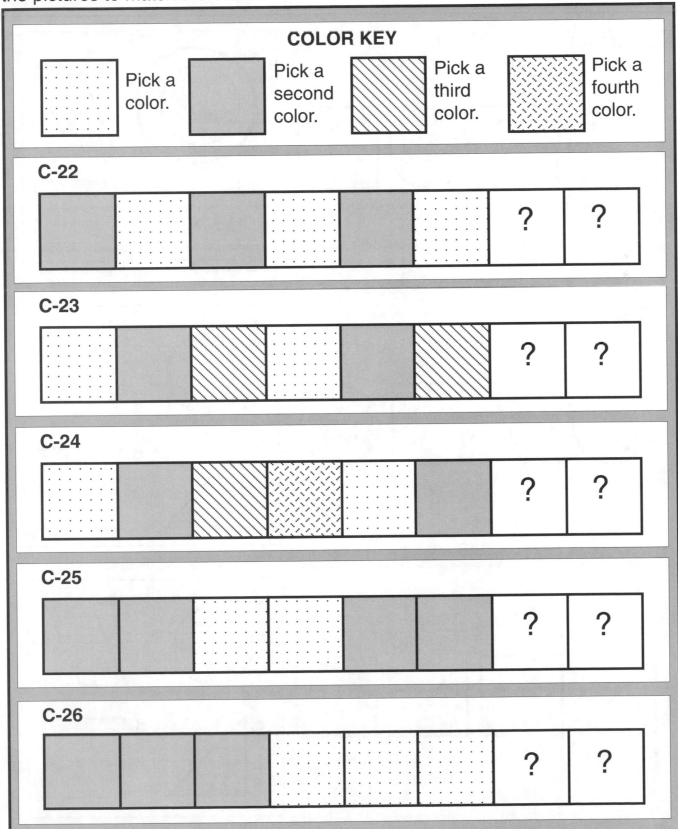

WHICH SHAPE COMES NEXT?—SELECT

DIRECTIONS: Circle the shape that comes next.

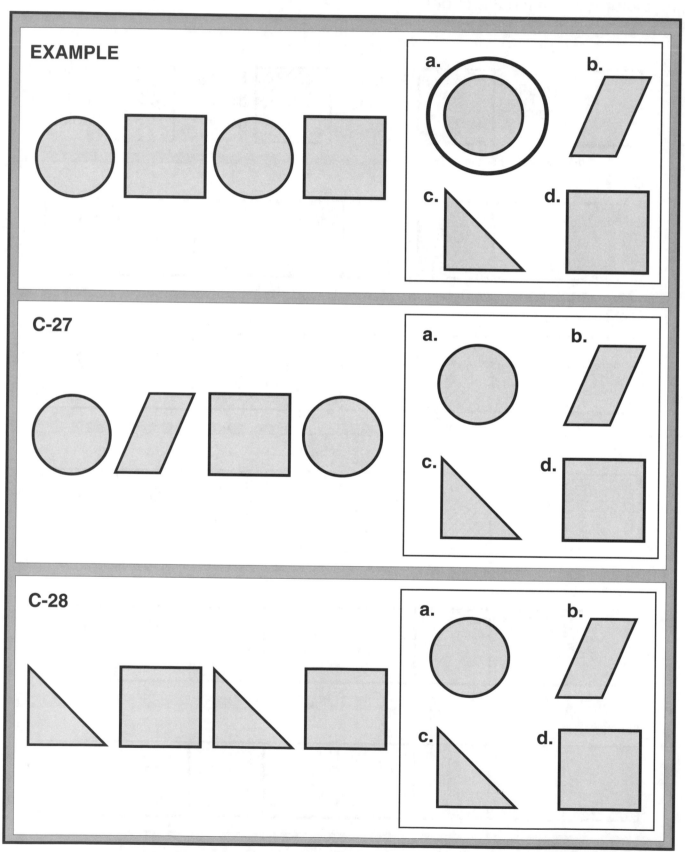

EXAMPLE

a. b. c. d.

C-27

a. b. c. d.

C-28

a. b. c. d.

WHICH SHAPE COMES NEXT?—SELECT

DIRECTIONS: Circle the shape that comes next.

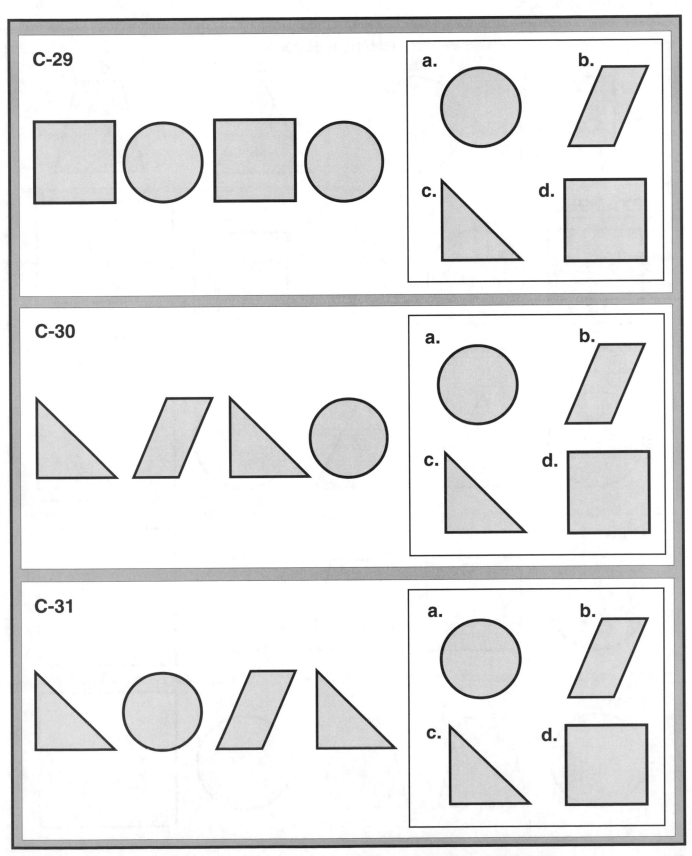

WHICH SHAPE COMES NEXT?—SELECT

DIRECTIONS: Each line contains a pattern of shapes. In the choice box, find the shape that continues the pattern. In the box at the right, write the letter that belongs to the correct shape.

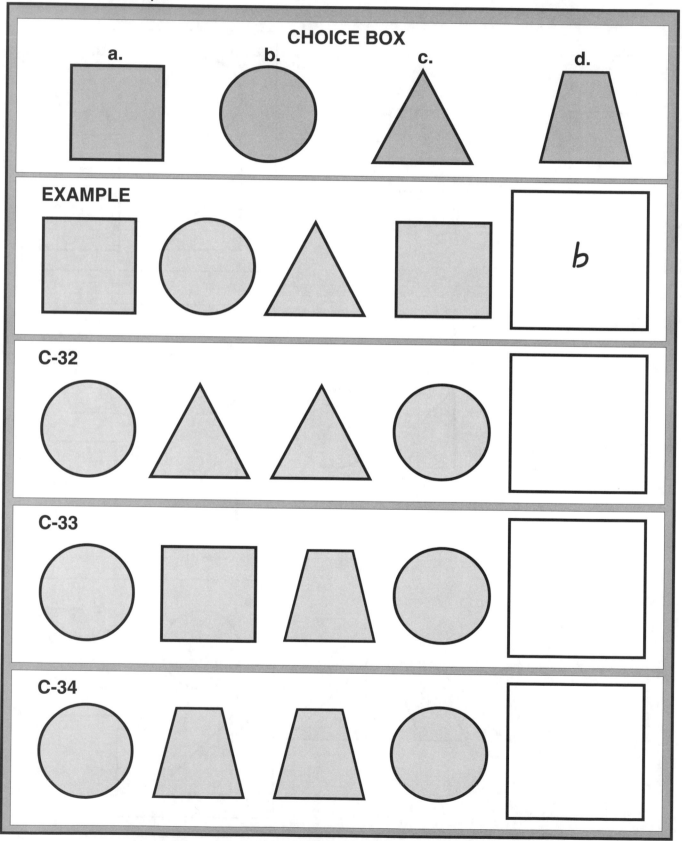

WHICH SHAPE COMES NEXT?—SELECT

DIRECTIONS: Each line contains a pattern of shapes. In the choice box, find the shape that continues the pattern. In the box at the right, write the letter that belongs to the correct shape.

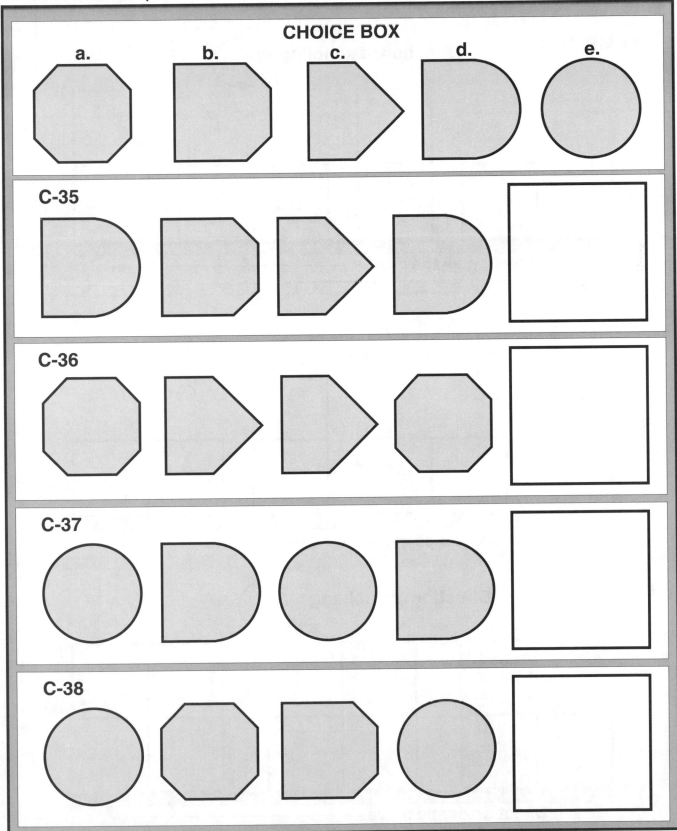

CHOICE BOX

a.   b.   c.   d.   e.

C-35

C-36

C-37

C-38

TUMBLING—COLORING

DIRECTIONS: As a shape tumbles along, the side that is on the ground changes. Build each figure with interlocking cubes of two different colors. Tumble the blocks as shown. Color the following figures to show how they look as they tumble.

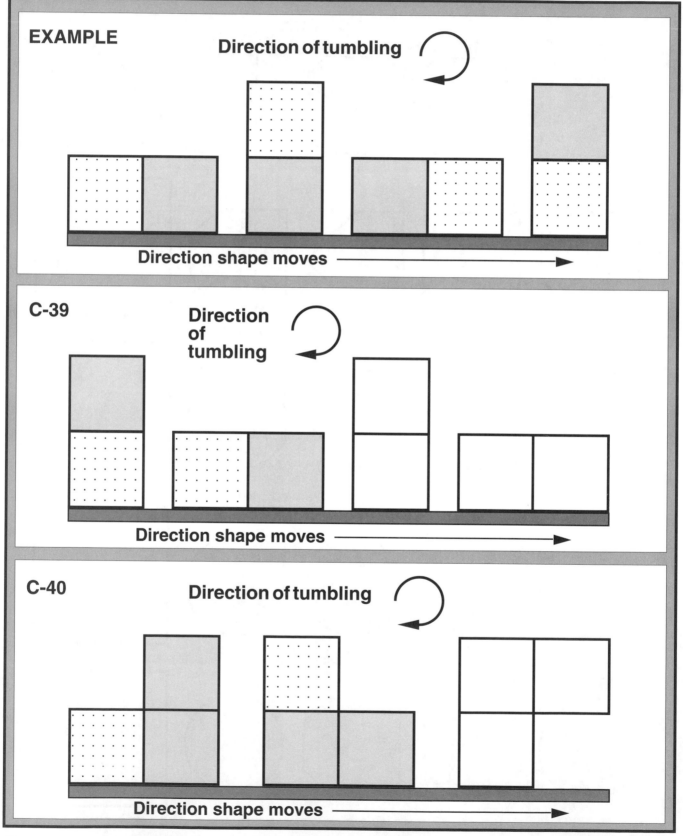

EXAMPLE

Direction of tumbling

Direction shape moves

C-39

Direction of tumbling

Direction shape moves

C-40

Direction of tumbling

Direction shape moves

TUMBLING—SHADING

DIRECTIONS: As a shape tumbles along, the side that is on the ground changes. Darken the final two figures to show how they look as they tumble across the page.

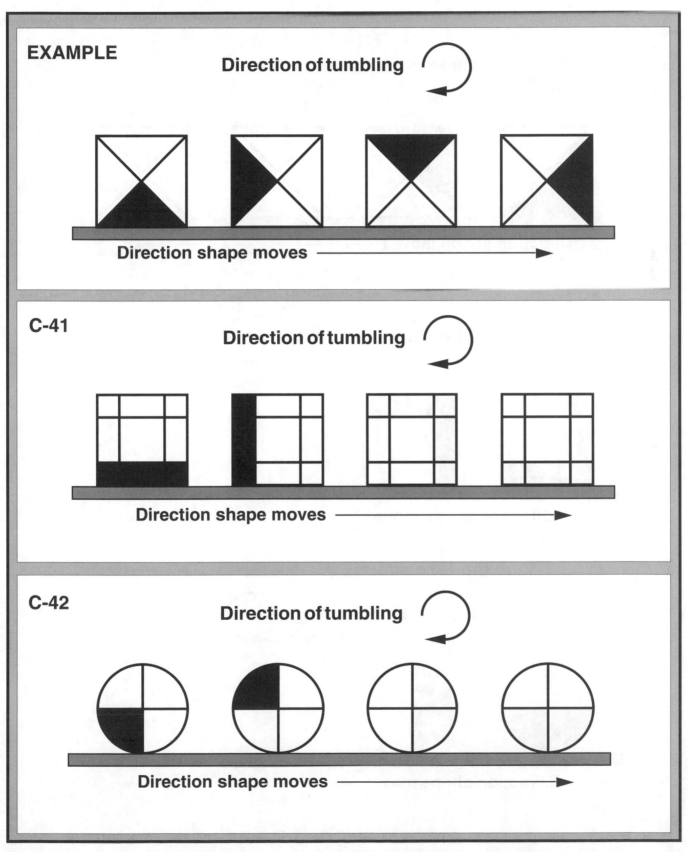

TUMBLING—SHADING

DIRECTIONS: As a shape tumbles along, the side that is on the ground changes. Darken the final two figures to show how they look as they tumble across the page.

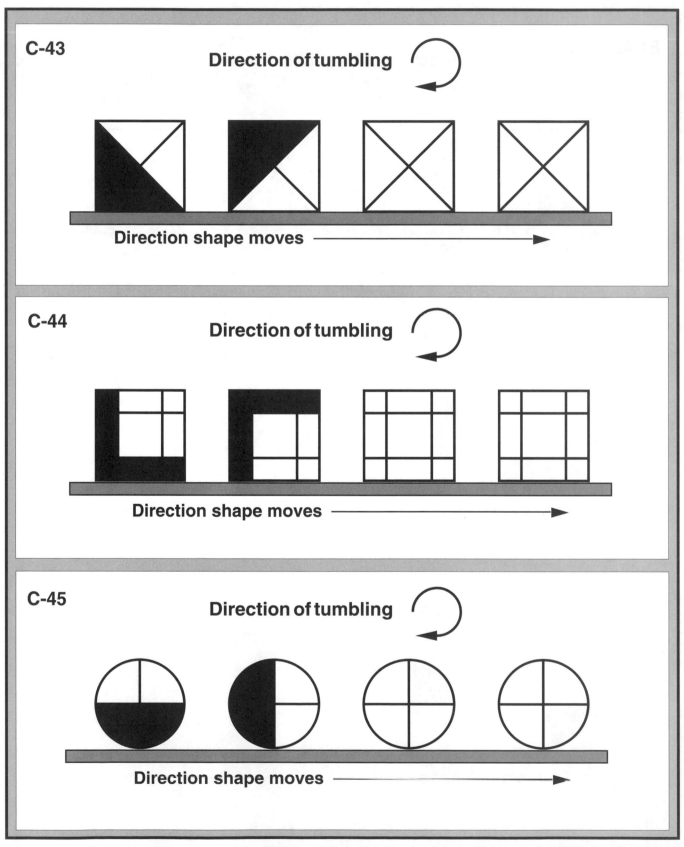

TUMBLING—DRAWING

DIRECTIONS: Build each figure with interlocking cubes of three different colors. Tumble the figure according to the directions in each box. Color your diagram.

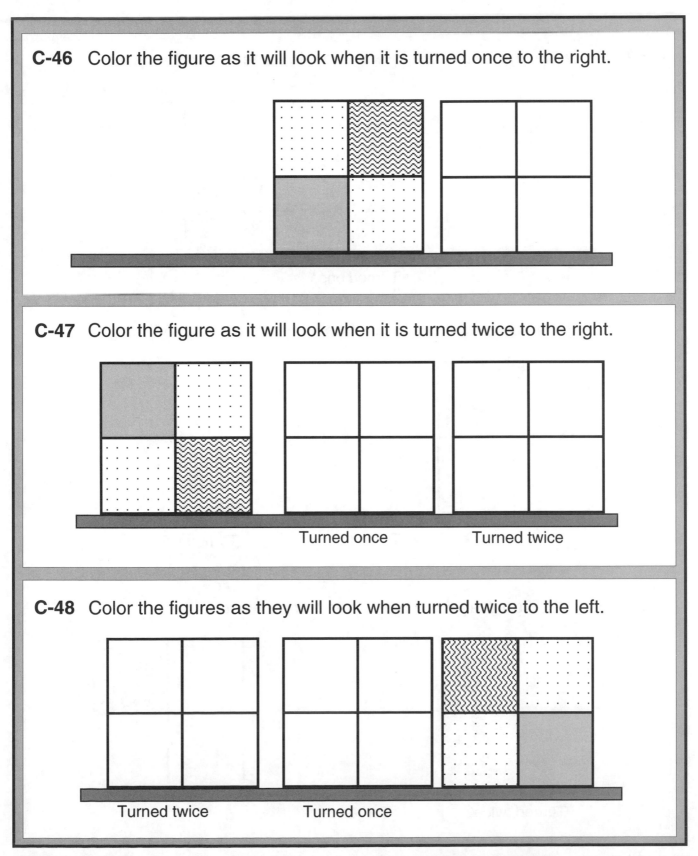

C-46 Color the figure as it will look when it is turned once to the right.

C-47 Color the figure as it will look when it is turned twice to the right.

Turned once   Turned twice

C-48 Color the figures as they will look when turned twice to the left.

Turned twice   Turned once

TUMBLING—DRAWING

DIRECTIONS: Build each figure with interlocking cubes of three different colors. Tumble the figure according to the directions in each box. Color your diagram.

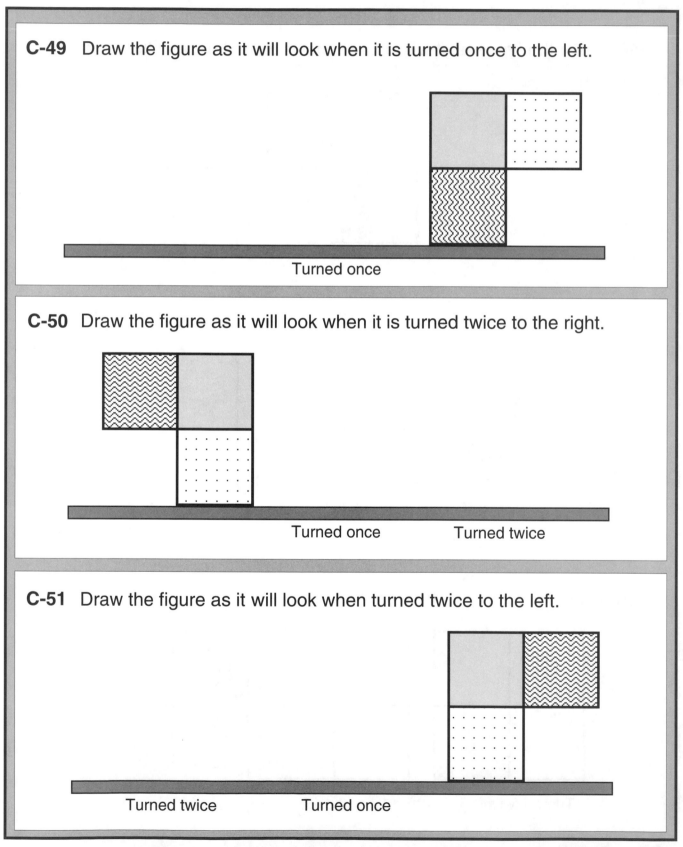

C-49 Draw the figure as it will look when it is turned once to the left.

Turned once

C-50 Draw the figure as it will look when it is turned twice to the right.

Turned once   Turned twice

C-51 Draw the figure as it will look when turned twice to the left.

Turned twice   Turned once

WHICH FIGURE COMES NEXT?—SELECT

DIRECTIONS: Circle the figure that comes next.

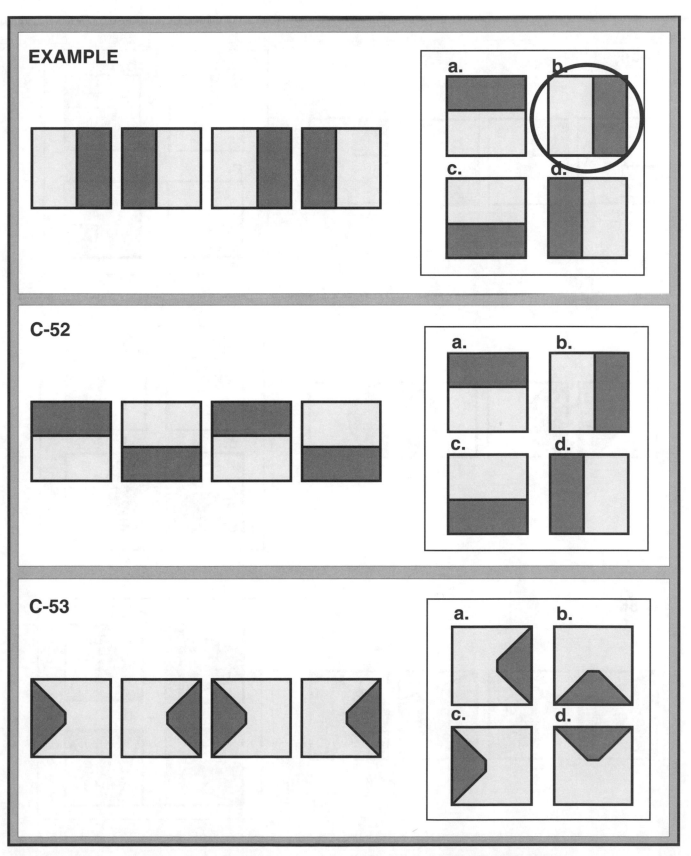

EXAMPLE

C-52

C-53

WHICH FIGURE COMES NEXT?—SELECT

DIRECTIONS: Circle the figure that comes next.

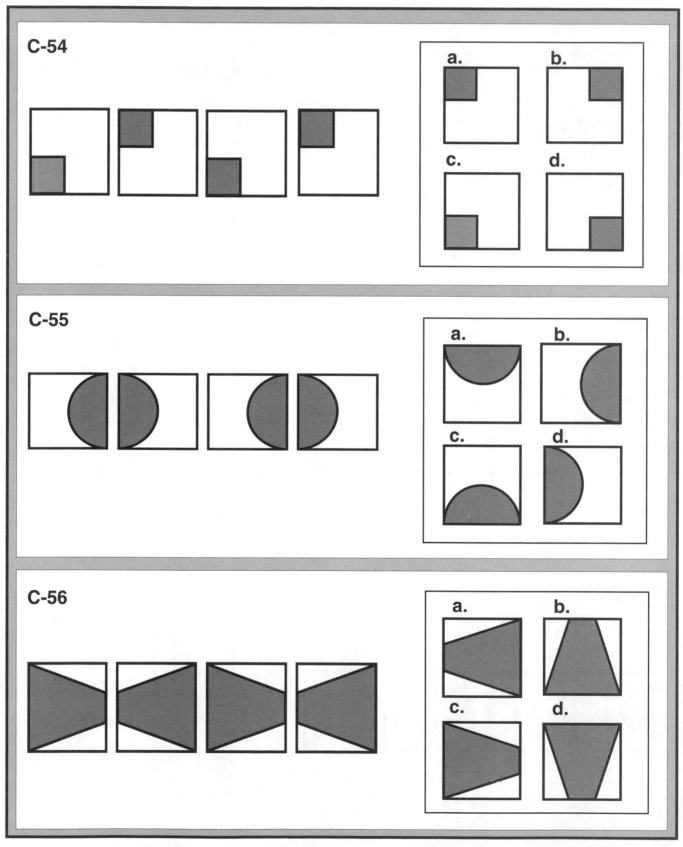

© 1997 CRITICAL THINKING BOOKS & SOFTWARE, P. O. BOX 448, PACIFIC GROVE, CA 93950 • 800-458-4849

WHICH FIGURE COMES NEXT?—SELECT

DIRECTIONS: Circle the figure that comes next.

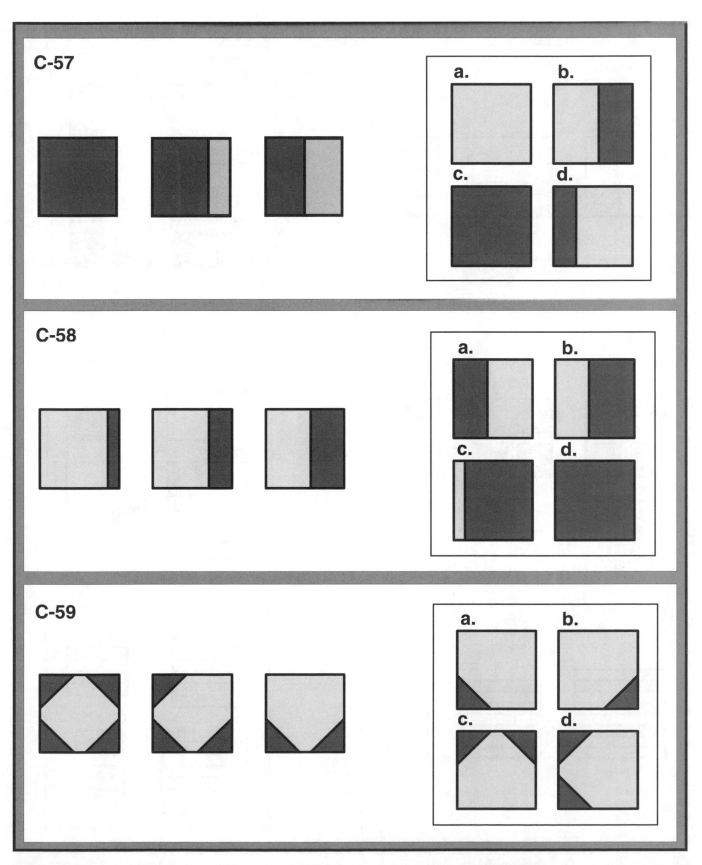

WHICH FIGURE COMES NEXT?—SELECT

DIRECTIONS: Circle the figure that comes next.

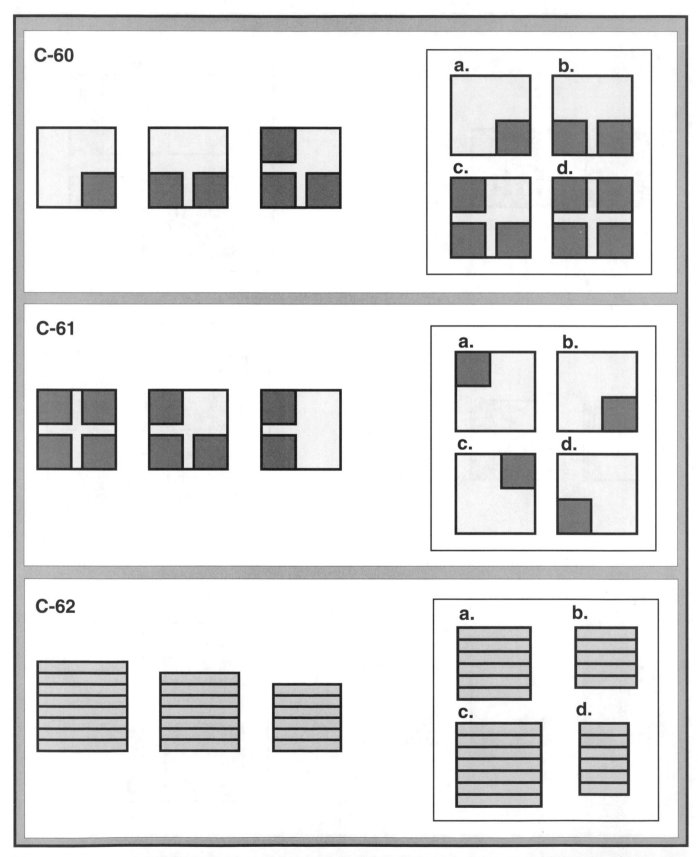

WHICH FIGURE COMES NEXT?—DRAW IT!

DIRECTIONS: Complete the sequence. Finish drawing the figure that comes next.

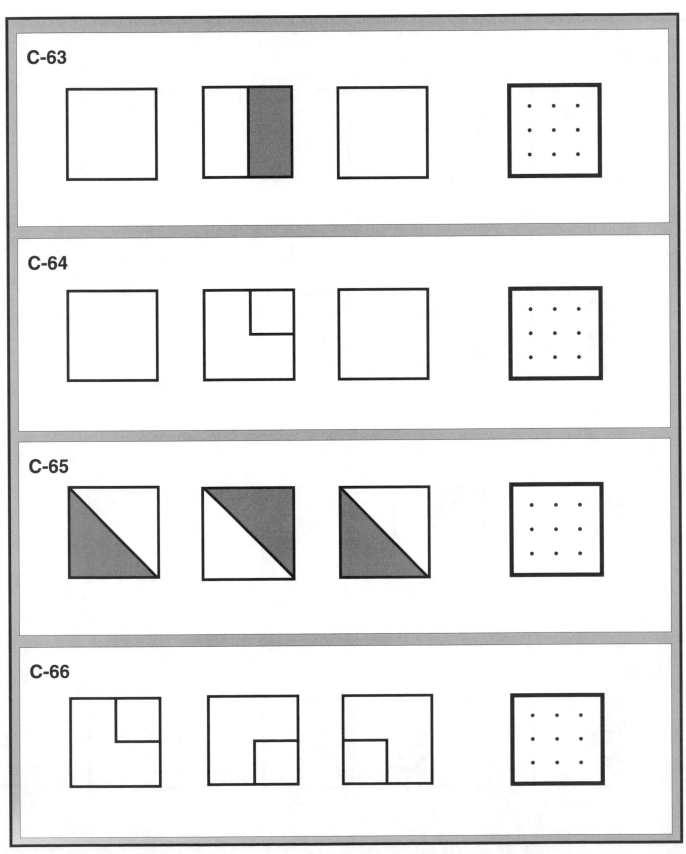

WHICH FIGURE COMES NEXT?—DRAW IT!

DIRECTIONS: Complete the sequence. Finish drawing the figure that comes next.

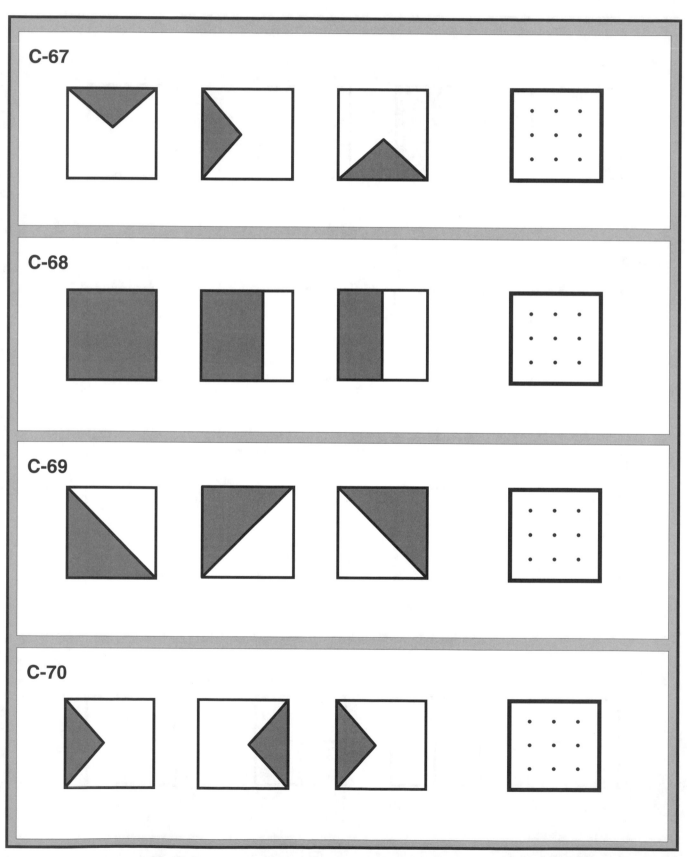

WHICH FIGURE COMES NEXT?—DRAW IT!

DIRECTIONS: Complete the sequence. Finish drawing the figure that comes next.

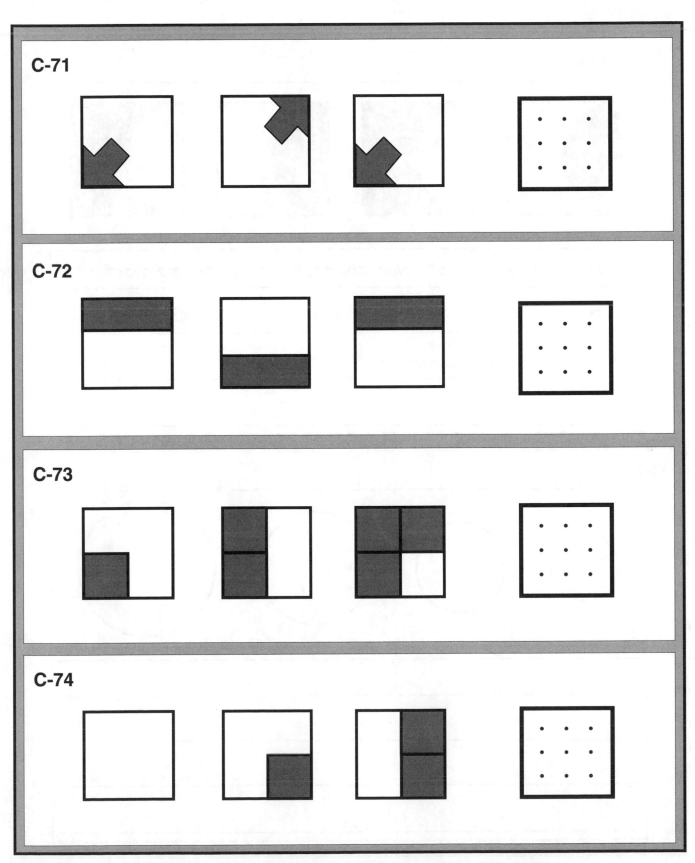

DESCRIBE A SEQUENCE

DIRECTIONS: Look at each sequence. Decide how the figures are changing. Write a description of the sequence on the lines below. Use complete sentences in your descriptions.

EXAMPLE

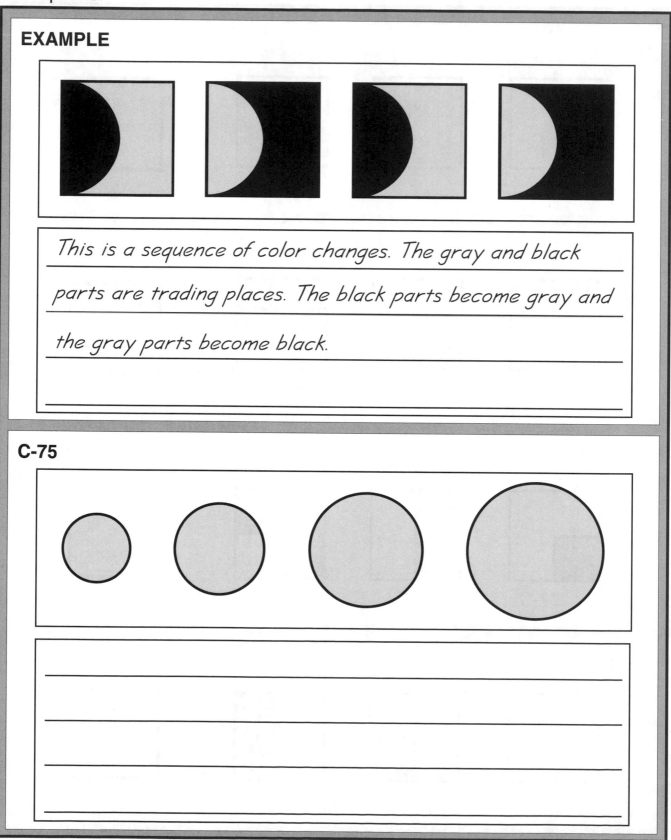

This is a sequence of color changes. The gray and black parts are trading places. The black parts become gray and the gray parts become black.

C-75

DESCRIBE A SEQUENCE

DIRECTIONS: Look at each sequence. Decide how the figures are changing. Write a description of the sequence on the lines below. Use complete sentences in your descriptions.

C-76

C-77

DESCRIBE A SEQUENCE

DIRECTIONS: Look at each sequence. Decide how the figures are changing. Write a description of the sequence on the lines below. Use complete sentences in your descriptions.

C-78

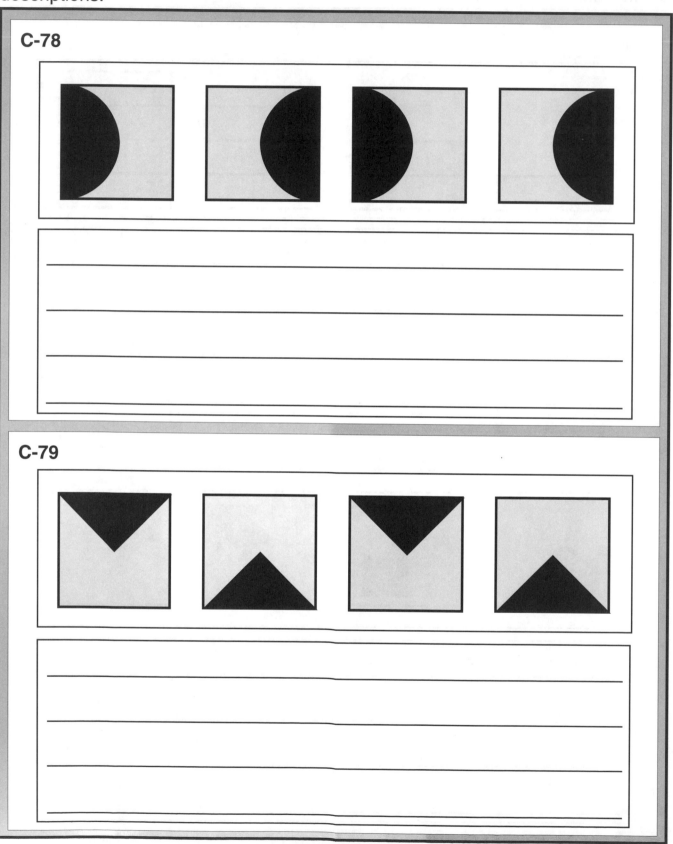

C-79

DESCRIBE A SEQUENCE

DIRECTIONS: Look at each sequence. Decide how the figures are changing. Write a description of the sequence on the lines below. Use complete sentences in your descriptions.

C-80

C-81

A SEQUENCE OF POLYGONS

DIRECTIONS: Look at the three polygons in the box. Cut the shapes apart. Arrange or draw them on the diagram.

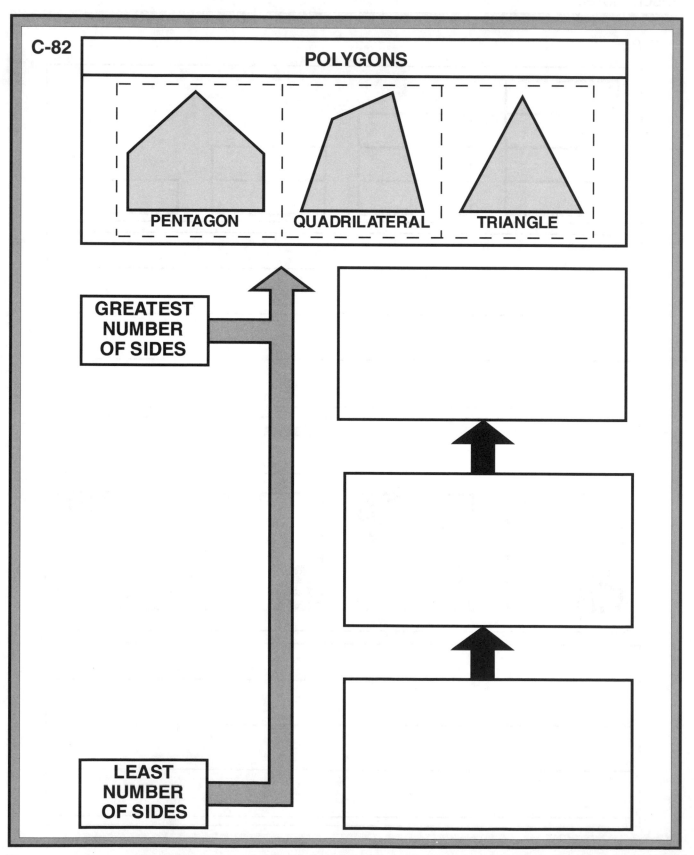

A SEQUENCE OF ANGLES

DIRECTIONS: Look at the three kinds of angles in the box. An angle is the shape made when two straight lines meet. On the diagram below, draw and label the angles from smallest to largest.

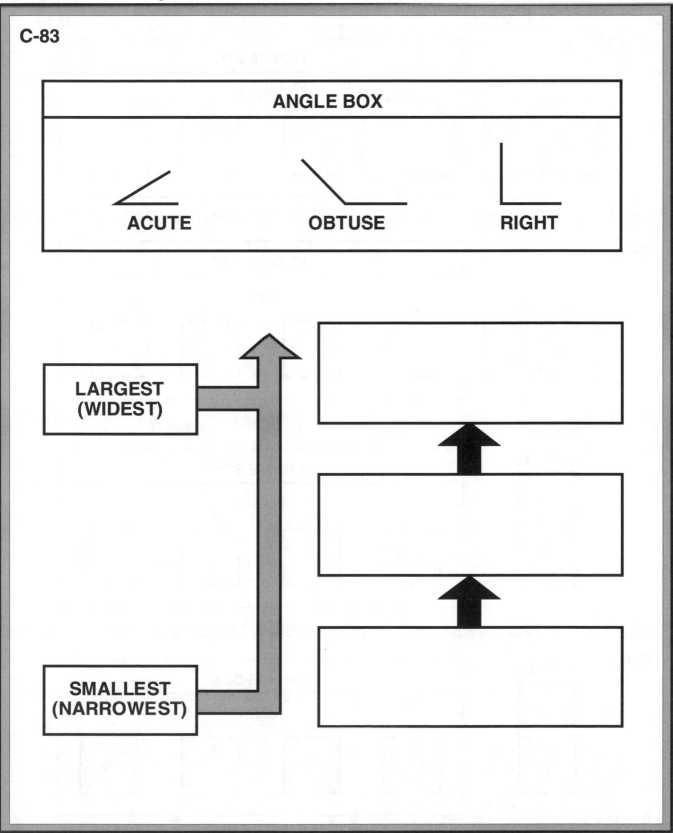

PAPER FOLDING—SELECT

DIRECTIONS: The figure on the left represents a sheet of paper with holes punched in it. How will the sheet look when folded along the dotted line? Circle the correct answer in the choice box.

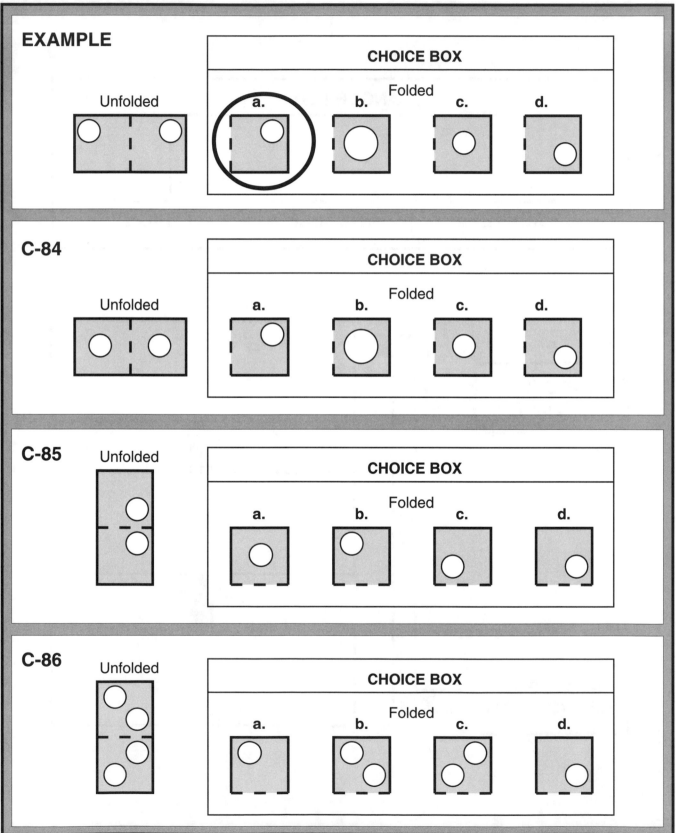

PAPER FOLDING—SELECT

DIRECTIONS: The figure on the left represents a sheet of paper with holes punched in it that has been folded along the dotted line. How will the sheet look when it is unfolded? Circle the correct answer in the choice box.

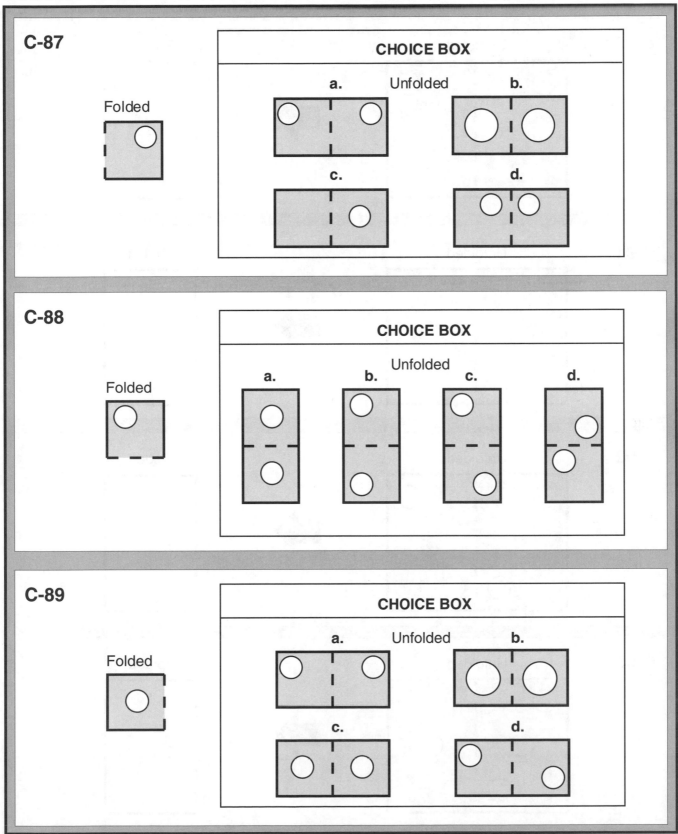

PAPER FOLDING—DRAW

DIRECTIONS: The figures on the left represent sheets of paper with holes punched in them. They are to be folded along the dotted line. Draw each sheet the way it will look after being folded.

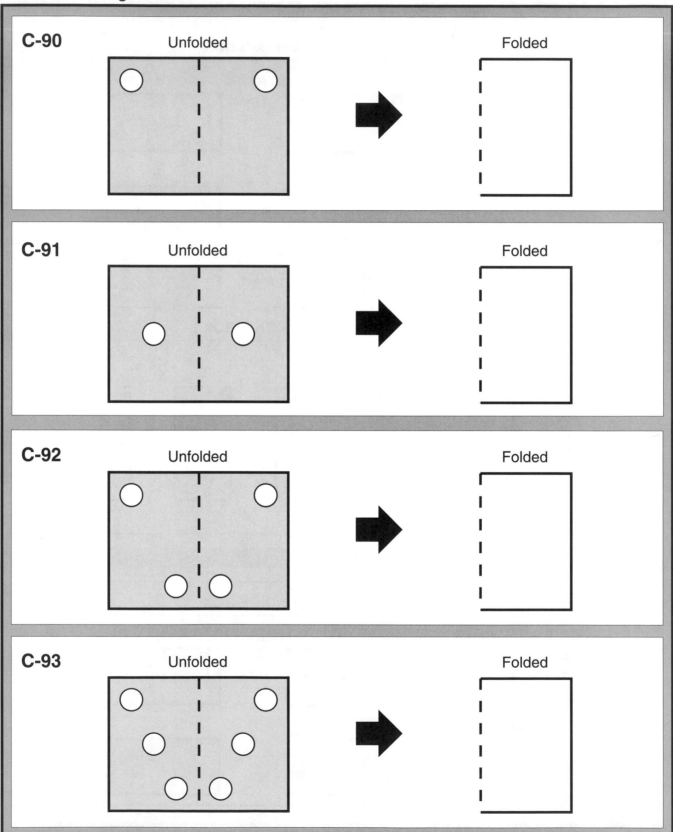

PAPER FOLDING—DRAW

DIRECTIONS: The figures on the left represent sheets of paper with holes punched in them. They are folded along the dotted line. Draw each sheet as it will look when it is unfolded.

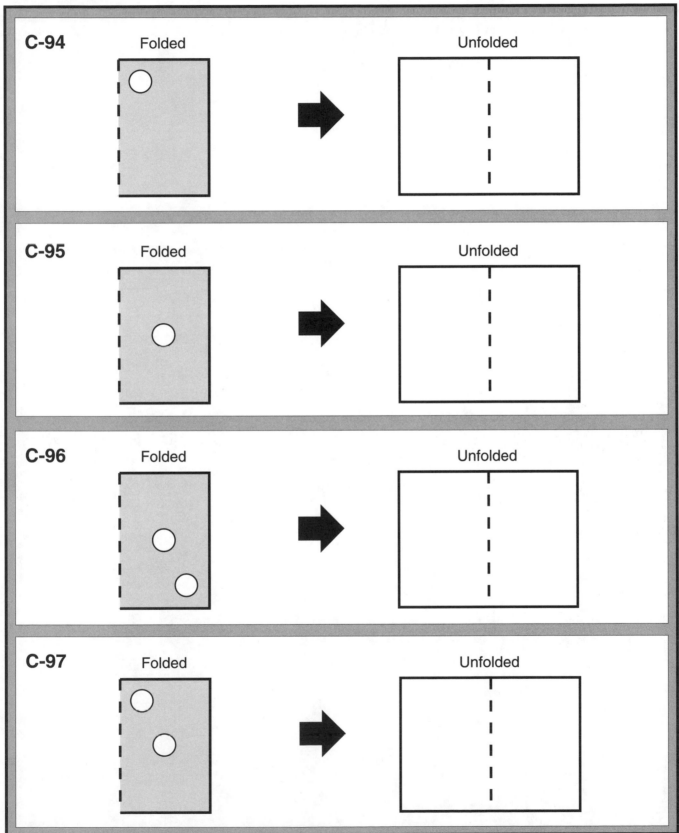

CHAPTER FOUR

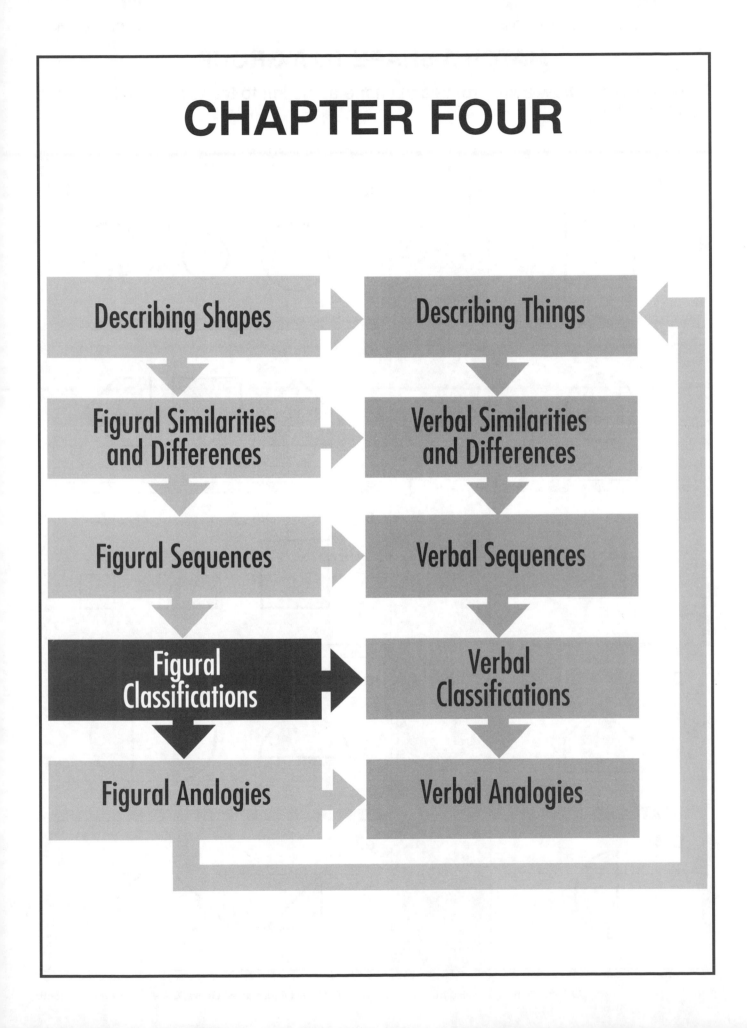

Describing Shapes → Describing Things

Figural Similarities and Differences → Verbal Similarities and Differences

Figural Sequences → Verbal Sequences

Figural Classifications → Verbal Classifications

Figural Analogies → Verbal Analogies

MATCH A SHAPE TO A GROUP

DIRECTIONS: Draw a line from each shape at the left to the group on the right in which it belongs.

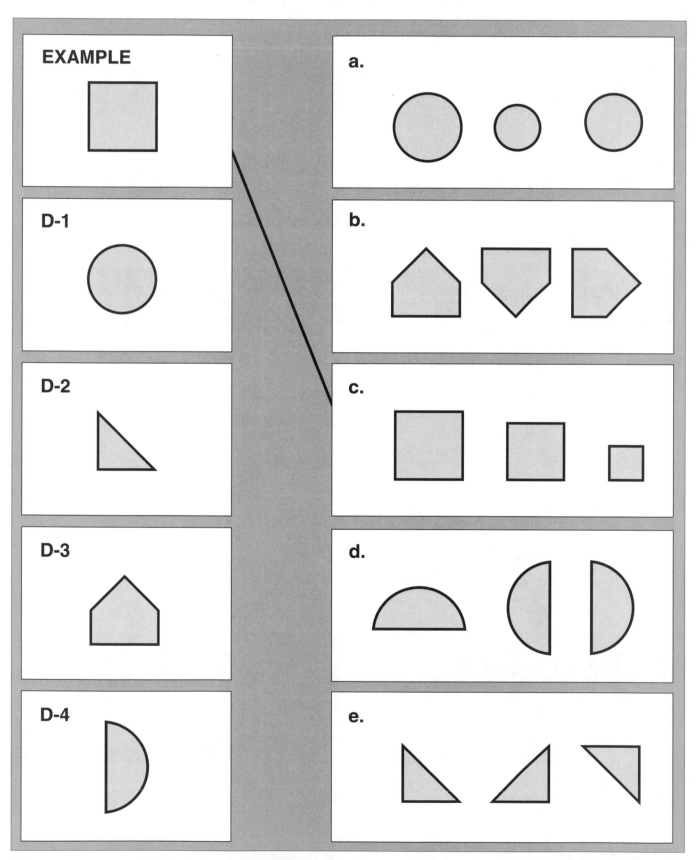

MATCH A SHAPE TO A GROUP

DIRECTIONS: Draw a line from each shape on the left to the group on the right in which it belongs.

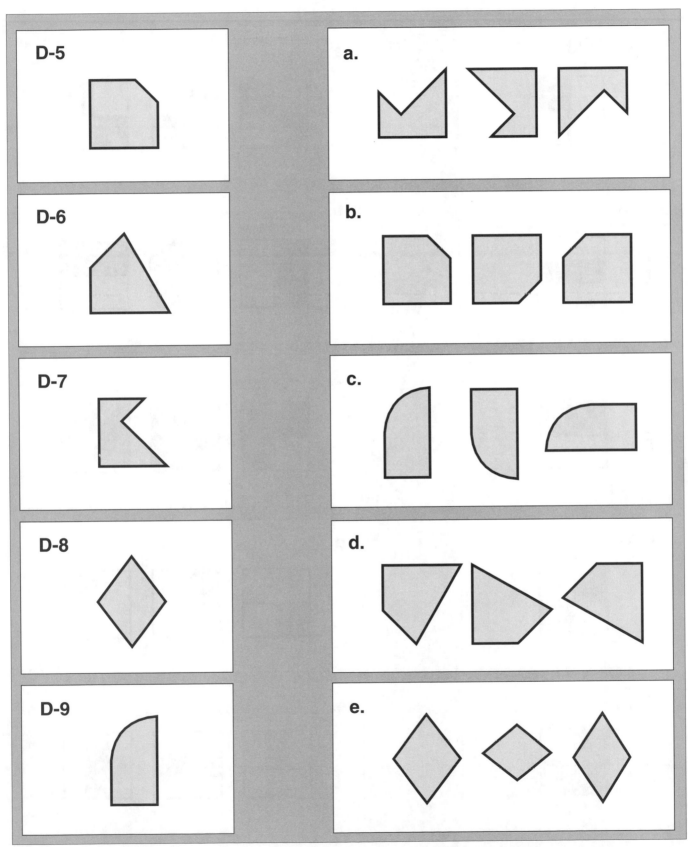

MATCH A PATTERN TO A GROUP

DIRECTIONS: Sometimes figures are grouped by patterns. Match each shape on the left with the correct group on the right by drawing a line from the shape to the group (class) having the same pattern.

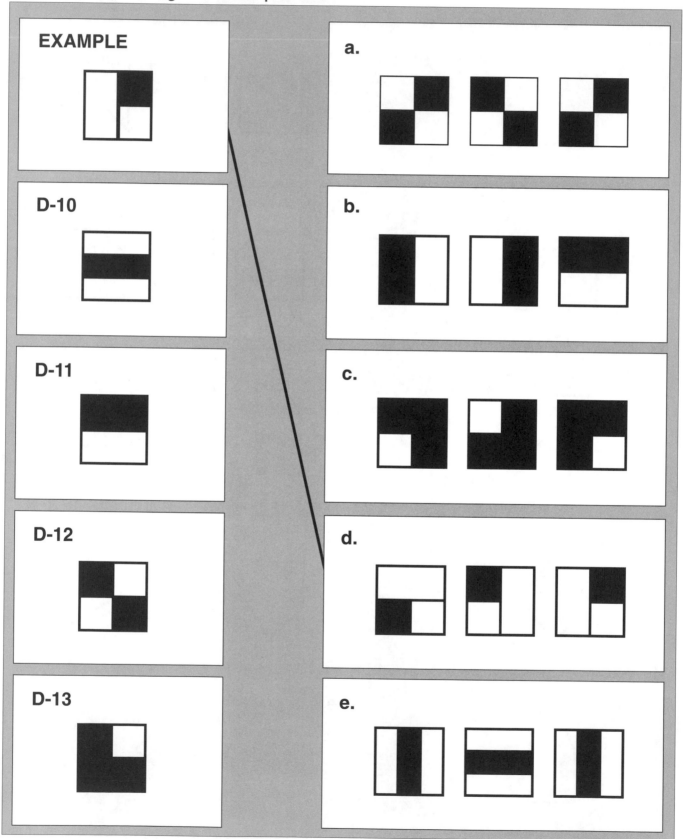

MATCH A PATTERN TO A GROUP

DIRECTIONS: Sometimes figures are grouped by patterns. Match each shape on the left with the correct group on the right by drawing a line from the shape to the group (class) having the same pattern.

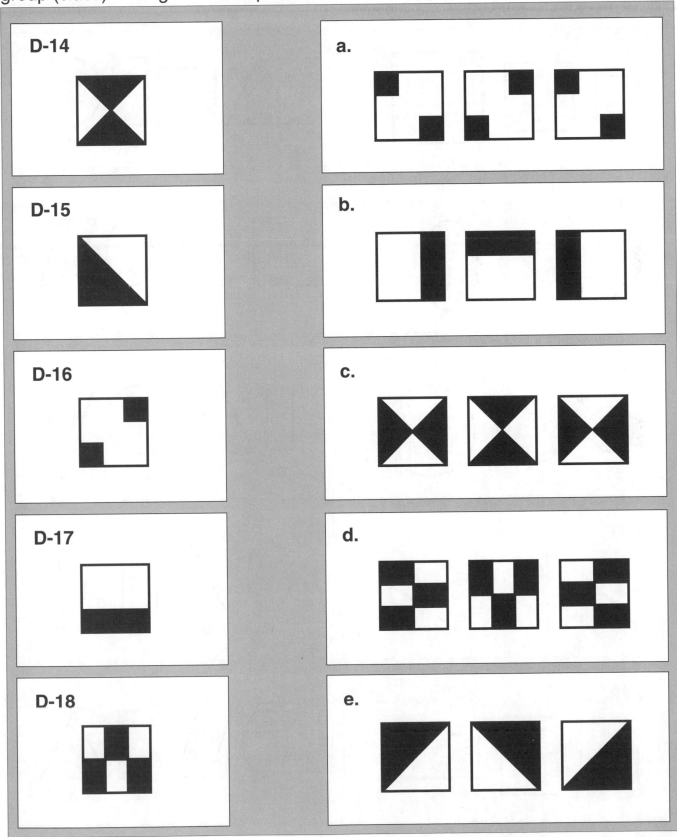

SELECT A SHAPE THAT BELONGS TO A GROUP

DIRECTIONS: The box on the left contains several figures of the same shape. The box on the right contains several lettered shapes. Check or circle the shape on the right that belongs to the group at the left.

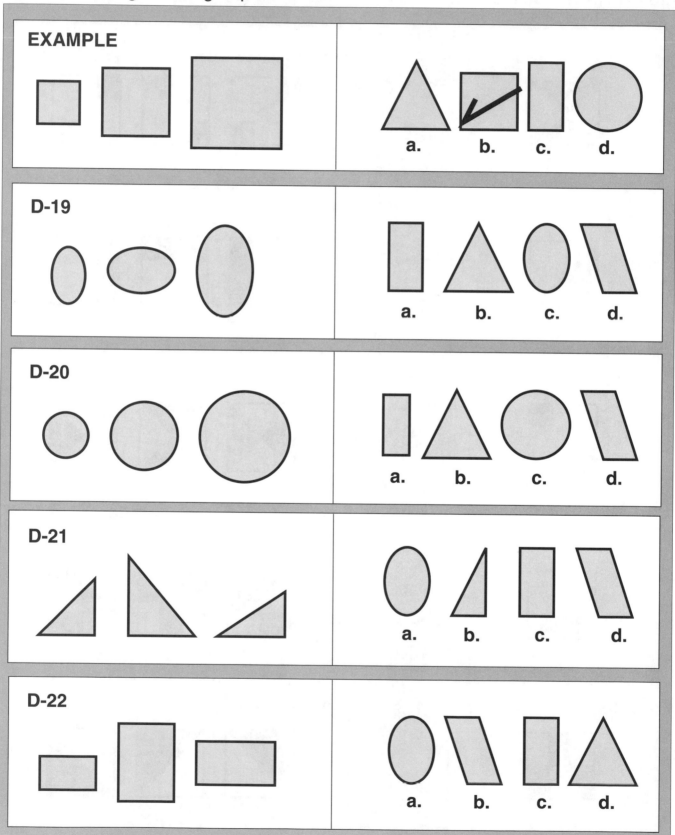

EXAMPLE

a. b. c. d.

D-19

a. b. c. d.

D-20

a. b. c. d.

D-21

a. b. c. d.

D-22

a. b. c. d.

SELECT A SHAPE THAT BELONGS TO A GROUP

DIRECTIONS: The box on the left contains several figures of the same shape. The box on the right contains several lettered shapes. Check or circle the shape on the right that belongs to the group at the left.

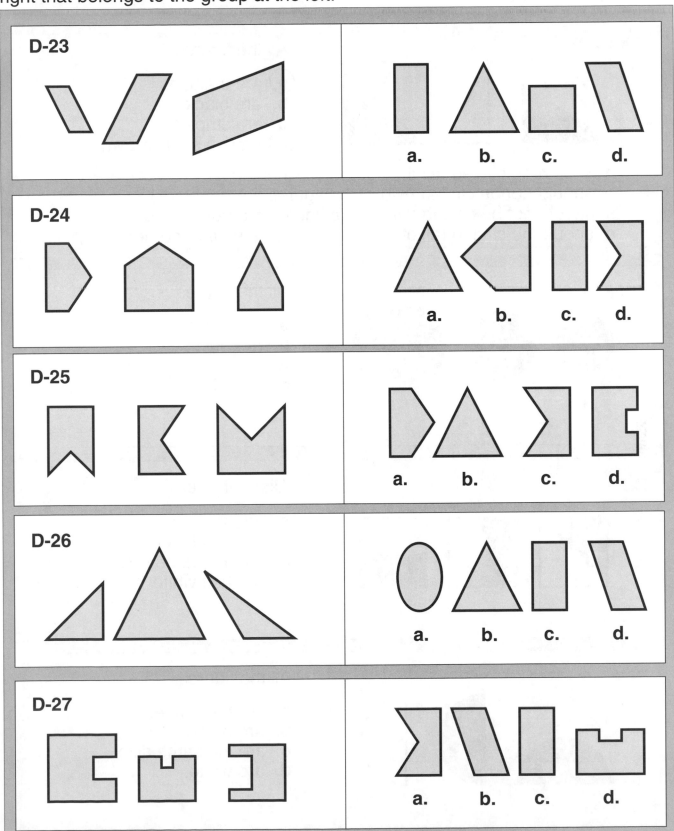

DESCRIBING CLASSES

DIRECTIONS: Circle the letter in front of each true statement.

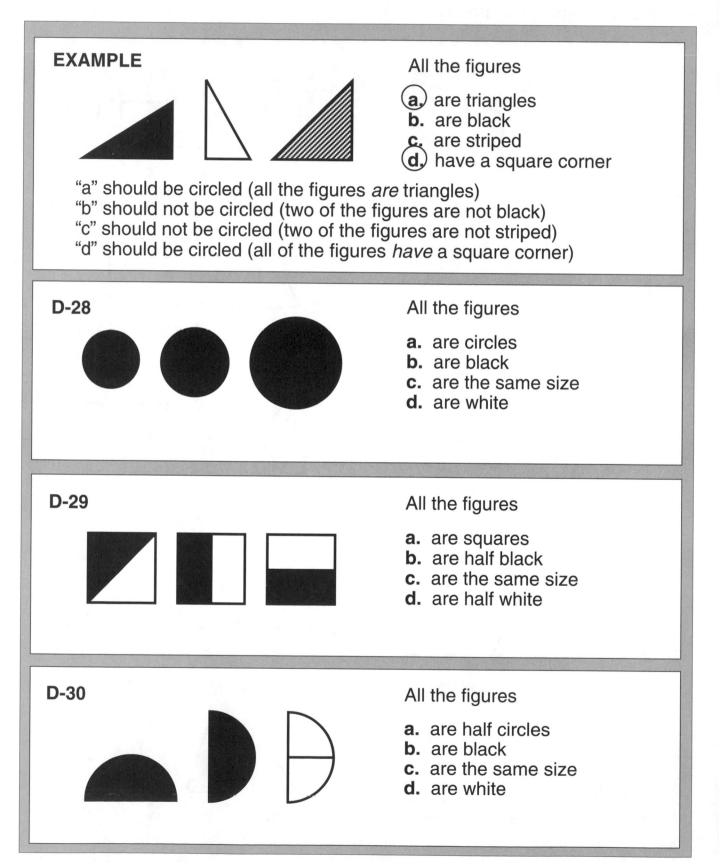

EXAMPLE

All the figures

a. are triangles
b. are black
c. are striped
d. have a square corner

"a" should be circled (all the figures *are* triangles)
"b" should not be circled (two of the figures are not black)
"c" should not be circled (two of the figures are not striped)
"d" should be circled (all of the figures *have* a square corner)

D-28

All the figures

a. are circles
b. are black
c. are the same size
d. are white

D-29

All the figures

a. are squares
b. are half black
c. are the same size
d. are half white

D-30

All the figures

a. are half circles
b. are black
c. are the same size
d. are white

DESCRIBING CLASSES

DIRECTIONS: Circle the letter in front of each true statement.

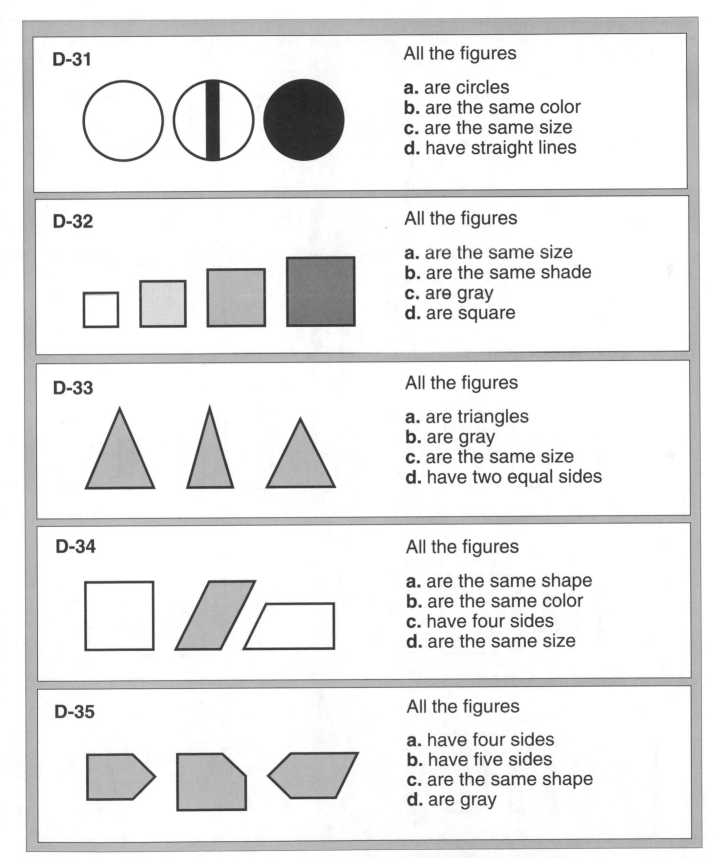

D-31

All the figures

a. are circles
b. are the same color
c. are the same size
d. have straight lines

D-32

All the figures

a. are the same size
b. are the same shade
c. are gray
d. are square

D-33

All the figures

a. are triangles
b. are gray
c. are the same size
d. have two equal sides

D-34

All the figures

a. are the same shape
b. are the same color
c. have four sides
d. are the same size

D-35

All the figures

a. have four sides
b. have five sides
c. are the same shape
d. are gray

MATCHING CLASSES BY SHAPE

DIRECTIONS: For every box on the left, there is a box on the right with the same shapes. Draw lines between boxes that have shapes of the same class.

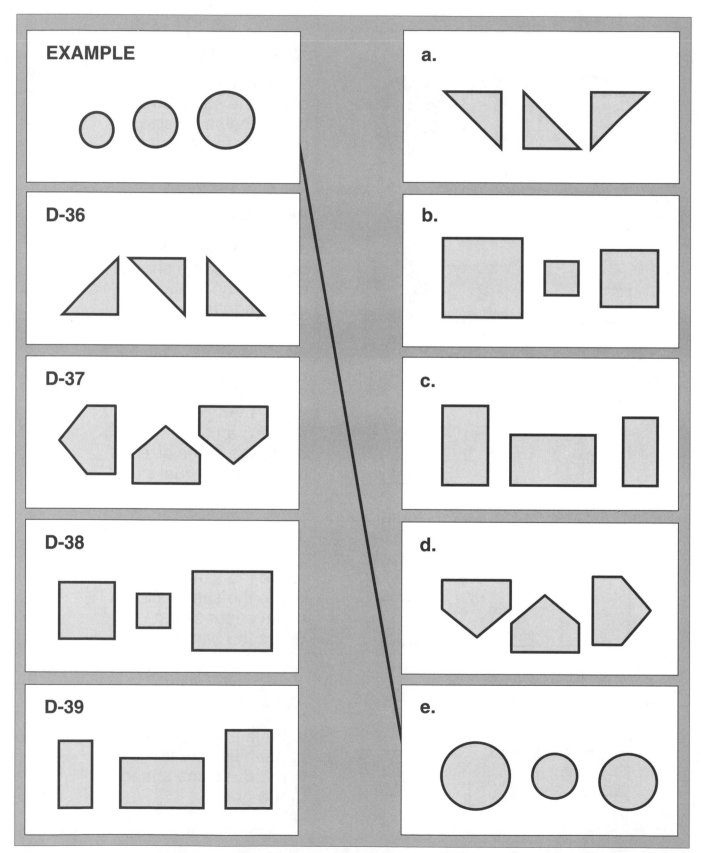

MATCHING CLASSES BY SHAPE

DIRECTIONS: Draw lines between boxes that have shapes that belong to the same class.

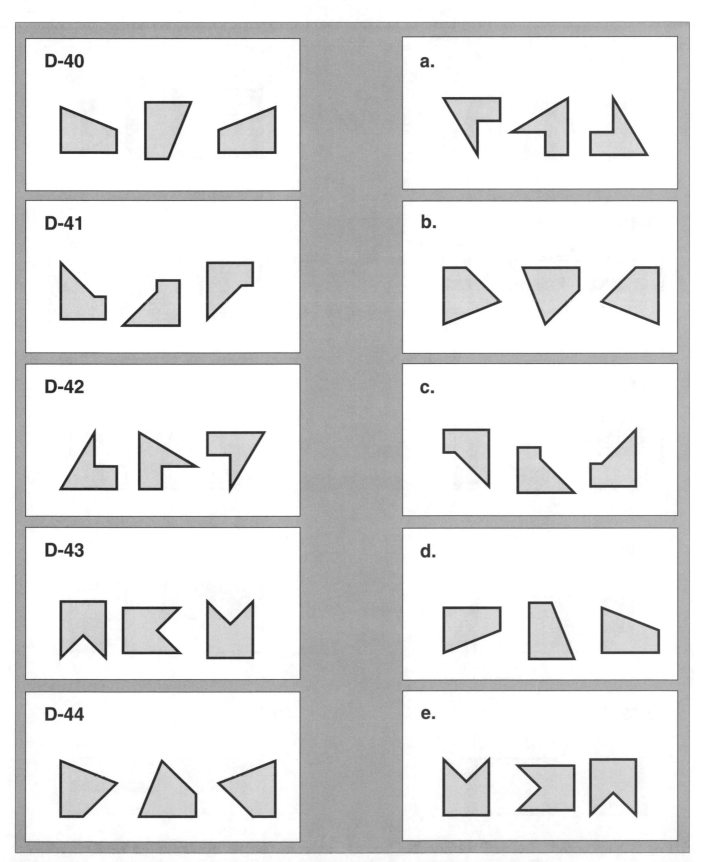

MATCHING CLASSES BY PATTERN

DIRECTIONS: Draw a line from each pattern on the left to a pattern on the right that belongs to the same class.

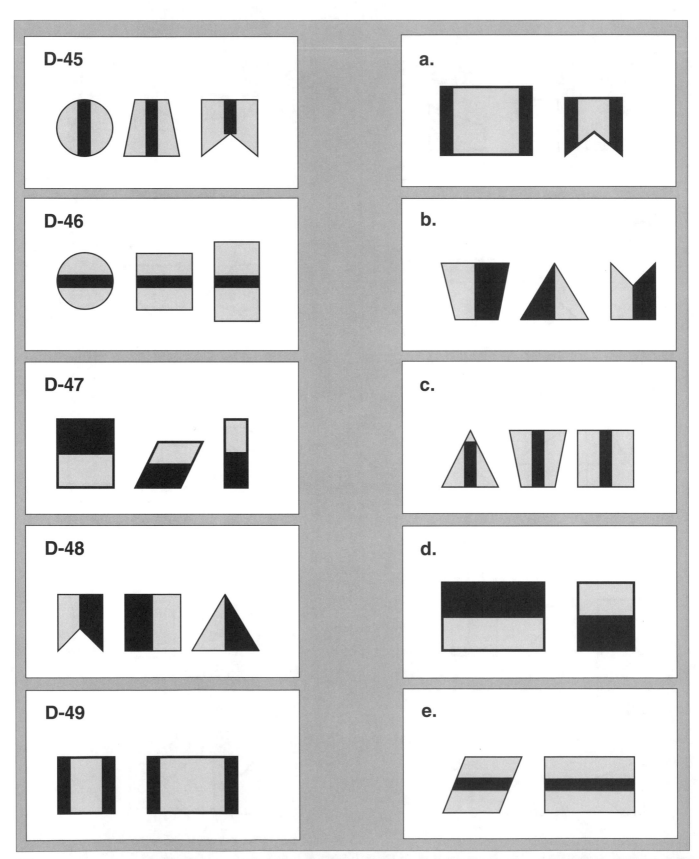

© 1997 CRITICAL THINKING BOOKS & SOFTWARE, P. O. BOX 448, PACIFIC GROVE, CA 93950 • 800-458-4849

CLASSIFYING BY SHAPE—FIND THE EXCEPTION

DIRECTIONS: In each row, cross out the shape that does <u>not</u> belong to the class.

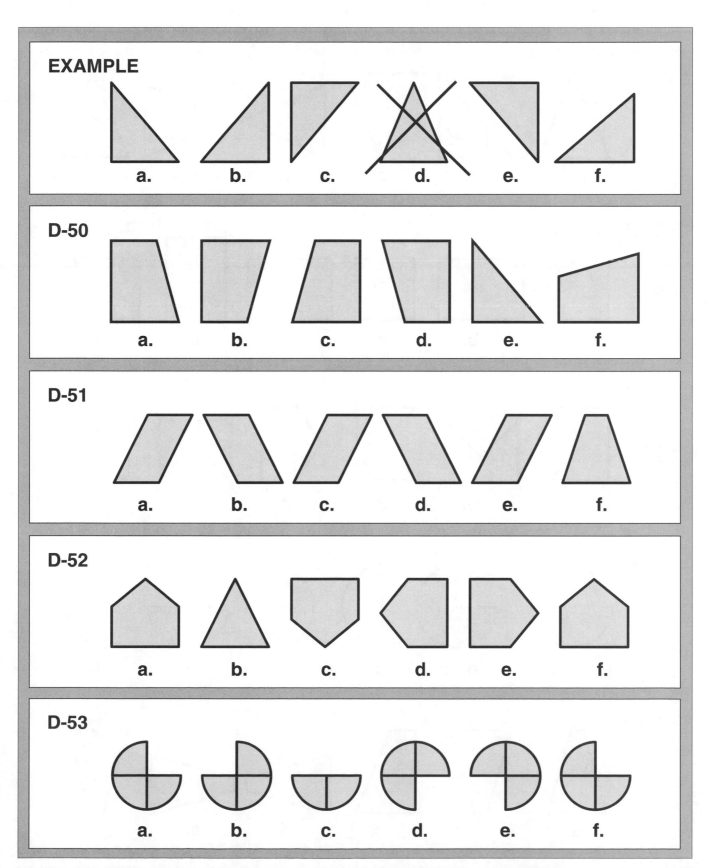

CLASSIFYING BY SHAPE—FIND THE EXCEPTION

DIRECTIONS: In each row, cross out the shape that does <u>not</u> belong to the class.

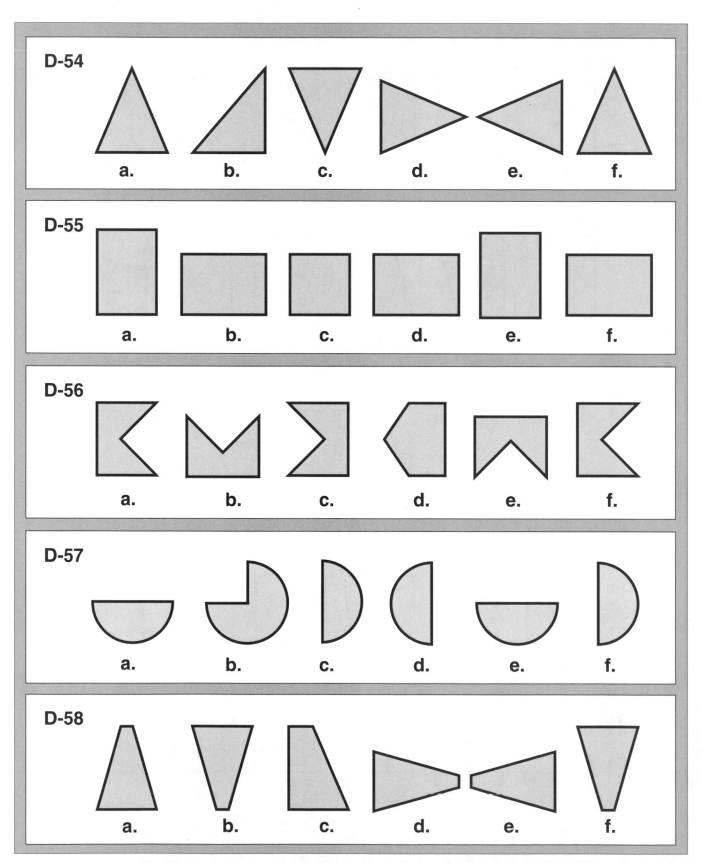

CLASSIFYING BY PATTERN—FIND THE EXCEPTION

DIRECTIONS: In each row, cross out the figure that does <u>not</u> belong to the class.

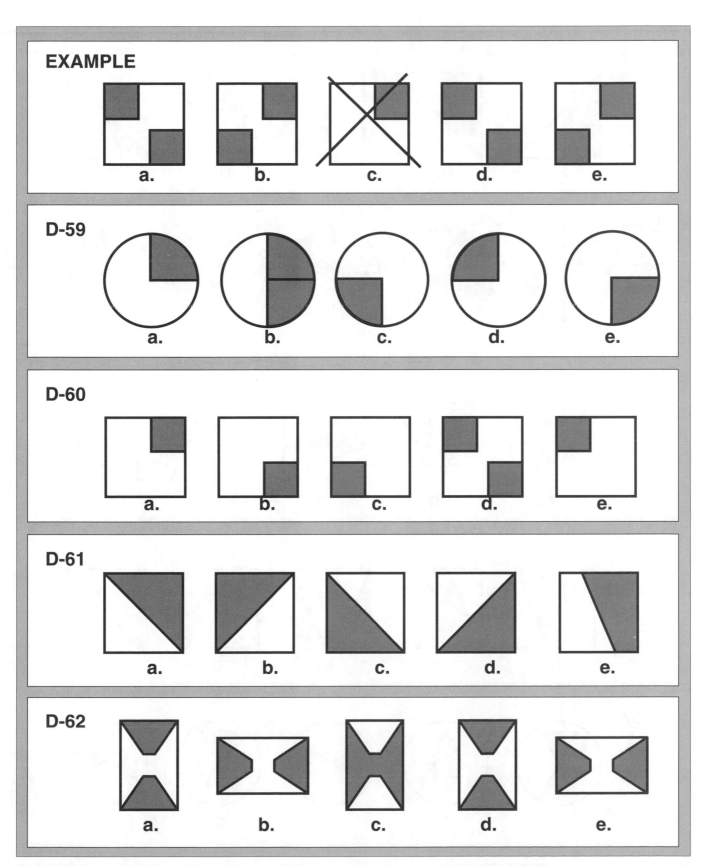

CLASSIFYING BY PATTERN—FIND THE EXCEPTION

DIRECTIONS: In each row, cross out the figure that does <u>not</u> belong to the class.

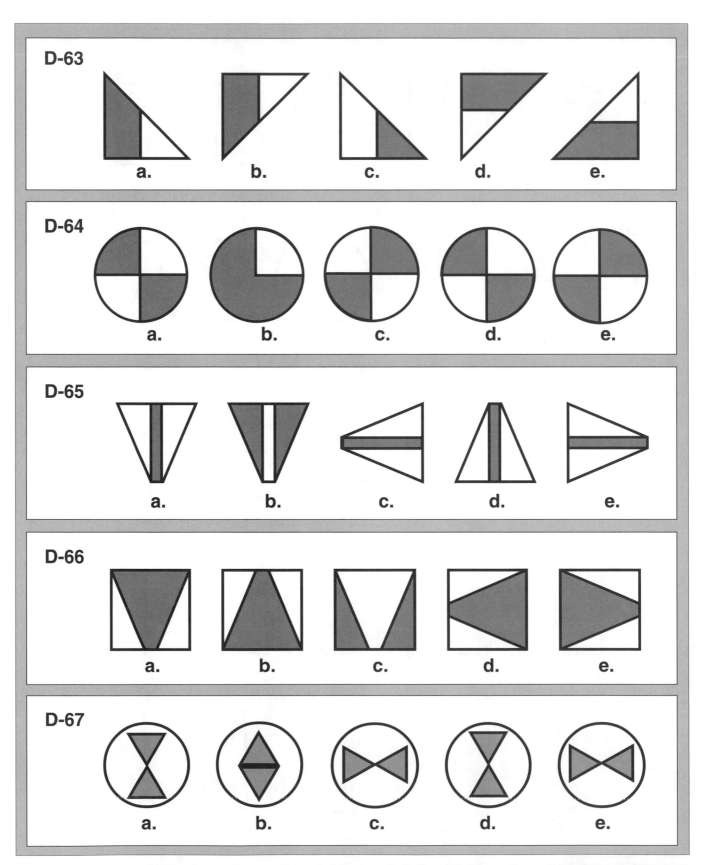

CLASSIFYING MORE THAN ONE WAY

DIRECTIONS: On the line beside each figure, write the letters of all classes to which the figure can belong. Classes are shown at the bottom of the page.

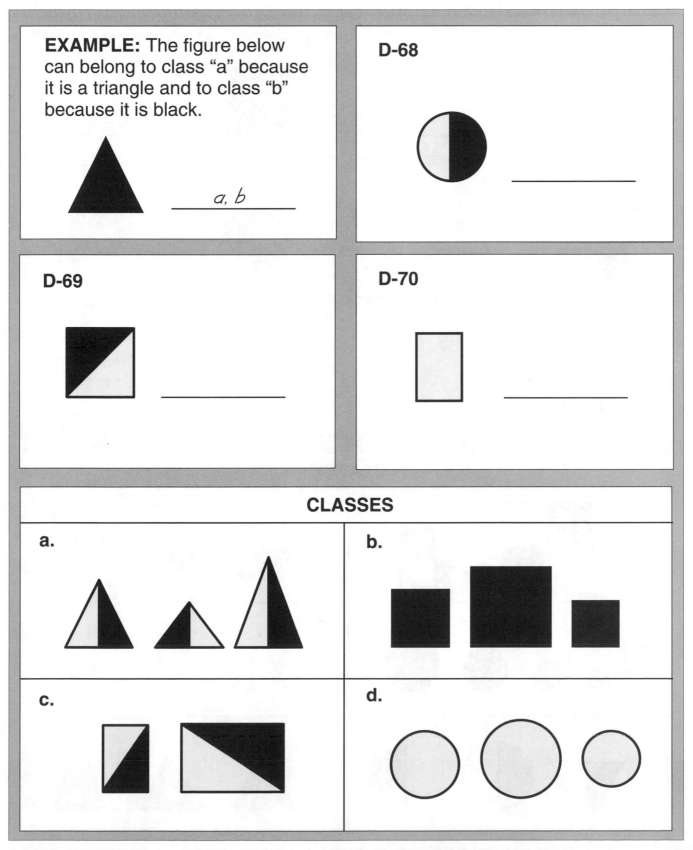

EXAMPLE: The figure below can belong to class "a" because it is a triangle and to class "b" because it is black.

a, b

D-68

D-69

D-70

CLASSES

a.

b.

c.

d.

CLASSIFYING MORE THAN ONE WAY

DIRECTIONS: On the line beside each figure, write the letters of all classes to which the figure can belong. Classes are shown at the bottom of the page.

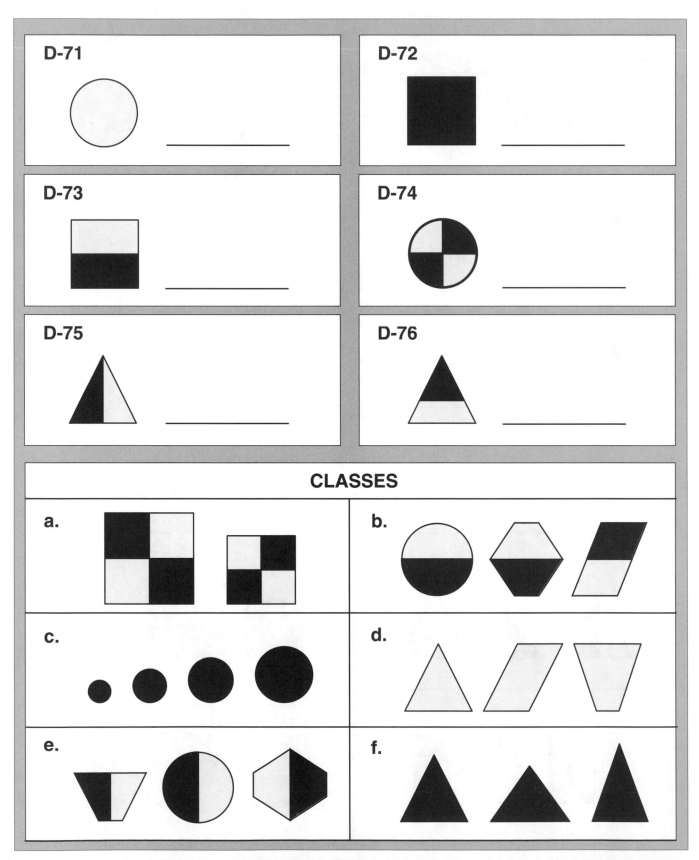

D-71

D-72

D-73

D-74

D-75

D-76

CLASSES

a.

b.

c.

d.

e.

f.

CLASSIFYING BY COLOR—SORTING

DIRECTIONS: Each shape below is made of several squares. Use two colors of interlocking cubes to build the shapes, placing one cube on each square. In the boxes at the bottom, draw and color the shapes that belong in each class.

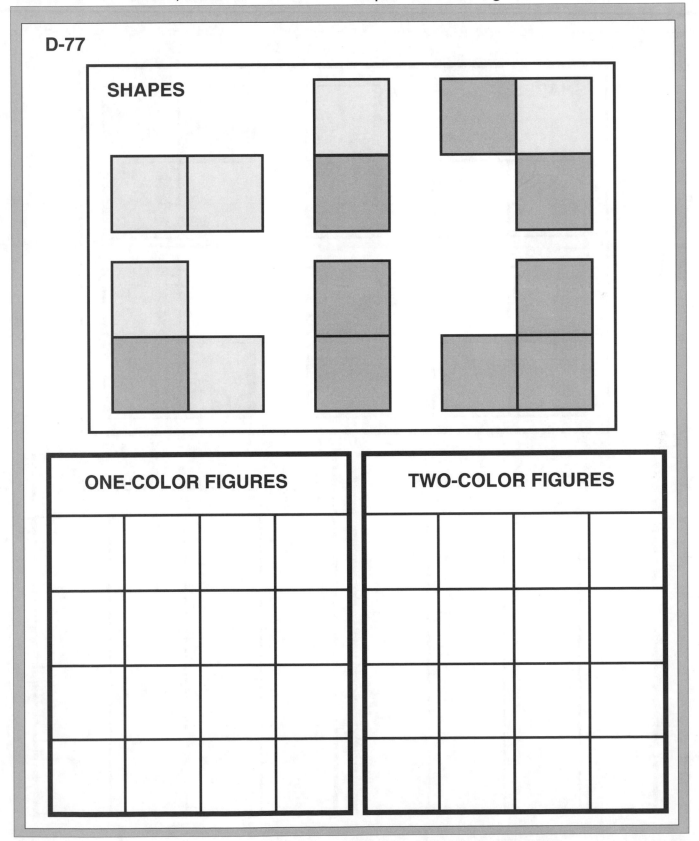

CLASSIFYING BY SHAPE—SORTING

DIRECTIONS: Each shape below is made of several squares. Use two colors of interlocking cubes to build the shapes, placing one cube on each square. In the boxes at the bottom, draw and color the shapes that belong in each class.

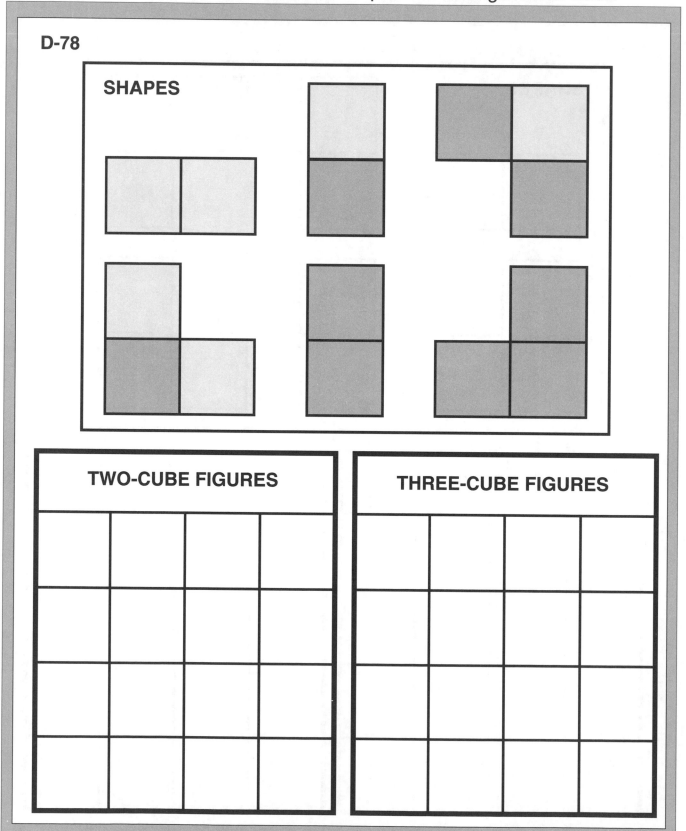

COMPLETE THE CLASS

DIRECTIONS: The shapes at the top of the page can be classified in many ways. At the bottom of the page, list the numbers of the shapes that complete each group.

EXAMPLES

1, 4, _____

Answer: 1, 4, ___7___

(The shapes numbered 1 and 4 are circles. Shape 7 is another shape in this class.)

2, 3, 4, _____ , _____

Answer: 2, 3, 4, ___1___ , ___5___

(Shapes 2, 3, and 4 are all gray. Shapes 1 and 5 are also gray shapes.)

D-79

2, 5, _____

D-80

6, 7, 8, _____

D-81

3, 6, _____

D-82

1, 3, 8, _____, _____, _____

COMPLETE THE CLASS

DIRECTIONS: The figures at the left can be classified in many ways. Fill in each blank with the number of the figure that completes the given group.

FIGURES FOR D-83 to D-88

D-83

1, 6, _____

D-84

1, 3, _____

D-85

2, 4, _____

D-86

2, 5, _____

D-87

7, 8, _____

D-88

3, 4, _____

FIGURES FOR D-89 to D-94

D-89

1, 2, _____

D-90

3, 6, _____

D-91

7, 8, _____

D-92

1, 4, _____

D-93

2, 5, _____

D-94

4, 5, _____

FORM A CLASS

DIRECTIONS: The figures at the left can be classified in many ways. Fill in each blank with the numbers of the figures that belong to the group described.

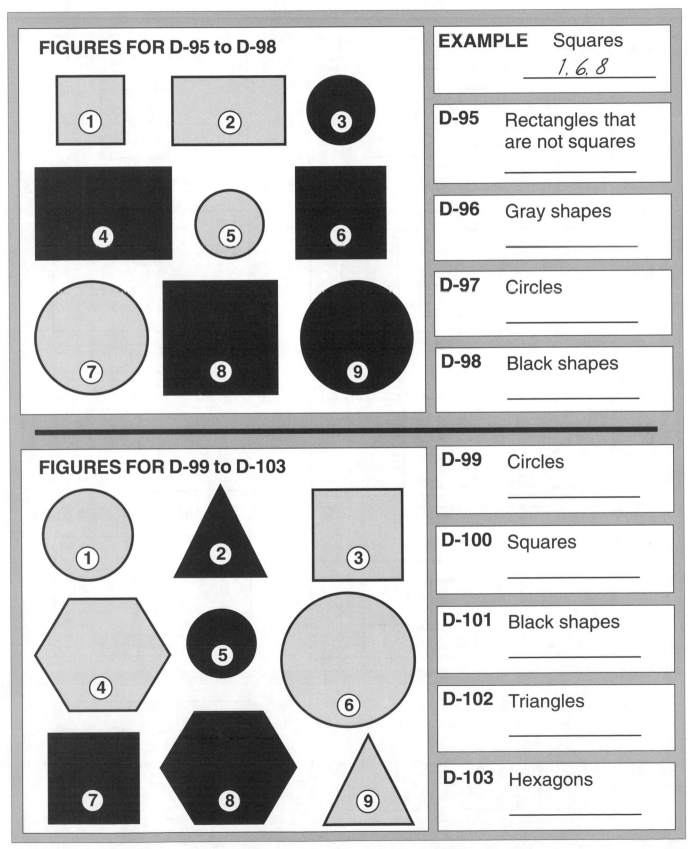

FIGURES FOR D-95 to D-98

① ② ③ ④ ⑤ ⑥ ⑦ ⑧ ⑨

FIGURES FOR D-99 to D-103

① ② ③ ④ ⑤ ⑥ ⑦ ⑧ ⑨

EXAMPLE	Squares	*1, 6, 8*
D-95	Rectangles that are not squares	_____
D-96	Gray shapes	_____
D-97	Circles	_____
D-98	Black shapes	_____
D-99	Circles	_____
D-100	Squares	_____
D-101	Black shapes	_____
D-102	Triangles	_____
D-103	Hexagons	_____

DRAW ANOTHER

DIRECTIONS: In each grid on the right, draw another figure that belongs to the group on the left.

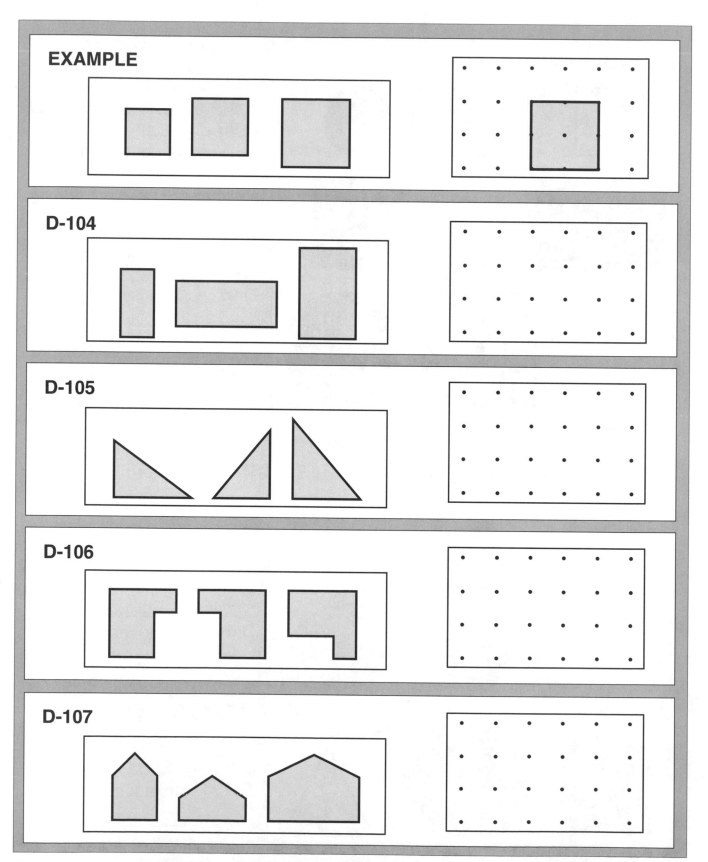

DRAW ANOTHER

DIRECTIONS: In each grid on the right, draw another figure that belongs to the group on the left.

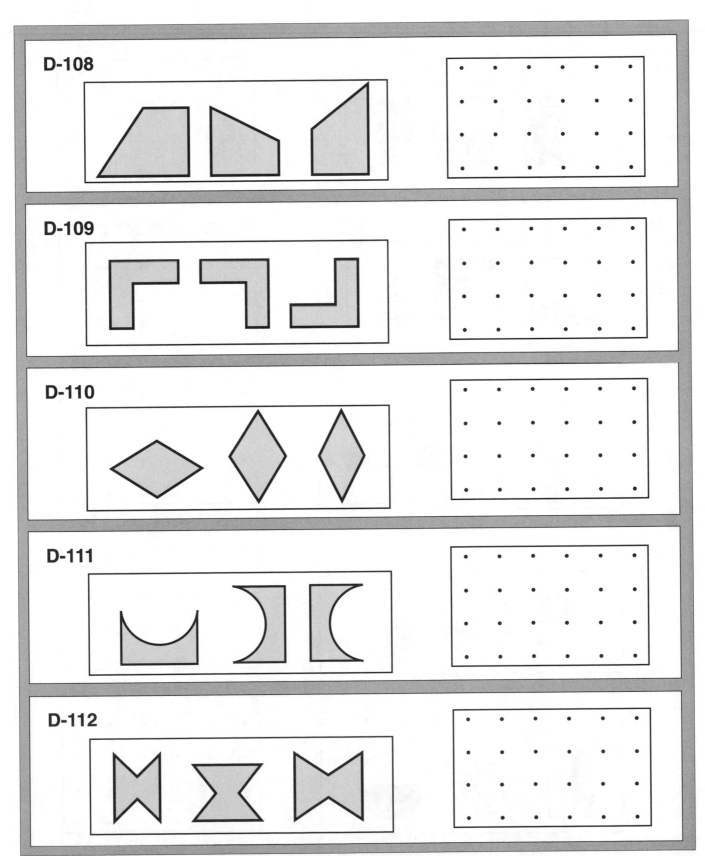

D-108

D-109

D-110

D-111

D-112

DRAW ANOTHER

DIRECTIONS: In each grid on the right, draw another figure that belongs to the group on the left.

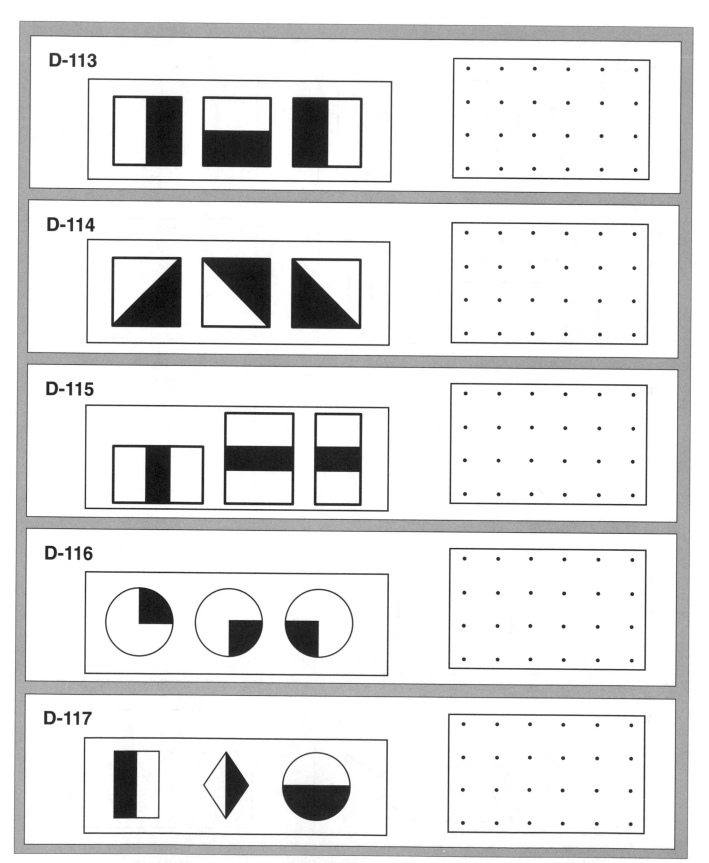

D-113

D-114

D-115

D-116

D-117

CLASSIFYING BY SHAPE—SORTING

DIRECTIONS: The figures at the top can be sorted into classes in more than one way. In the boxes at the bottom, draw and color the figures that belong in each class.

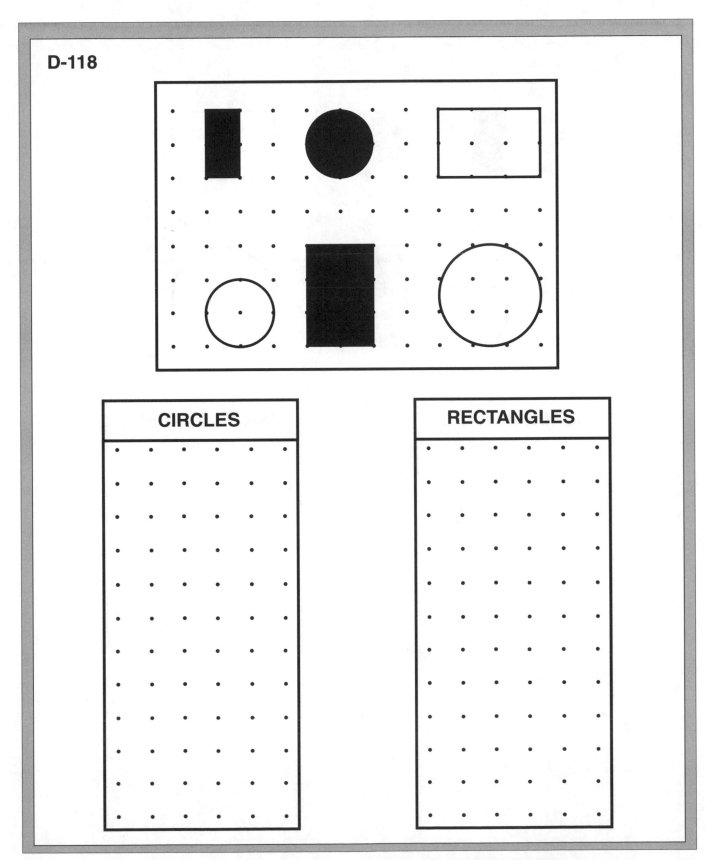

CLASSIFYING BY COLOR—SORTING

DIRECTIONS: The figures at the top can be sorted into classes in more than one way. In the boxes at the bottom, draw and color the figures that belong in each class.

D-119

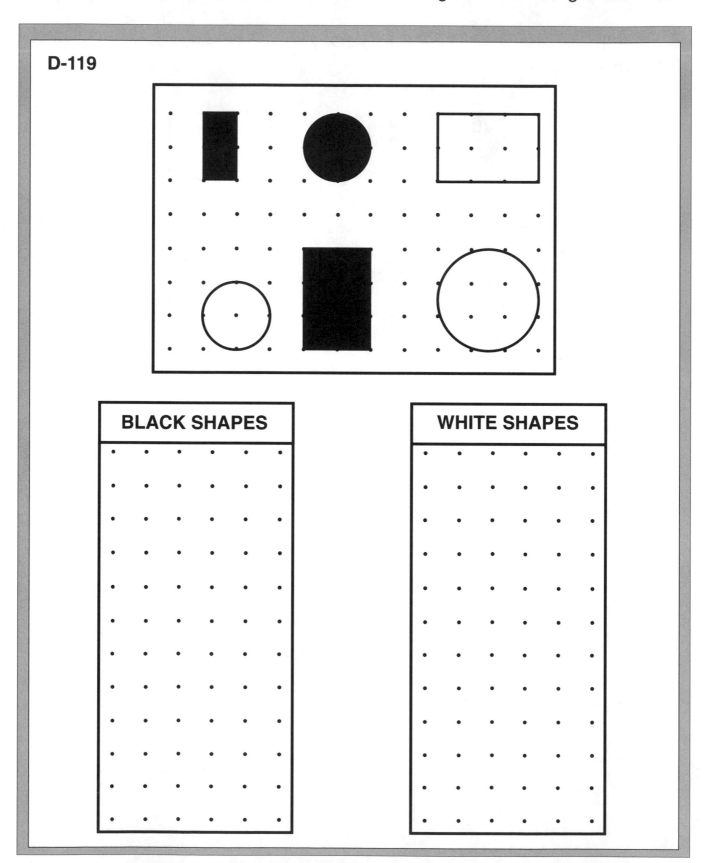

| BLACK SHAPES | WHITE SHAPES |

CLASSIFYING BY SIZE—SORTING

DIRECTIONS: The figures at the top can be sorted into classes in more than one way. In the boxes at the bottom, draw and color the figures that belong in each class.

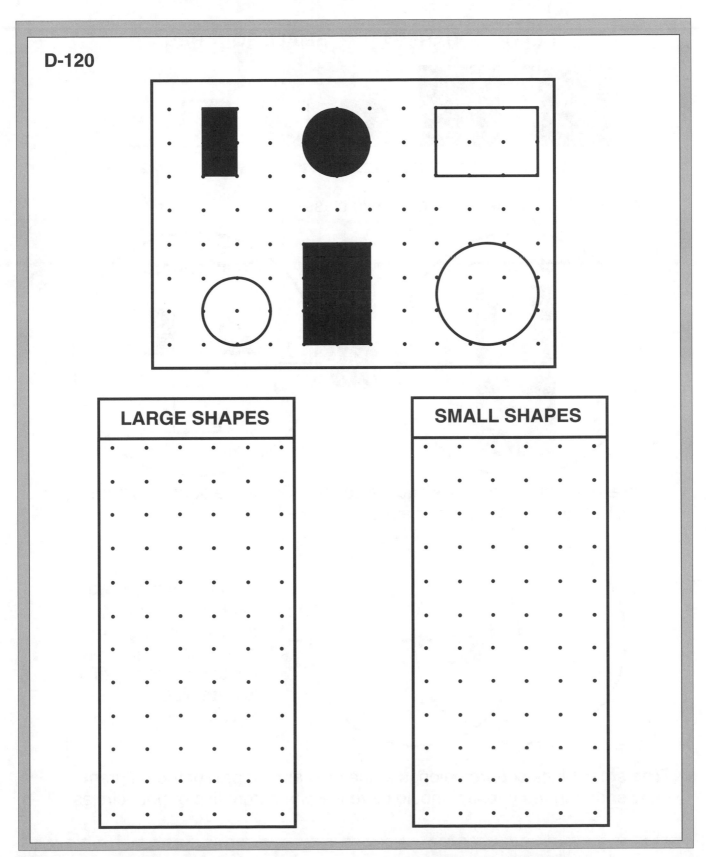

OVERLAPPING CLASSES—INTERSECTION

This group of squares can be sorted by color and size.

BLACK SQUARES   **SMALL SQUARES**

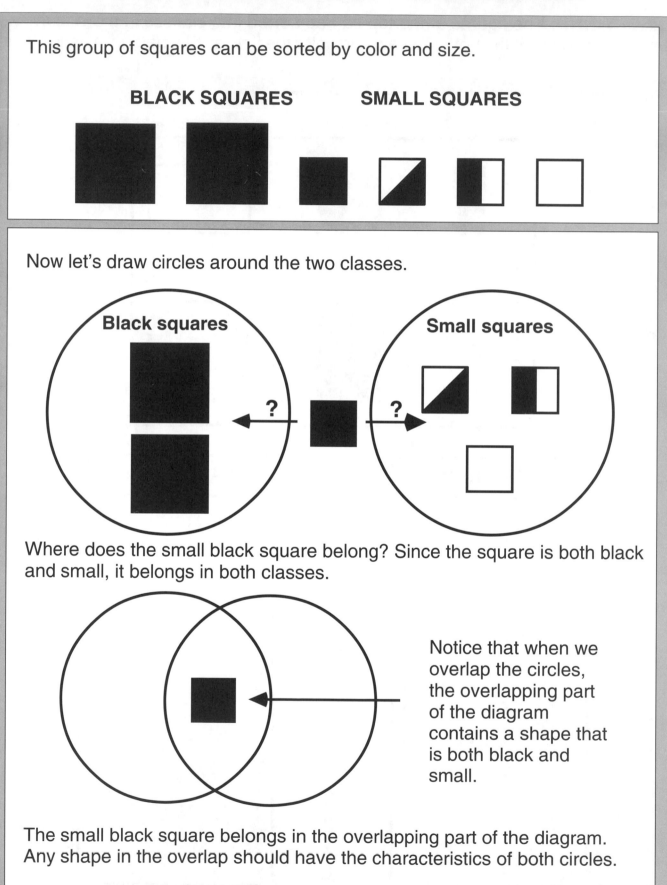

Now let's draw circles around the two classes.

Where does the small black square belong? Since the square is both black and small, it belongs in both classes.

Notice that when we overlap the circles, the overlapping part of the diagram contains a shape that is both black and small.

The small black square belongs in the overlapping part of the diagram. Any shape in the overlap should have the characteristics of both circles.

OVERLAPPING CLASSES—INTERSECTION

DIRECTIONS: Notice where the shapes are placed in the circles at the top. In the exercises below, use your pencil to darken the part of the circles diagram to which the figure belongs (see example).

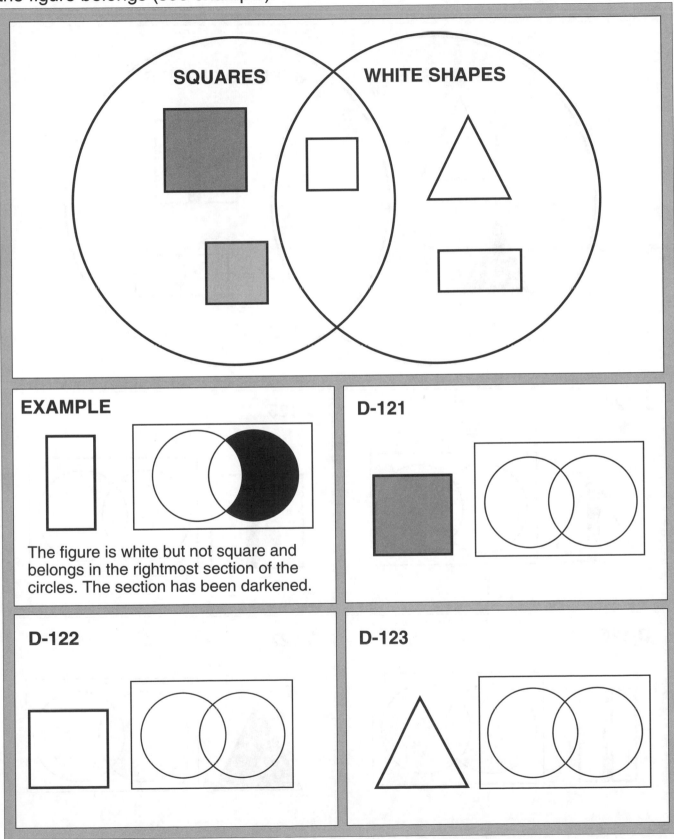

EXAMPLE

The figure is white but not square and belongs in the rightmost section of the circles. The section has been darkened.

D-121

D-122

D-123

OVERLAPPING CLASSES—INTERSECTION

DIRECTIONS: Notice where the shapes are placed in the circles at the top. In the exercises below, use your pencil to darken the part of the circles diagram to which the figure belongs.

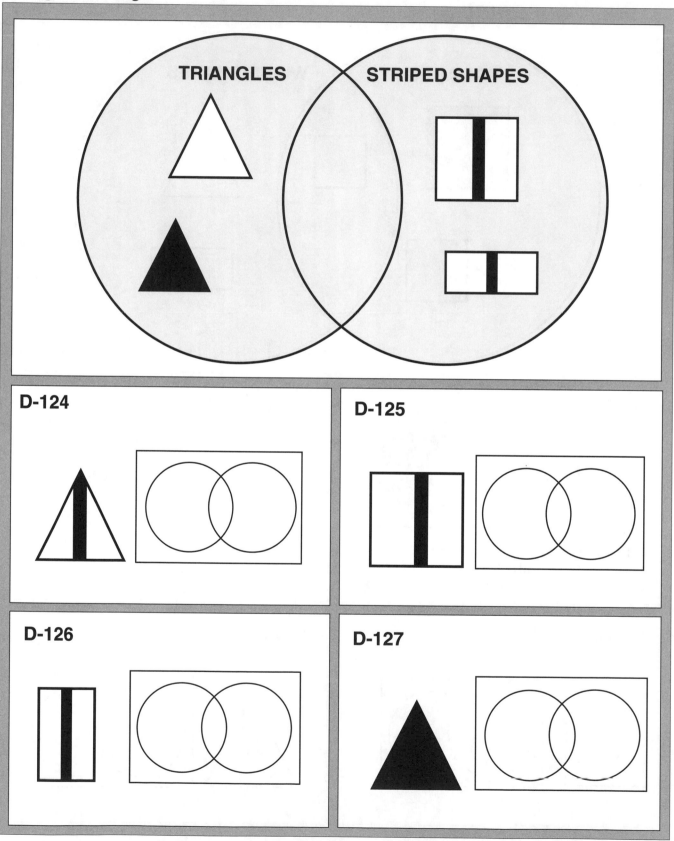

OVERLAPPING CLASSES—INTERSECTION

DIRECTIONS: Notice where the shapes are placed in the circles at the top. In the exercises below, use your pencil to darken the part of the circles diagram to which the figure belongs.

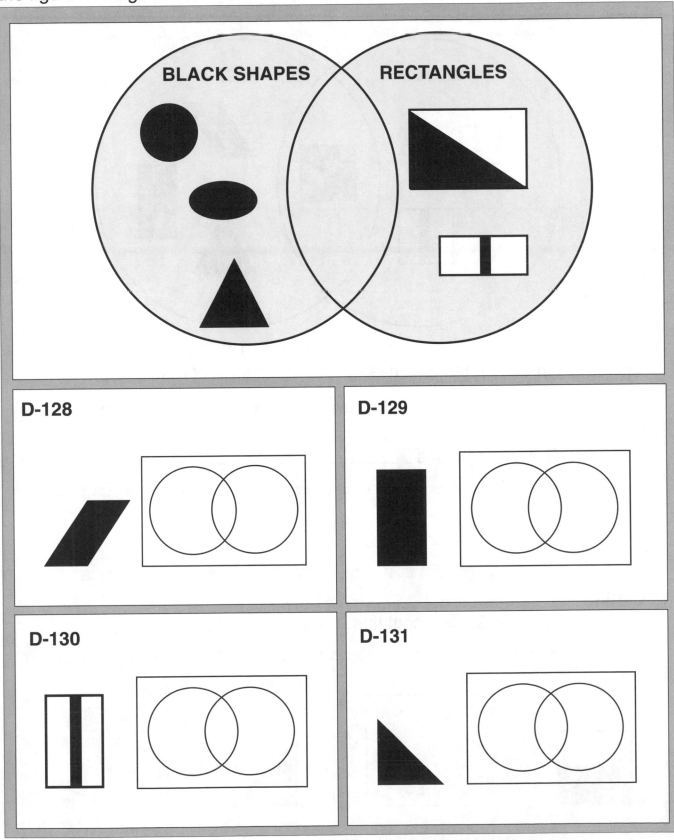

OVERLAPPING CLASSES—INTERSECTION

DIRECTIONS: Read the information about the circles and complete the exercises below. In each blank, write the characteristics for the group. In each small circles diagram, darken the part where the given shape belongs.

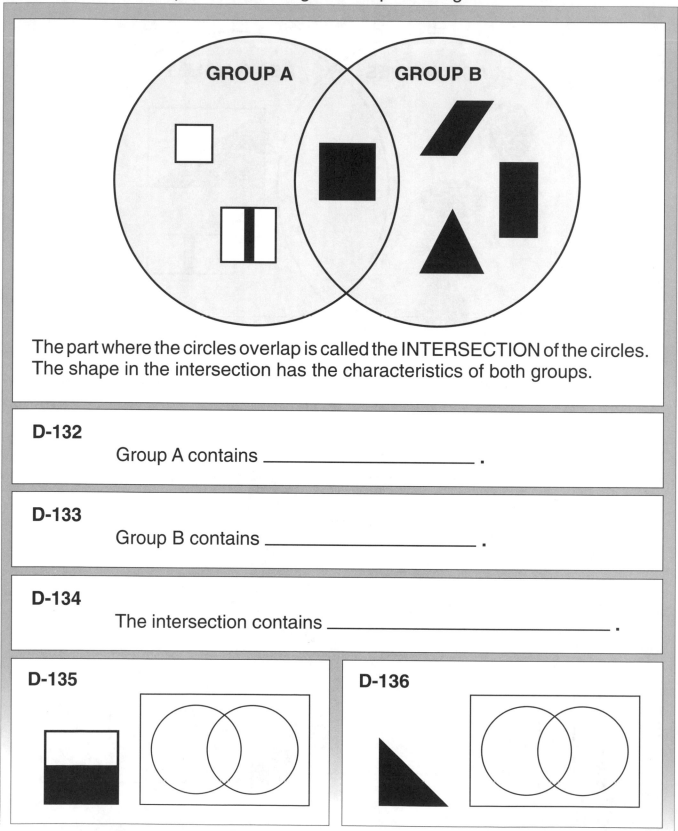

The part where the circles overlap is called the INTERSECTION of the circles. The shape in the intersection has the characteristics of both groups.

D-132

Group A contains _____ .

D-133

Group B contains _____ .

D-134

The intersection contains _____ .

D-135

D-136

OVERLAPPING CLASSES—MATRIX

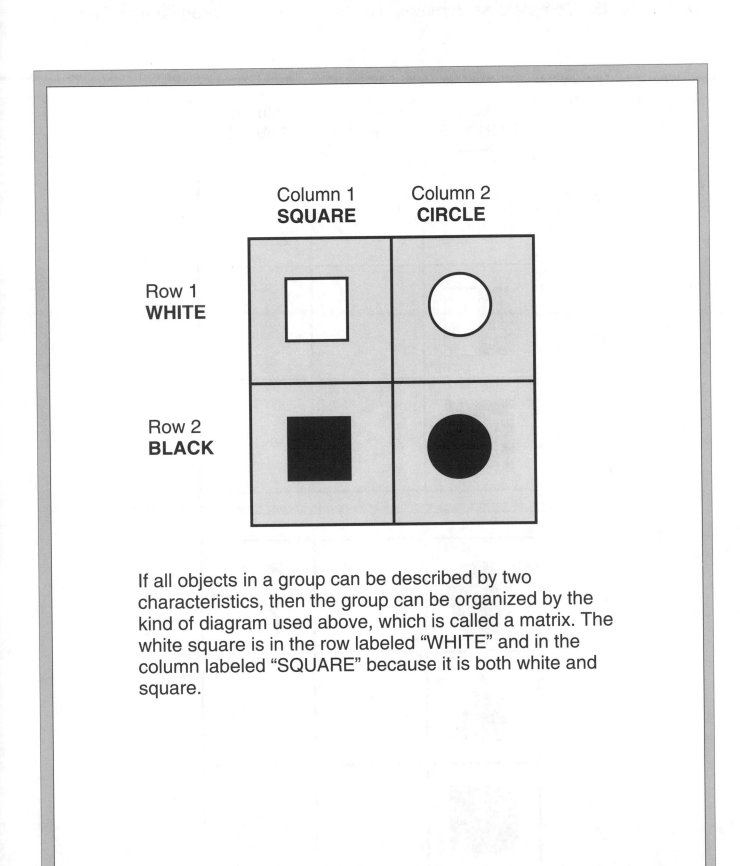

If all objects in a group can be described by two characteristics, then the group can be organized by the kind of diagram used above, which is called a matrix. The white square is in the row labeled "WHITE" and in the column labeled "SQUARE" because it is both white and square.

OVERLAPPING CLASSES—MATRIX

DIRECTIONS: Complete each matrix. The first matrix has been labeled for you.

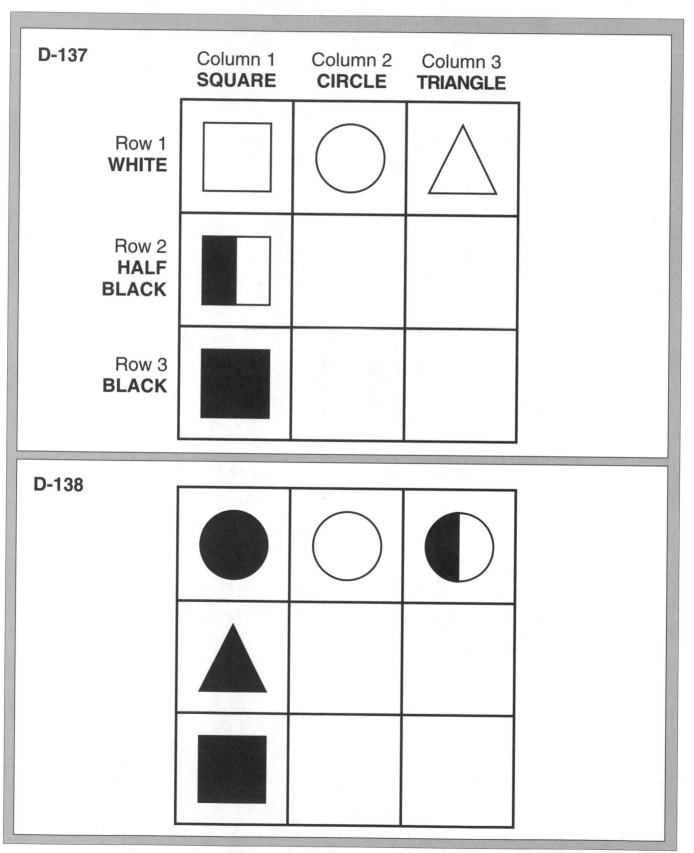

OVERLAPPING CLASSES—MATRIX

DIRECTIONS: Complete each matrix.

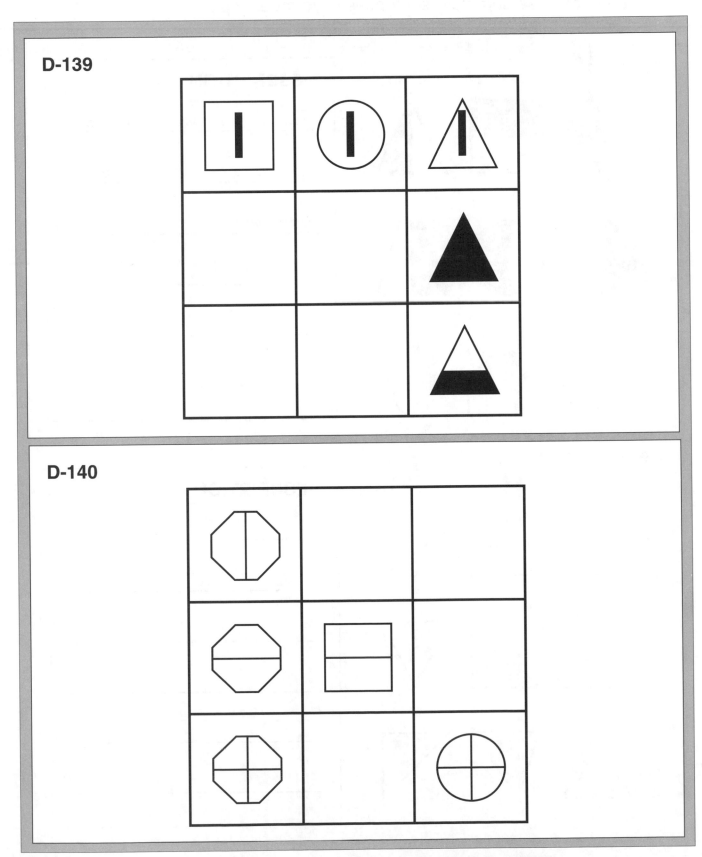

D-139

D-140

WRITING DESCRIPTIONS OF CLASSES

DIRECTIONS: Look at each group (class) of figures. Decide what characteristics all the figures have in common. Write a description of each class of figures in the description box. Use complete sentences in your description.

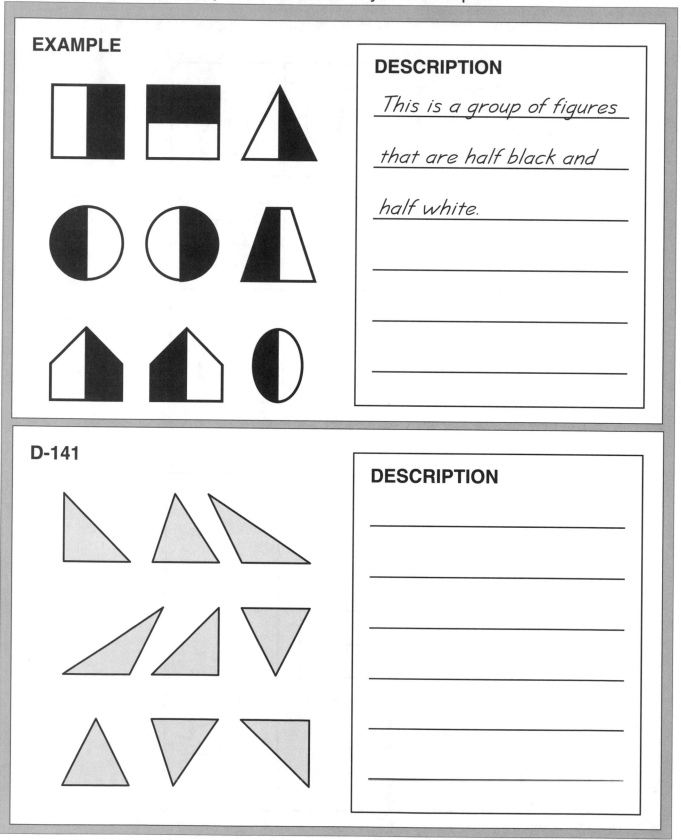

EXAMPLE

DESCRIPTION

This is a group of figures that are half black and half white.

D-141

DESCRIPTION

WRITING DESCRIPTIONS OF CLASSES

DIRECTIONS: Look at each group (class) of figures. Decide what characteristics all the figures have in common. Write a description of each class of figures in the description box. Use complete sentences in your description.

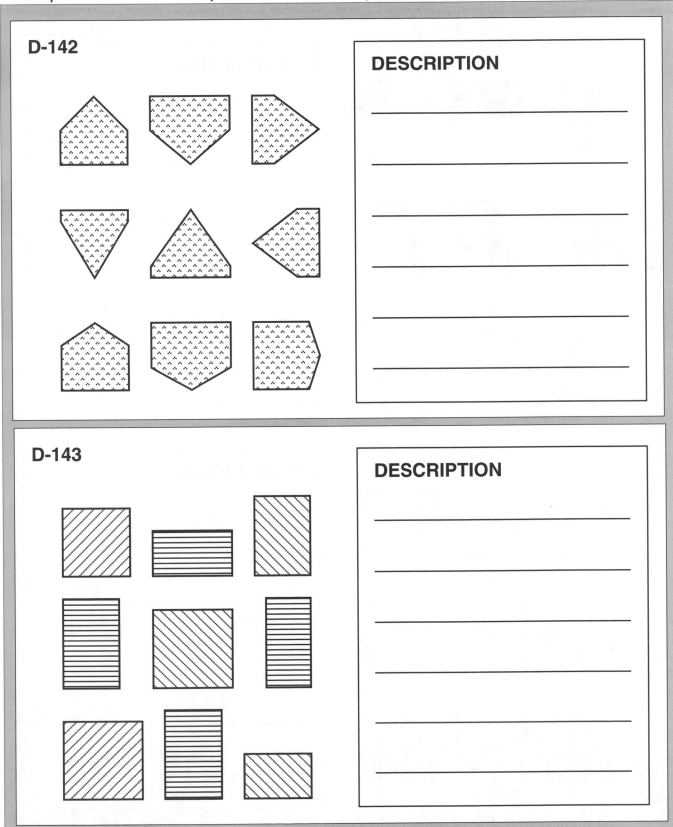

D-142

DESCRIPTION

_____

_____

_____

_____

_____

_____

D-143

DESCRIPTION

_____

_____

_____

_____

_____

WRITING DESCRIPTIONS OF CLASSES

DIRECTIONS: Look at each group (class) of figures. Decide what characteristics all the figures have in common. Write a description of each class of figures in the description box. Use complete sentences in your description.

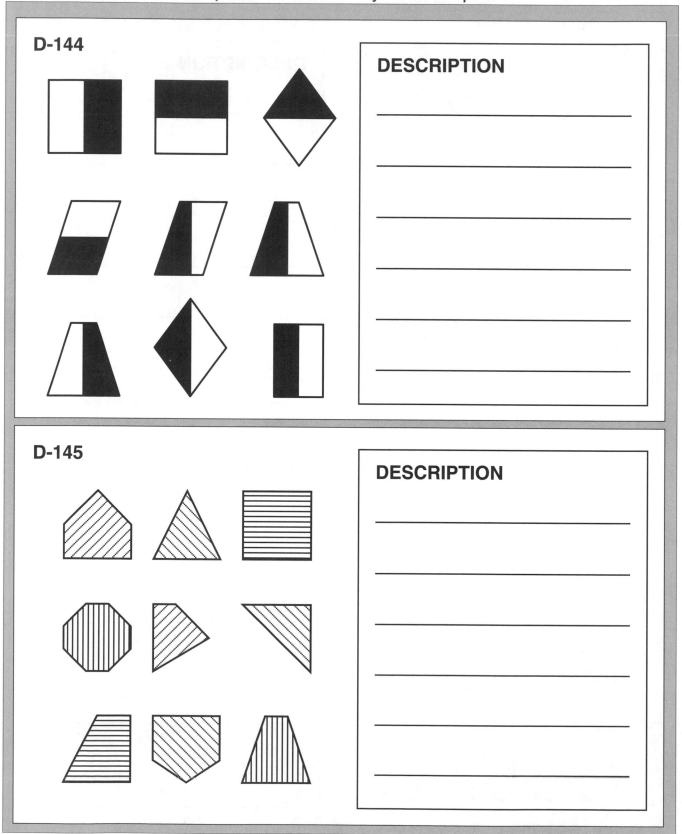

D-144

DESCRIPTION

D-145

DESCRIPTION

CHAPTER FIVE

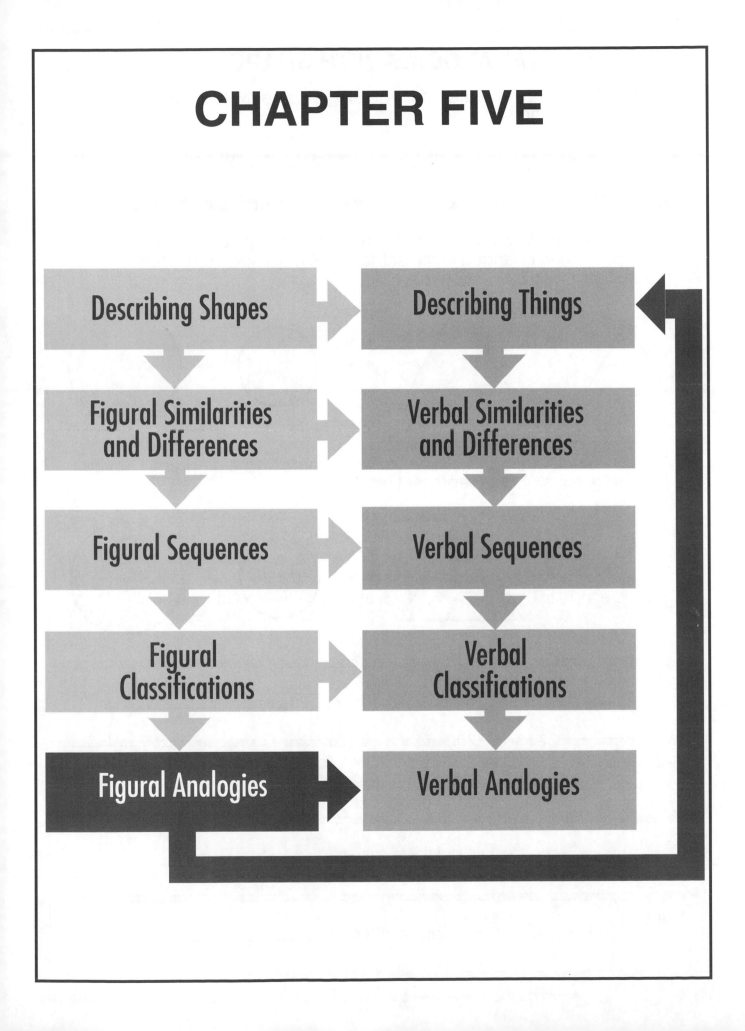

Describing Shapes → Describing Things

Figural Similarities and Differences → Verbal Similarities and Differences

Figural Sequences → Verbal Sequences

Figural Classifications → Verbal Classifications

Figural Analogies → Verbal Analogies

ANALOGIES WITH SHAPES

DIRECTIONS: Use the information in the diagrams below to fill in the blanks at the bottom of the page.

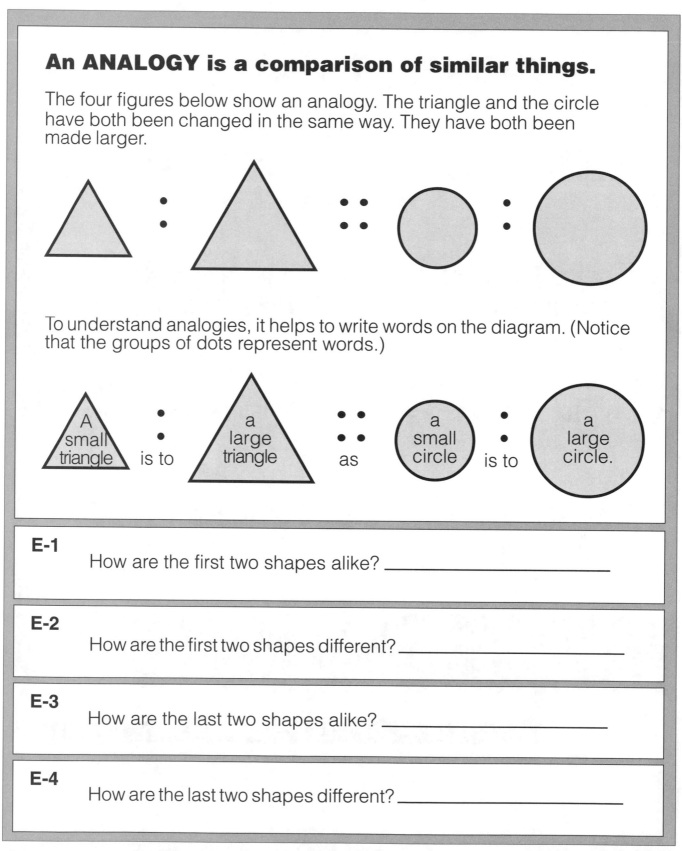

An ANALOGY is a comparison of similar things.

The four figures below show an analogy. The triangle and the circle have both been changed in the same way. They have both been made larger.

To understand analogies, it helps to write words on the diagram. (Notice that the groups of dots represent words.)

A small triangle : is to a large triangle as a small circle : is to a large circle.

E-1 How are the first two shapes alike? _____

E-2 How are the first two shapes different? _____

E-3 How are the last two shapes alike? _____

E-4 How are the last two shapes different? _____

BUILDING ANALOGIES WITH BLOCKS

DIRECTIONS: On another sheet of paper, arrange attribute blocks to copy the analogies shown. Trace and color the figures. Then fill in the blanks to complete each sentence (the first one is done for you).

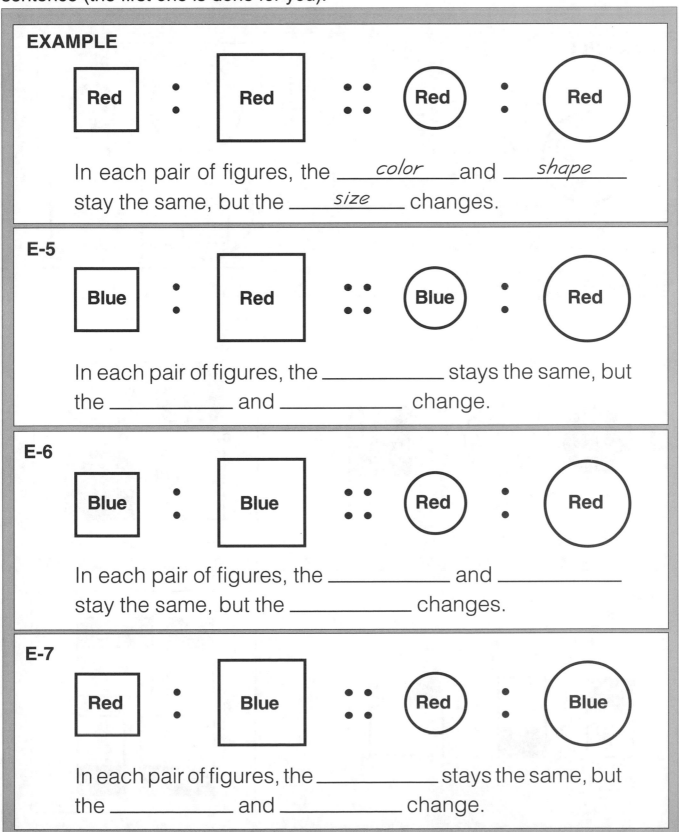

EXAMPLE

In each pair of figures, the ___*color*___ and ___*shape*___ stay the same, but the ___*size*___ changes.

E-5

In each pair of figures, the _____ stays the same, but the _____ and _____ change.

E-6

In each pair of figures, the _____ and _____ stay the same, but the _____ changes.

E-7

In each pair of figures, the _____ stays the same, but the _____ and _____ change.

ANALOGIES WITH SHAPES—SELECT

DIRECTIONS: Circle the figure that completes the analogy.

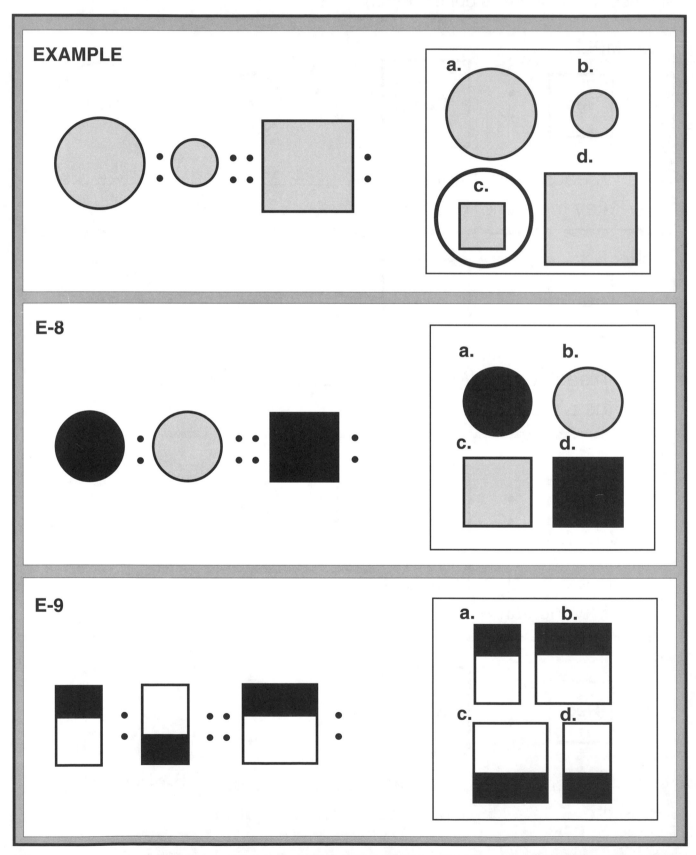

ANALOGIES WITH SHAPES—SELECT

DIRECTIONS: Circle the figure that completes the analogy.

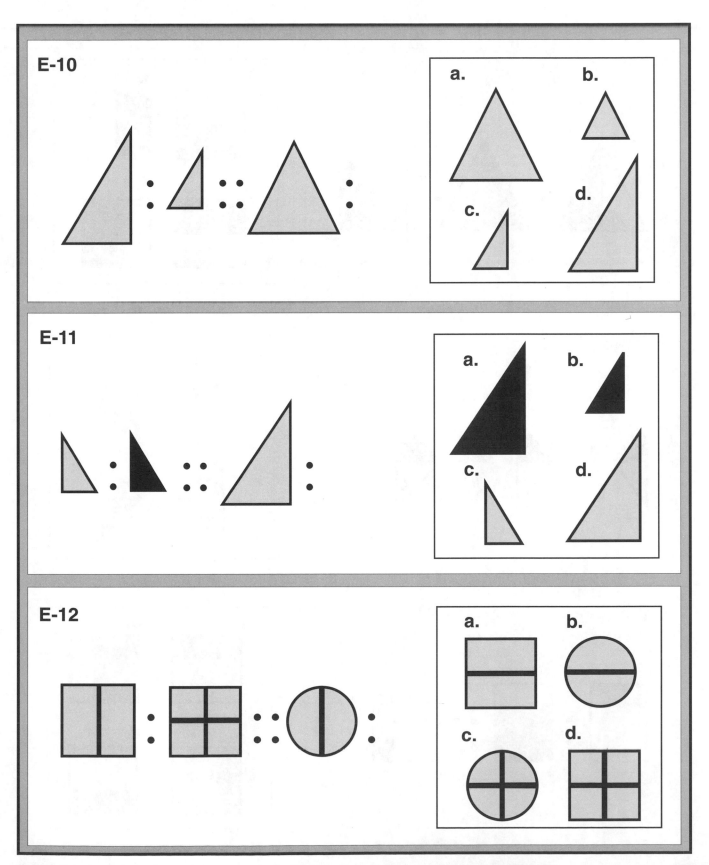

ANALOGIES WITH SHAPES—SELECT

DIRECTIONS: Circle the figure that completes the analogy.

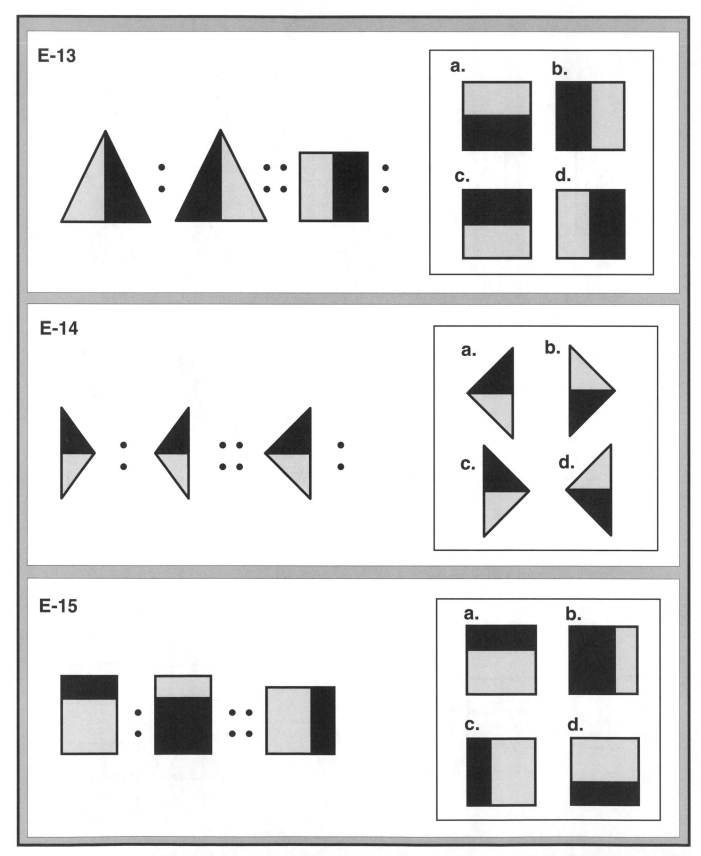

ANALOGIES WITH SHAPES—SELECT

DIRECTIONS: Circle the figure that completes the analogy.

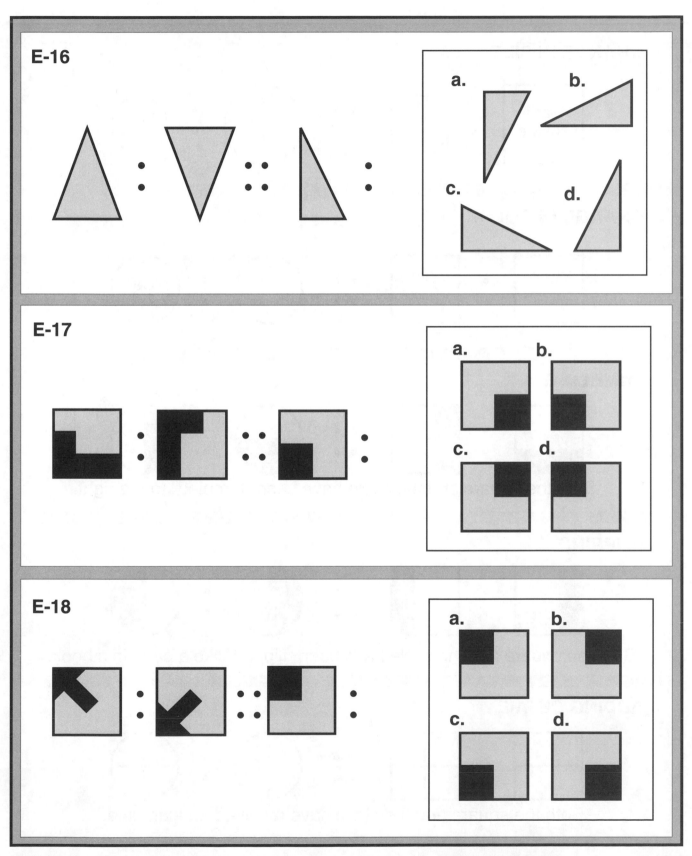

KINDS OF ANALOGIES

DIRECTIONS: Study the five types of analogies illustrated below.

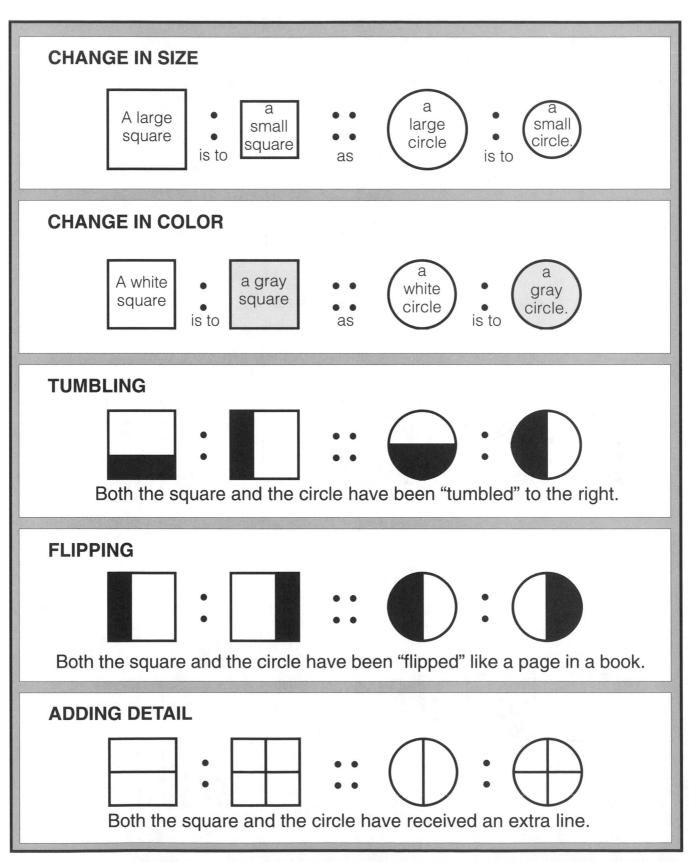

CHANGE IN SIZE

A large square **:** a small square **::** a large circle **:** a small circle.
is to   as   is to

CHANGE IN COLOR

A white square **:** a gray square **::** a white circle **:** a gray circle.
is to   as   is to

TUMBLING

Both the square and the circle have been "tumbled" to the right.

FLIPPING

Both the square and the circle have been "flipped" like a page in a book.

ADDING DETAIL

Both the square and the circle have received an extra line.

ANALOGIES WITH SHAPES—COMPLETE

DIRECTIONS: In the grid at the end of each row, draw the last figure to complete the analogy. As you draw the figure, think about what has changed.

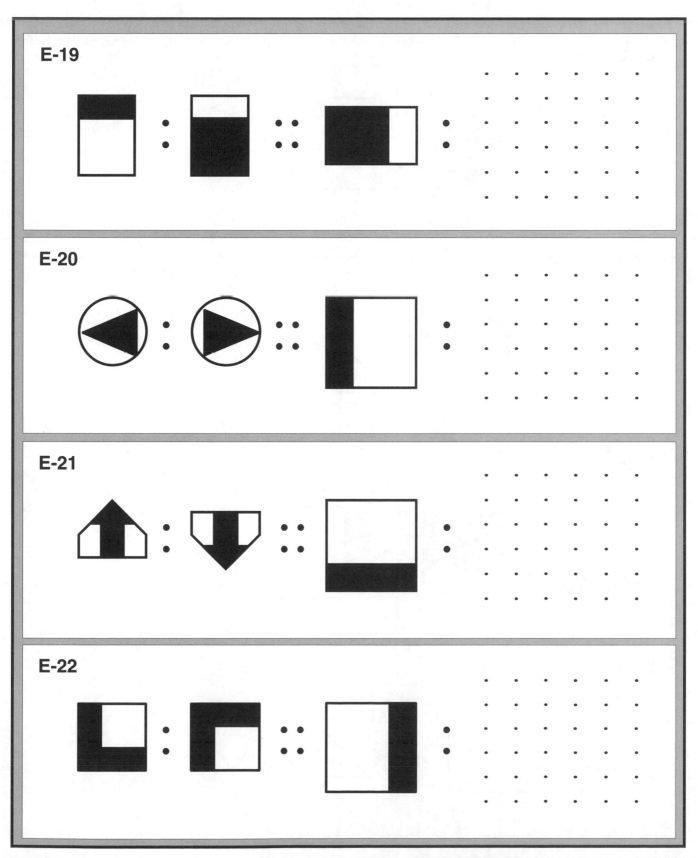

ANALOGIES WITH SHAPES—COMPLETE

DIRECTIONS: In the grid at the end of each row, draw the last figure to complete the analogy. As you draw the figure, think about what has changed.

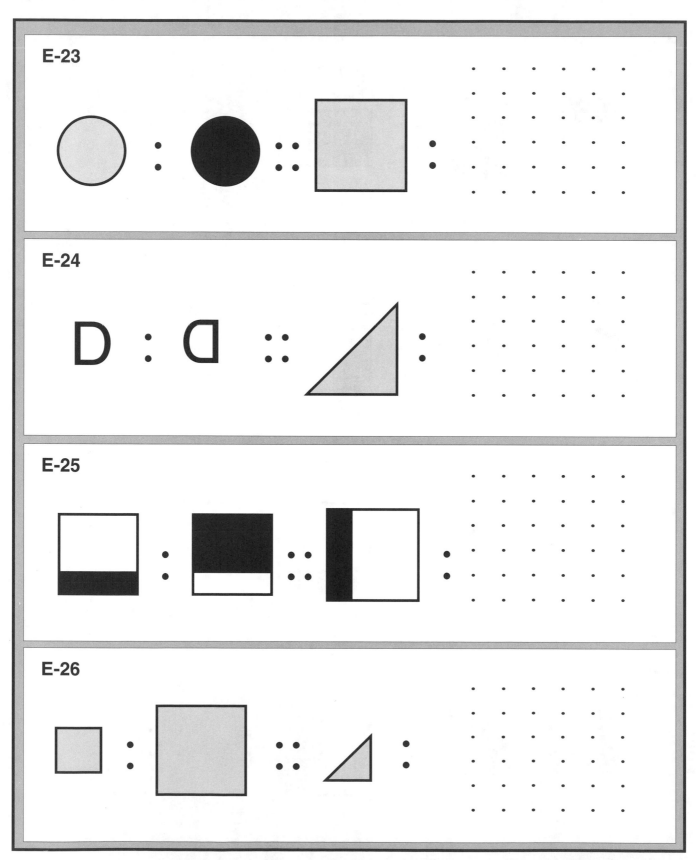

ANALOGIES WITH SHAPES—COMPLETE

DIRECTIONS: In the grid at the end of each row, draw the last figure to complete the analogy. As you draw the figure, think about what has changed.

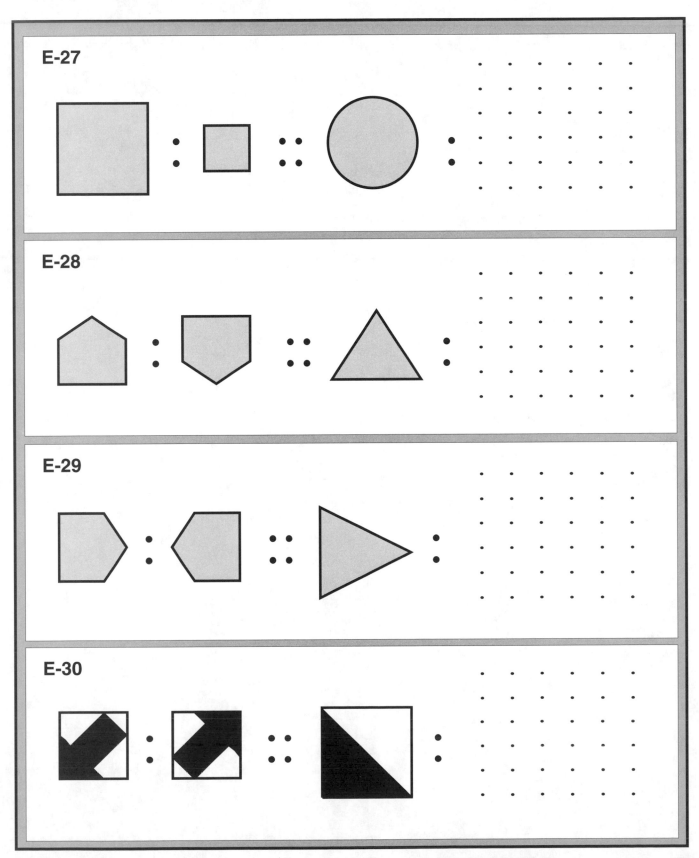

CHAPTER SIX

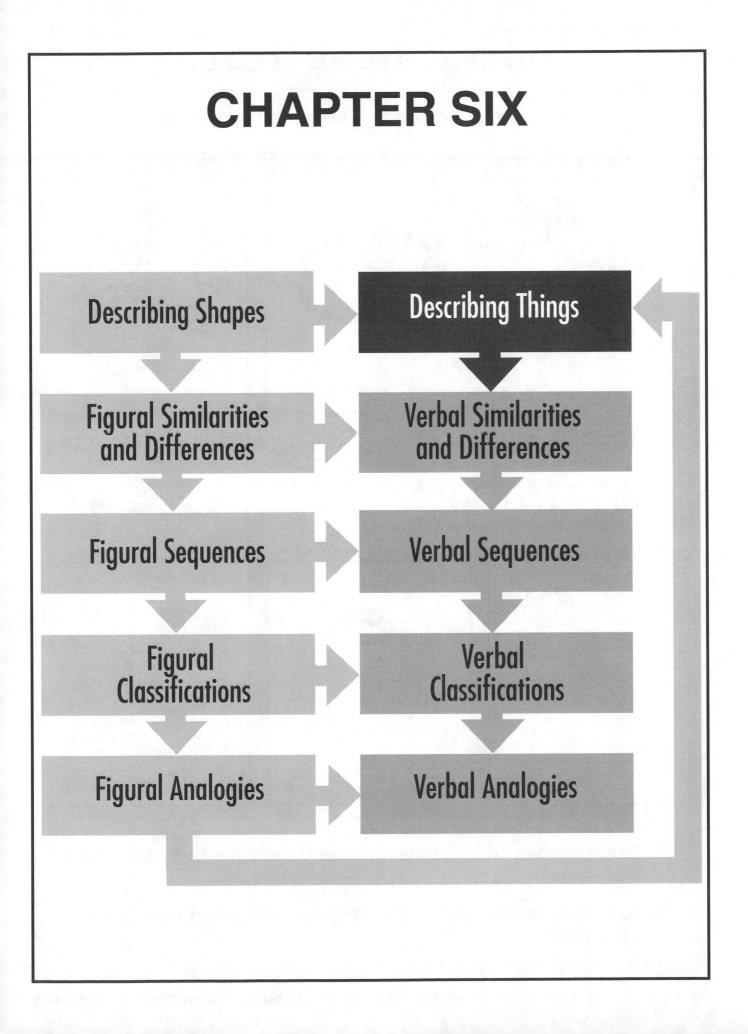

Describing Shapes

Describing Things

Figural Similarities and Differences

Verbal Similarities and Differences

Figural Sequences

Verbal Sequences

Figural Classifications

Verbal Classifications

Figural Analogies

Verbal Analogies

DESCRIBING FOODS—SELECT

DIRECTIONS: Look at the three pictures of foods. Read each description below the pictures and decide which of the pictures it describes. Write the letter of the correct picture on the line.

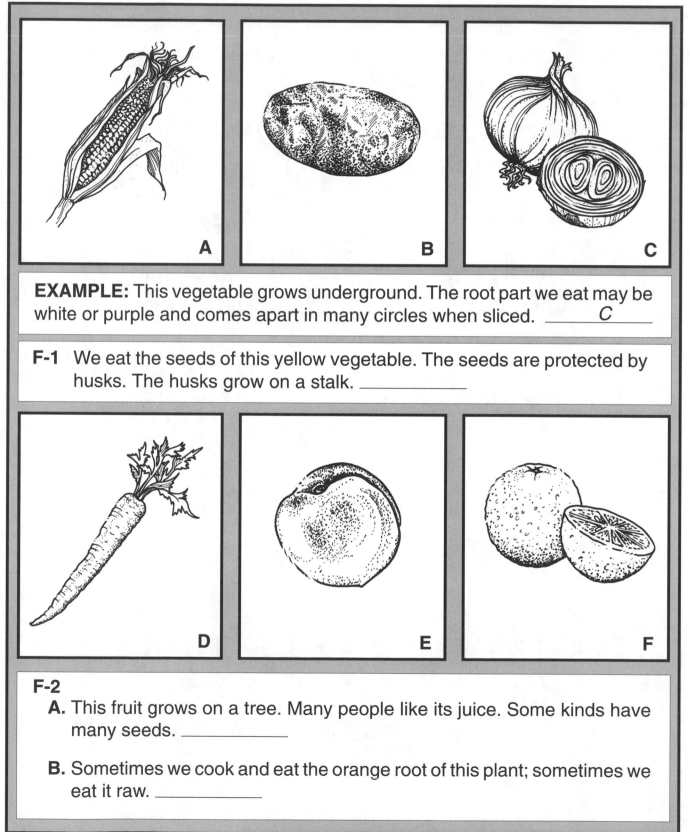

A

B

C

EXAMPLE: This vegetable grows underground. The root part we eat may be white or purple and comes apart in many circles when sliced. _____*C*_____

F-1 We eat the seeds of this yellow vegetable. The seeds are protected by husks. The husks grow on a stalk. _____

D

E

F

F-2

   A. This fruit grows on a tree. Many people like its juice. Some kinds have many seeds. _____

   B. Sometimes we cook and eat the orange root of this plant; sometimes we eat it raw. _____

DESCRIBING ANIMALS—SELECT

DIRECTIONS: Look at the three pictures of animals. Read each description below the pictures and decide which of the pictures it describes. Write the letter of the correct picture on the line.

G   H   I

F-3

   A. This wide-eyed bird has large feathers. It uses its beak to prey on small animals. _____

   B. This bird is a good swimmer and uses its bill to scoop up food in the water.

_____

J   K   L

F-4

   A. This striped, horselike animal is a native of Africa. In the United States, it is seen only in zoos. _____

   B. This African animal eats the leaves from the tops of tall trees.

_____

DESCRIBING VEHICLES—SELECT

DIRECTIONS: Look at the three pictures of vehicles. Read each description below the pictures and decide which of the pictures it describes. Write the letter of the correct picture on the line.

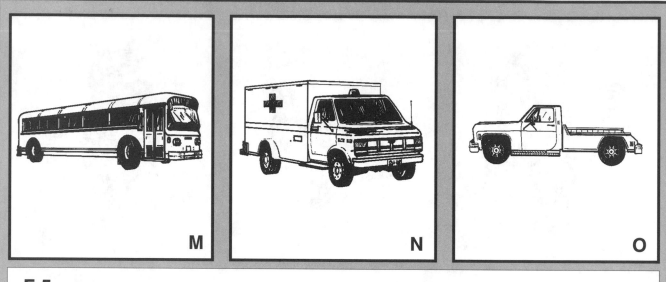

M   N   O

F-5

   A. This vehicle is used to take injured or sick people to the hospital.
_____

   B. This vehicle is used for hauling large objects or material. _____

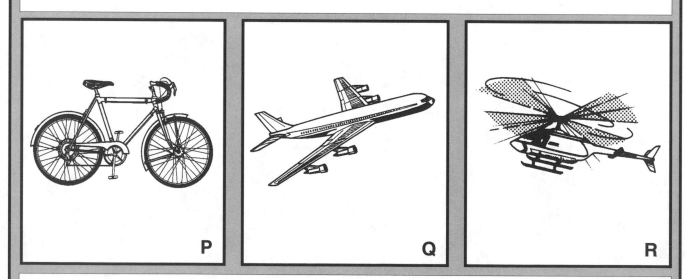

P   Q   R

F-6

   A. This aircraft takes off and lands on an airport runway. It has wings and is moved by propellers or by jet engines. _____

   B. This aircraft can take off straight up and land in very small areas. It is used for police patrol and sightseeing. _____

DESCRIBING PLACES—SELECT

DIRECTIONS: Look at the three pictures of places. Read each description and decide which of the pictures it describes. On the line, write the letter of the correct picture.

S   T   U

F-7

A. Food is grown and animals are raised here. Workers use machinery to plant and harvest the food. _____

B. Food is cooked and served to people here. _____

V   W   X

F-8

A. People come here to buy fuel for their vehicles. _____

B. Police officers keep their vehicles and equipment here. _____

DESCRIBING OCCUPATIONS—SELECT

DIRECTIONS: Look at the three pictures of people working. Read each description and decide which of the pictures it describes. On the line, write the letter of the correct picture.

F-9

A. This person may work in an office or clinic. He or she cares for teeth and teaches people about dental care. _____

B. This person works in a school. He or she talks to children to help them learn. _____

F-10

A. This public worker works longs hours and sometimes sleeps above the garage where his or her truck and equipment are stored. _____

B. This public worker protects people and property and helps prevent crime. He or she sometimes rides in a car or on a motorcycle. _____

DESCRIBING FOODS—EXPLAIN

DIRECTIONS: In each box, describe the food in the picture.

F-11　　DESCRIPTION

_____

_____

_____

_____

_____

_____

_____

F-12　　DESCRIPTION

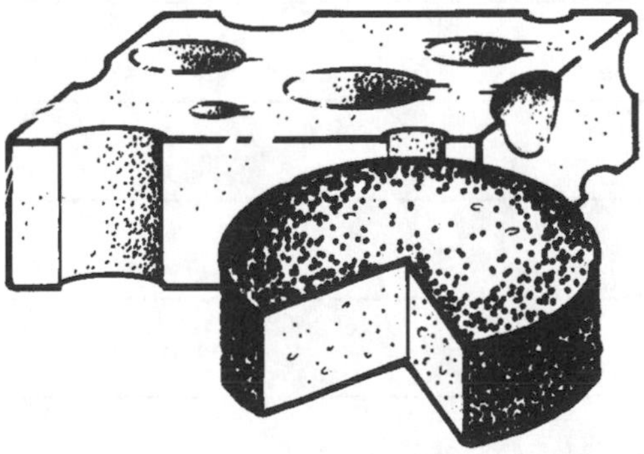

_____

_____

_____

_____

_____

_____

_____

DESCRIBING PLACES—EXPLAIN

DIRECTIONS: In each box, describe the building in the picture.

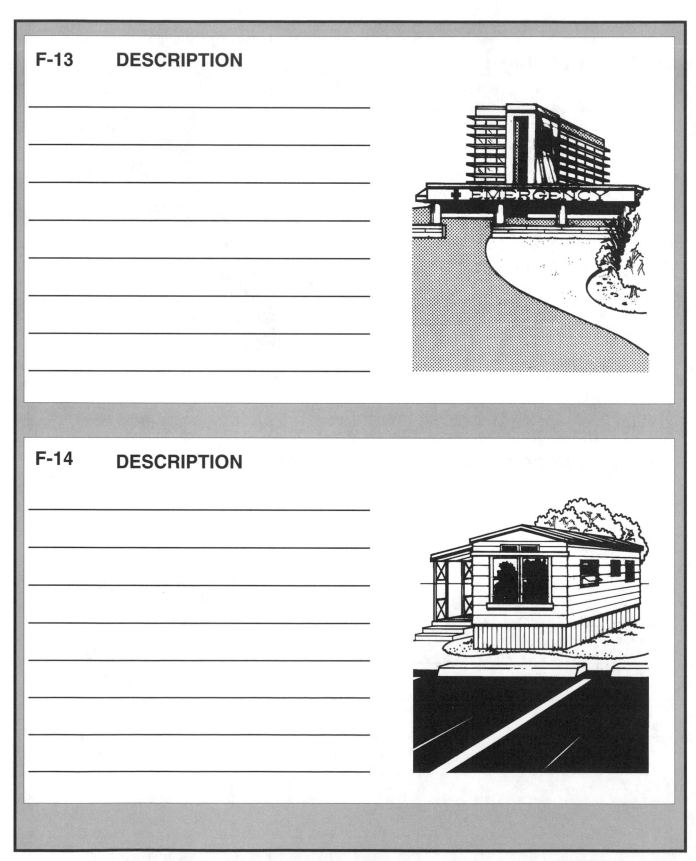

F-13   DESCRIPTION

_____

_____

_____

_____

_____

_____

F-14   DESCRIPTION

_____

_____

_____

_____

_____

_____

DESCRIBING PLACES ON EARTH—EXPLAIN

DIRECTIONS: In each box, describe the land form in the picture.

F-15   DESCRIPTION

_____

_____

_____

_____

_____

_____

F-16   DESCRIPTION

_____

_____

_____

_____

_____

_____

DESCRIBING ANIMALS—EXPLAIN

DIRECTIONS: In each box, describe the animal in the picture.

F-17   **DESCRIPTION**

_____

_____

_____

_____

_____

_____

_____

F-18   **DESCRIPTION**

_____

_____

_____

_____

_____

_____

_____

_____

DESCRIBING OCCUPATIONS—EXPLAIN

DIRECTIONS: In each box, describe the job of the person in the picture.

F-19   DESCRIPTION

_____

_____

_____

_____

_____

_____

_____

F-20   DESCRIPTION

_____

_____

_____

_____

_____

_____

_____

DESCRIBING WORDS—SELECT

DIRECTIONS: Each exercise contains three words used in social studies followed by descriptions of two of the words. For each description, select the matching word and write it in the blank.

F-21

WORD CHOICES: country, map, photograph

Example: A drawing of all or part of the surface of the earth

_____ *map* _____

A. A picture taken by a camera _____

F-22

WORD CHOICES: lake, river, ocean

A. A body of water completely surrounded by land

_____

B. The body of salt water that covers a large part of the surface of the earth _____

F-23

WORD CHOICES: continent, country, state

A. A nation made up of states _____

B. A land mass made up of countries _____

DESCRIBING WORDS—SELECT

DIRECTIONS: Each exercise contains three words used in social studies followed by descriptions of two of the words. For each description, select the matching word and write it in the blank.

F-24

WORD CHOICES: blade, leaf, needle

A. The long, thin, pointed leaf of a pine tree

_____

B. The broad leaf of a grass plant _____

F-25

WORD CHOICES: cloud, rainbow, star

A. A large, fluffy mass of water vapor in the sky _____

B. A half circle of colors that sometimes appears in the sky. It is formed by the light of the sun passing through rain droplets.

_____

F-26

WORD CHOICES: clock, thermometer, yardstick

A. A measuring device that is three feet long. It is divided into thirty-six parts. _____

B. A measuring device made of a glass tube containing a liquid. The liquid expands when heated and shows changes in temperature.

_____

NAME THE ANIMAL—SUPPLY

DIRECTIONS: Each exercise contains a description of an animal. Read each description, then decide what is being described. Write the answer in the blank.

F-27

This large bird is raised to be eaten. It is often purchased for holiday celebrations. Many meat products are made from this bird.

_____

F-28

This large cat is a good hunter. It is tan or light brown with a large mane on its head. _____

F-29

This large fish lives in the ocean. The meat from this fish is often canned and used to make salad-type sandwiches. _____

F-30

This beast of burden has two humps and can go days between drinks of water. _____

F-31

This insect builds hives and makes honey. _____

F-32

This reptile has two surfaces of hard shell. Its head and legs come out of the shell. _____

NAME THE PLANT—SUPPLY

DIRECTIONS: Each exercise contains a description of a plant. Read each description, then decide what is being described. Write the answer in the blank.

F-33

This dark-green leafy vegetable is eaten cooked or served as a salad.

_____

F-34

This long yellow fruit is peeled before being eaten. It grows in bunches in warm countries. _____

F-35

This grain is grown on huge farms in the center of the United States. It is made into bread, baking flour, and many breakfast cereals.

_____

F-36

This large tree has beautiful hard wood which is used to make furniture. Its seeds are called acorns. _____

F-37

This plant grows in the desert. It has many long, sharp points.

_____

F-38

This tree has soft wood which is used as lumber to build houses. Its seeds grow in a bunch called a "cone." Young trees of this kind are decorated at Christmas. _____

NAME THE VEHICLE/PLACE—SUPPLY

DIRECTIONS: Each exercise below contains a description of a vehicle or a place. Read each description, then decide what is being described. Write the answer in the blank.

F-39

This vehicle is used on farms to plow fields and tend the land.

_____

F-40

This vehicle is used to take injured or sick people to the hospital.

_____

F-41

This large vehicle flies through the air at 500 miles an hour by pushing hot gas out of a tube. It carries more than one hundred passengers.

_____

F-42

People come here to buy stamps and mail letters and packages.

_____

F-43

People come here to put money in their accounts. You can cash a check here. You can store valuable papers here. _____

F-44

This very large building contains a few large department stores and many small shops. _____

NAME THE OCCUPATION—SUPPLY

DIRECTIONS: Each exercise contains a description of a worker in a particular occupation. Read each description, then decide what worker is being described. Write the answer in the blank.

F-45

This public worker delivers letters and packages to homes.

_____

F-46

This person washes, cuts, and combs hair. _____

F-47

This person works in an office where he or she examines, cleans, fills, or removes teeth. _____

F-48

This person grows the food that we eat. _____

F-49

This person works in a store and sells food. _____

F-50

This person works in a restaurant and prepares the food that we eat at the restaurant. _____

F-51

This person works in a school and helps children learn.

_____

F-52

This person works in an office or hospital. He or she finds out why a person is sick and gives advice on what medicine the person should take. _____

IDENTIFYING CHARACTERISTICS

DIRECTIONS: Read the passage about frogs. Identify the characteristics of a frog and write them in the blanks.

F-53

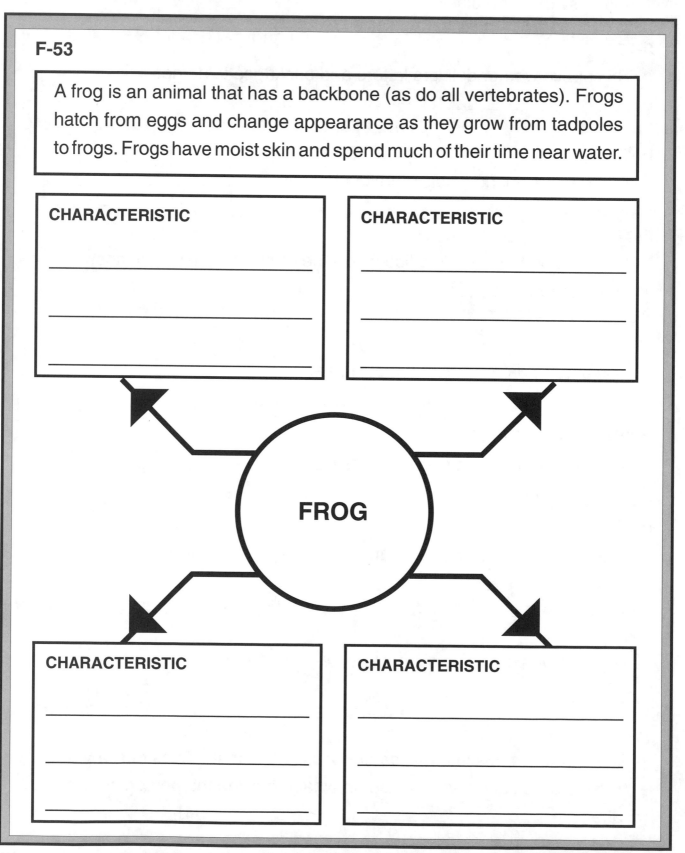

A frog is an animal that has a backbone (as do all vertebrates). Frogs hatch from eggs and change appearance as they grow from tadpoles to frogs. Frogs have moist skin and spend much of their time near water.

CHARACTERISTIC

CHARACTERISTIC

FROG

CHARACTERISTIC

CHARACTERISTIC

CHAPTER SEVEN

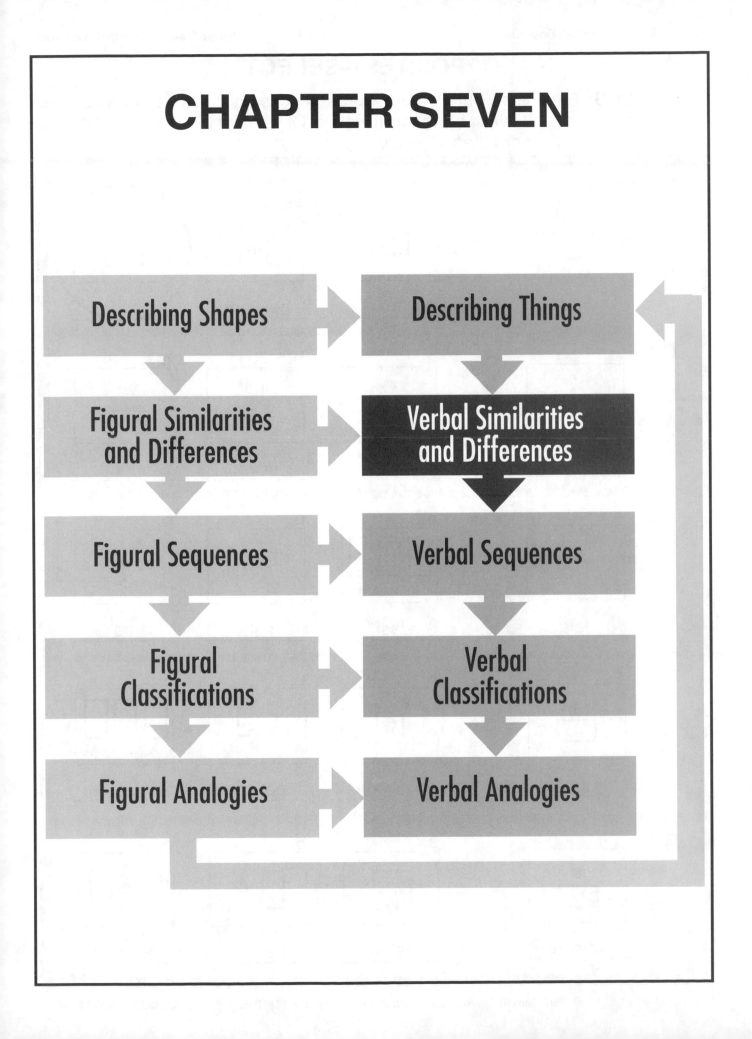

Describing Shapes → Describing Things

Figural Similarities and Differences → Verbal Similarities and Differences

Figural Sequences → Verbal Sequences

Figural Classifications → Verbal Classifications

Figural Analogies → Verbal Analogies

OPPOSITES—SELECT

DIRECTIONS: Each line contains four words describing directions or locations. Read the first word and think about what it means. Of the next three words, circle the opposite word or the word that is <u>most</u> <u>unlike</u> the first word.

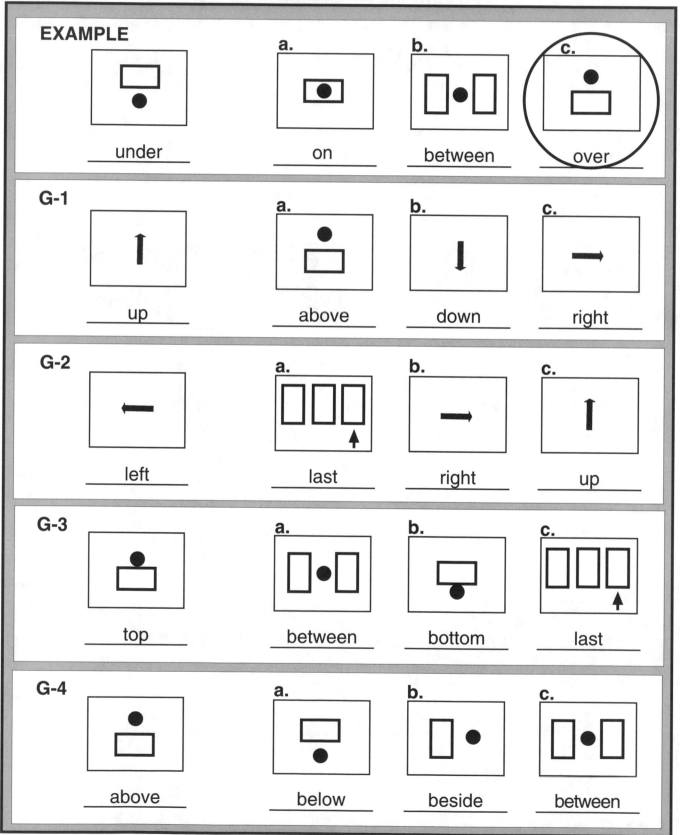

EXAMPLE

under   **a.** on   **b.** between   **c.** over

G-1 up   **a.** above   **b.** down   **c.** right

G-2 left   **a.** last   **b.** right   **c.** up

G-3 top   **a.** between   **b.** bottom   **c.** last

G-4 above   **a.** below   **b.** beside   **c.** between

OPPOSITES—SELECT

DIRECTIONS: Each line contains four words. Read the first word and think about what it means. One of the next three words will mean the <u>opposite</u> of the first word. Circle the word that is opposite or <u>most</u> <u>unlike</u> the first word.

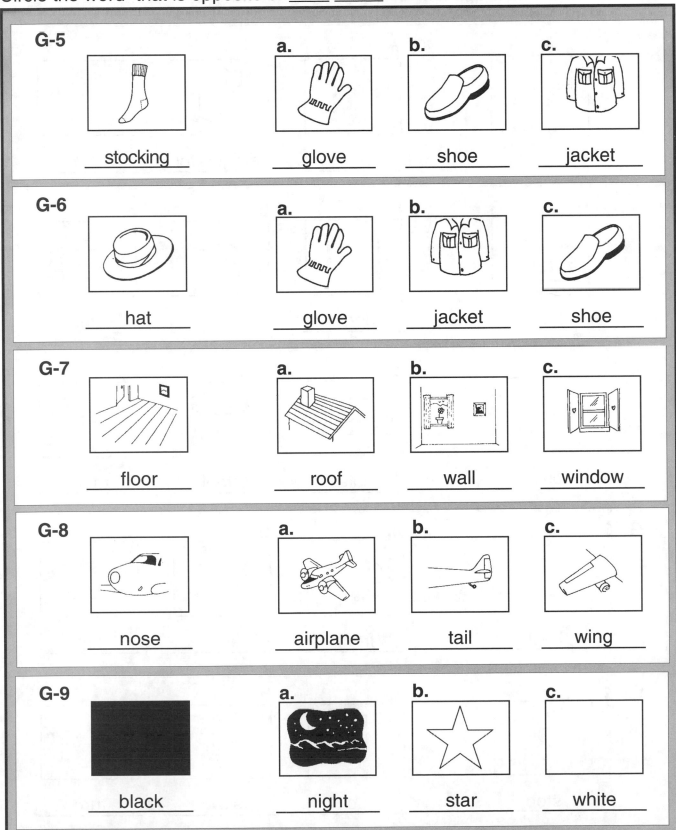

G-5

stocking

a. glove

b. shoe

c. jacket

G-6

hat

a. glove

b. jacket

c. shoe

G-7

floor

a. roof

b. wall

c. window

G-8

nose

a. airplane

b. tail

c. wing

G-9

black

a. night

b. star

c. white

OPPOSITES—SELECT

DIRECTIONS: Each line contains four words. Read the first word and think about what it means. One of the next three words will mean the <u>opposite</u> of the first word. Circle the word that is opposite or <u>most</u> <u>unlike</u> the first word.

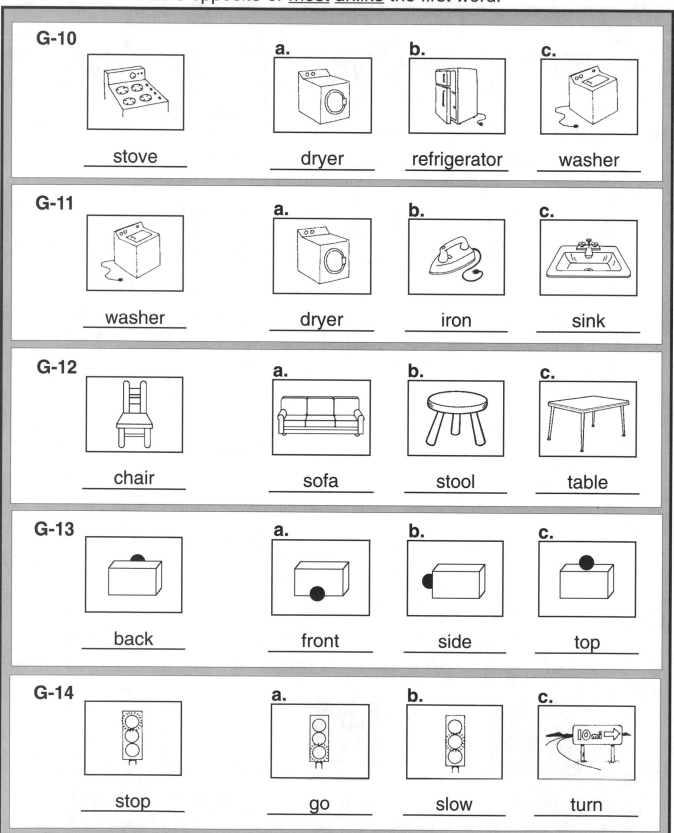

G-10

stove   **a.** dryer   **b.** refrigerator   **c.** washer

G-11

washer   **a.** dryer   **b.** iron   **c.** sink

G-12

chair   **a.** sofa   **b.** stool   **c.** table

G-13

back   **a.** front   **b.** side   **c.** top

G-14

stop   **a.** go   **b.** slow   **c.** turn

OPPOSITES—SELECT

DIRECTIONS: Each line contains four words we use in science. Read the first word and think about what it means. One of the next three words will mean the <u>opposite</u> of the first word. Circle the word that is opposite or <u>most</u> <u>unlike</u> the first word.

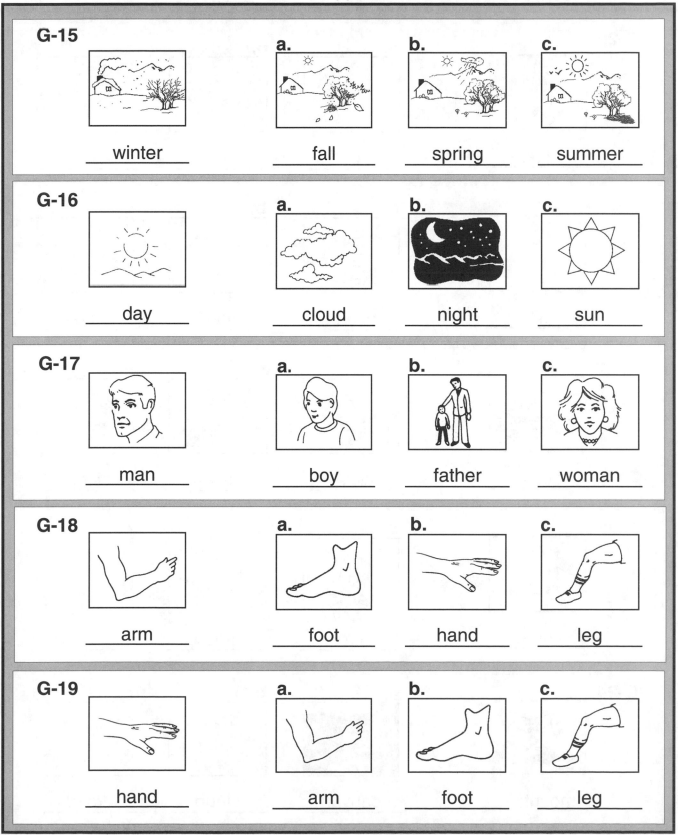

G-15
winter   **a.** fall   **b.** spring   **c.** summer

G-16
day   **a.** cloud   **b.** night   **c.** sun

G-17
man   **a.** boy   **b.** father   **c.** woman

G-18
arm   **a.** foot   **b.** hand   **c.** leg

G-19
hand   **a.** arm   **b.** foot   **c.** leg

OPPOSITES—SELECT

DIRECTIONS: Each line contains four words we use in science. Read the first word and think about what it means. One of the next three words will mean the <u>opposite</u> of the first word. Circle the word that is opposite or <u>most</u> <u>unlike</u> the first word.

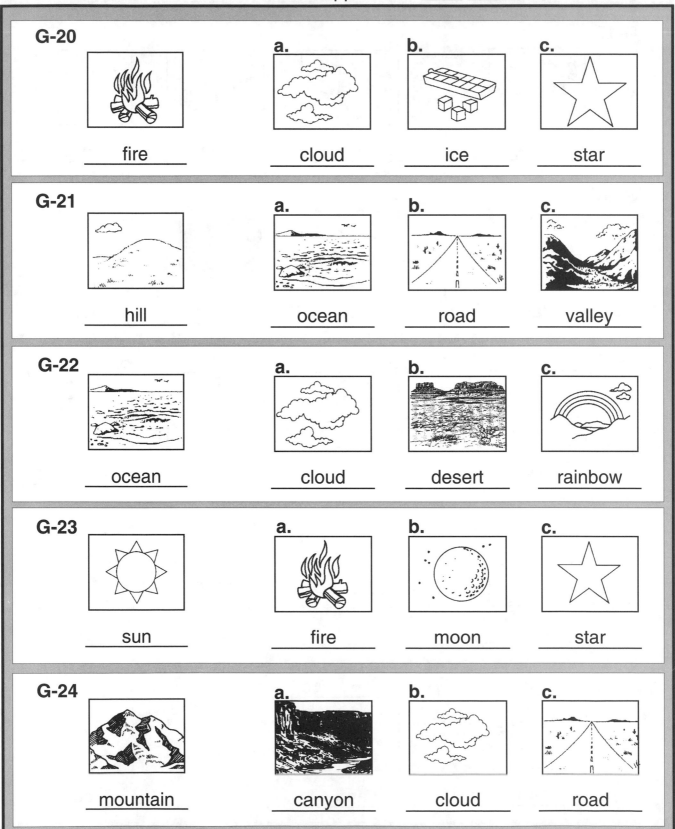

G-20

fire

a. cloud

b. ice

c. star

G-21

hill

a. ocean

b. road

c. valley

G-22

ocean

a. cloud

b. desert

c. rainbow

G-23

sun

a. fire

b. moon

c. star

G-24

mountain

a. canyon

b. cloud

c. road

OPPOSITES—SELECT

DIRECTIONS: Each line contains four words. Read the first word and think about what it means. One of the next three words will mean the <u>opposite</u> of the first word. Underline the word that is the opposite of the first word.

G-25

    clean   **a.** dirty   **b.** new   **c.** old

G-26

    lost   **a.** found   **b.** gone   **c.** look

G-27

    catch   **a.** ball   **b.** play   **c.** throw

G-28

    die   **a.** live   **b.** old   **c.** sick

G-29

    enter   **a.** leave   **b.** open   **c.** stay

G-30

    hard   **a.** difficult   **b.** easy   **c.** problem

G-31

    dull   **a.** boring   **b.** exciting   **c.** long

G-32

    hard   **a.** brittle   **b.** sharp   **c.** soft

G-33

    dull   **a.** blunt   **b.** sharp   **c.** worn

OPPOSITES—SELECT

DIRECTIONS: Each line contains four "direction" words. Read the first word and think about what it means. One of the next three words will mean the <u>opposite</u> of the first word. Underline the word that is the opposite of the first word.

G-34

back   **a.** bone   **b.** end   **c.** front

G-35

upper   **a.** class   **b.** lower   **c.** story

G-36

begin   **a.** end   **b.** go   **c.** start

G-37

north   **a.** east   **b.** south   **c.** west

G-38

give   **a.** present   **b.** receive   **c.** rent

G-39

right   **a.** above   **b.** below   **c.** left

G-40

head   **a.** first   **b.** foot   **c.** strong

G-41

leave   **a.** arrive   **b.** exit   **c.** run

G-42

go   **a.** come   **b.** exit   **c.** leave

OPPOSITES—SELECT

DIRECTIONS: Each line contains four science or weather words. Read the first word and think about what it means. One of the next three words will mean the <u>opposite</u> of the first word. Underline the word that is the opposite of the first word.

G-43

    dry   **a.** bright   **b.** hot   **c.** wet

G-44

    clear   **a.** bright   **b.** cloudy   **c.** sunny

G-45

    hot   **a.** cold   **b.** heat   **c.** warm

G-46

    sunny   **a.** bright   **b.** cloudy   **c.** hot

G-47

    rainy   **a.** cloudy   **b.** cold   **c.** sunny

G-48

    big   **a.** large   **b.** little   **c.** tall

G-49

    warm   **a.** bright   **b.** clothes   **c.** cool

G-50

    boiling   **a.** baking   **b.** cooking   **c.** freezing

G-51

    heavy   **a.** firm   **b.** light   **c.** weight

OPPOSITES—SELECT

DIRECTIONS: Each line contains four words about amount or time. Read the first word and think about what it means. One of the next three words will mean the <u>opposite</u> of the first word. Underline the word that is the opposite of the first word.

G-52

often   **a.** again   **b.** repeat   **c.** seldom

G-53

always   **a.** never   **b.** often   **c.** some

G-54

tight   **a.** loose   **b.** close   **c.** sharp

G-55

none   **a.** empty   **b.** nothing   **c.** some

G-56

all   **a.** every   **b.** none   **c.** some

G-57

now   **a.** here   **b.** often   **c.** then

G-58

many   **a.** all   **b.** few   **c.** none

G-59

past   **a.** before   **b.** future   **c.** then

G-60

everything   **a.** all   **b.** nothing   **c.** something

OPPOSITES—SELECT

DIRECTIONS: Each line contains four words used in art lessons. Read the first word and think about what it means. One of the next three words will mean the <u>opposite</u> of the first word. Underline the word that is the opposite of the first.

G-61

dark   **a.** dim   **b.** heavy   **c.** light

G-62

small   **a.** heavy   **b.** large   **c.** little

G-63

dull   **a.** bright   **b.** dim   **c.** light

G-64

smooth   **a.** glass   **b.** rough   **c.** slick

G-65

tall   **a.** high   **b.** short   **c.** round

G-66

easy   **a.** soft   **b.** simple   **c.** hard

G-67

fine   **a.** coarse   **b.** dim   **c.** soft

G-68

thick   **a.** fat   **b.** thin   **c.** wide

G-69

zigzag   **a.** bumpy   **b.** straight   **c.** up and down

OPPOSITES—SUPPLY

DIRECTIONS: Each line contains a word. Read the given word and think about what it means. Think of a word that means the <u>opposite</u>. Write the word that you think of. (If you can think of other opposites, write them all down.)

G-70

fast _____

G-71

love _____

G-72

leader _____

G-73

clean _____

G-74

happy _____

G-75

whisper _____

G-76

lost _____

G-77

work _____

G-78

asleep _____

OPPOSITES—SUPPLY

DIRECTIONS: Each line contains a "direction" word. Read the given word and think about what it means. Think of a word that means the <u>opposite</u>. Write the word that you think of. (If you can think of other opposites, write them all down.)

G-79

close _____

G-80

start _____

G-81

true _____

G-82

ahead _____

G-83

front _____

G-84

top _____

G-85

later _____

G-86

remember _____

G-87

receive _____

OPPOSITES—SUPPLY

DIRECTIONS: Each line contains a word about action, amount, or order. Read the given word and think about what it means. Think of a word that means the <u>opposite</u> and write it. (If you can think of other opposites, write them all down.)

G-88

dark _____

G-89

go _____

G-90

run _____

G-91

many _____

G-92

none _____

G-93

more _____

G-94

after _____

G-95

last _____

G-96

never _____

SIMILARITIES—SELECT

DIRECTIONS: Each line contains four words. Read the first word and think about what it means. One of the next three words will mean almost the same thing. Circle the word that is <u>most</u> <u>like</u> the first word.

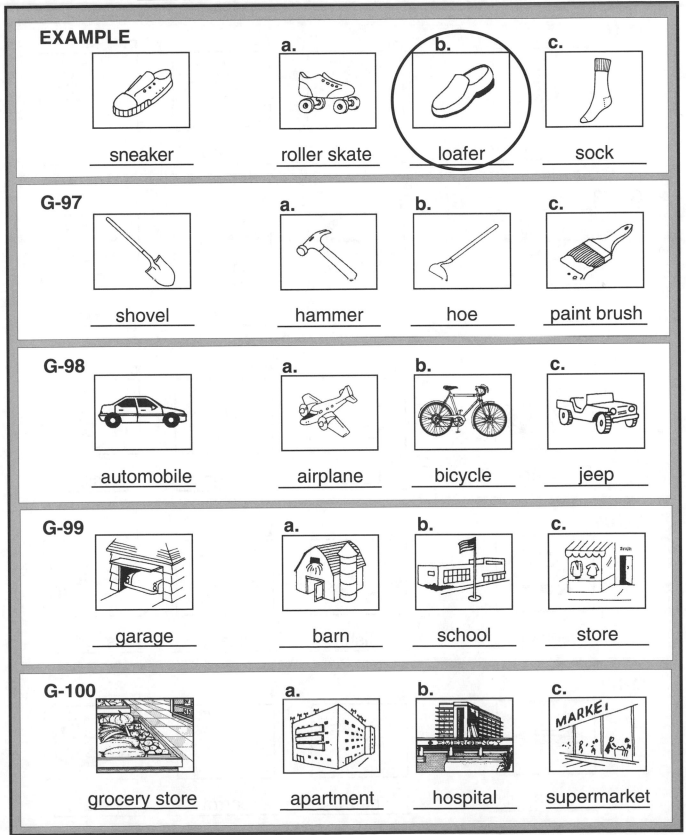

EXAMPLE

	a.	b.	c.
sneaker	roller skate	loafer	sock

G-97

	a.	b.	c.
shovel	hammer	hoe	paint brush

G-98

	a.	b.	c.
automobile	airplane	bicycle	jeep

G-99

	a.	b.	c.
garage	barn	school	store

G-100

	a.	b.	c.
grocery store	apartment	hospital	supermarket

SIMILARITIES—SELECT

DIRECTIONS: Each line contains four science or health words. Read the first word and think about what it means. One of the next three words will mean almost the same thing. Circle the word that is <u>most</u> <u>like</u> the first word.

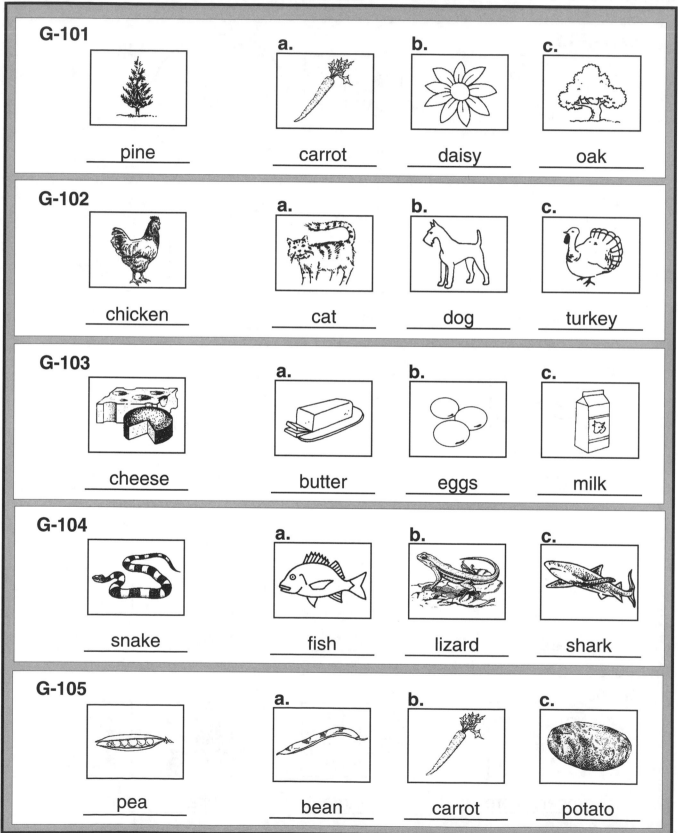

G-101

pine

a. carrot

b. daisy

c. oak

G-102

chicken

a. cat

b. dog

c. turkey

G-103

cheese

a. butter

b. eggs

c. milk

G-104

snake

a. fish

b. lizard

c. shark

G-105

pea

a. bean

b. carrot

c. potato

SIMILARITIES—SELECT

DIRECTIONS: Each line contains four words that tell what you do at school. Read the first word and think about what it means. One of the next three words will mean almost the same thing. Underline the word that is <u>most</u> <u>like</u> the first word.

G-106

listen   **a.** hear   **b.** speak   **c.** talk

G-107

talk   **a.** read   **b.** say   **c.** sing

G-108

draw   **a.** around   **b.** color   **c.** work

G-109

study   **a.** learn   **b.** lesson   **c.** talk

G-110

act   **a.** do   **b.** relax   **c.** rest

G-111

learn   **a.** discover   **b.** reply   **c.** show

G-112

ask   **a.** about   **b.** receive   **c.** question

G-113

answer   **a.** hear   **b.** reply   **c.** question

G-114

solve   **a.** ask   **b.** figure out   **c.** problem

SIMILARITIES—SELECT

DIRECTIONS: Each line contains four household words. Read the first word and think about what it means. One of the next three words will mean almost the same thing. Underline the word that is <u>most</u> <u>like</u> the first word.

G-115

    newspaper   **a.** book   **b.** dictionary   **c.** magazine

G-116

    cook   **a.** bake   **b.** dinner   **c.** soup

G-117

    fix   **a.** build   **b.** repair   **c.** wreck

G-118

    door   **a.** gate   **b.** roof   **c.** window

G-119

    rug   **a.** carpet   **b.** floor   **c.** sweeper

G-120

    curtains   **a.** drapes   **b.** door   **c.** window

G-121

    clean   **a.** clothes   **b.** house   **c.** wash

G-122

    meal   **a.** cook   **b.** dinner   **c.** vegetable

G-123

    broom   **a.** sponge   **b.** handle   **c.** sweeper

SIMILARITIES—SELECT

DIRECTIONS: Each line contains four action words. Read the first word and think about what it means. One of the next three words will mean almost the same thing. Underline the word that is <u>most</u> <u>like</u> the first word.

G-124			
pay	**a.** owe	**b.** spend	**c.** take

G-125			
run	**a.** jog	**b.** sit	**c.** walk

G-126			
look	**a.** hear	**b.** talk	**c.** watch

G-127			
stay	**a.** go	**b.** leave	**c.** remain

G-128			
call	**a.** say	**b.** shout	**c.** tell

G-129			
take	**a.** carry	**b.** give	**c.** keep

G-130			
throw	**a.** toss	**b.** catch	**c.** hit

G-131			
build	**a.** fix	**b.** make	**c.** repair

G-132			
hide	**a.** cover	**b.** seek	**c.** show

SIMILARITIES—SELECT

DIRECTIONS: Each line contains four words from science. Read the first word and think about what it means. One of the next three words will mean almost the same thing. Underline the word that is <u>most</u> <u>like</u> the first word.

G-133

| sound | **a.** noise | **b.** quiet | **c.** silence |

G-134

| heat | **a.** light | **b.** stove | **c.** warmth |

G-135

| sun | **a.** beam | **b.** shine | **c.** star |

G-136

| rock | **a.** mountain | **b.** ocean | **c.** stone |

G-137

| fog | **a.** cloud | **b.** ice | **c.** snow |

G-138

| beak | **a.** bill | **b.** claw | **c.** wing |

G-139

| baby | **a.** brother | **b.** child | **c.** sister |

G-140

| earth | **a.** continent | **b.** country | **c.** world |

G-141

| map | **a.** country | **b.** drawing | **c.** photograph |

SIMILARITIES—SUPPLY

DIRECTIONS: Each line contains a word used to describe something. Read the word and think about what it means. Think of a word or phrase that means <u>almost</u> the same and write it down. Write as many similar words as you can think of.

G-142

short   _____

G-143

big   _____

G-144

friendly   _____

G-145

heavy   _____

G-146

happy   _____

G-147

good   _____

G-148

sweet   _____

G-149

beautiful   _____

G-150

safe   _____

SIMILARITIES—SUPPLY

DIRECTIONS: Each line contains an action word. Read the word and think about what it means. Think of a word or phrase that means <u>almost</u> the same and write it down. Write as many similar words as you can think of.

G-151

touch _____

G-152

see _____

G-153

hear _____

G-154

speak _____

G-155

work _____

G-156

study _____

G-157

build _____

G-158

fix _____

G-159

destroy _____

SIMILARITIES—SUPPLY

DIRECTIONS: Each line contains a word used in instructions. Read the word and think about what it means. Think of a word or phrase that means almost the same and write it down. Write as many similar words as you can think of.

G-160

    leave   _____

G-161

    above   _____

G-162

    enter   _____

G-163

    below   _____

G-164

    continue   _____

G-165

    stop   _____

G-166

    choose   _____

G-167

    listen   _____

G-168

    fasten   _____

HOW ALIKE?—SELECT

DIRECTIONS: Each activity contains two pictures. Think about the ways these two things are alike. Circle the letters of the sentences that are true of both items.

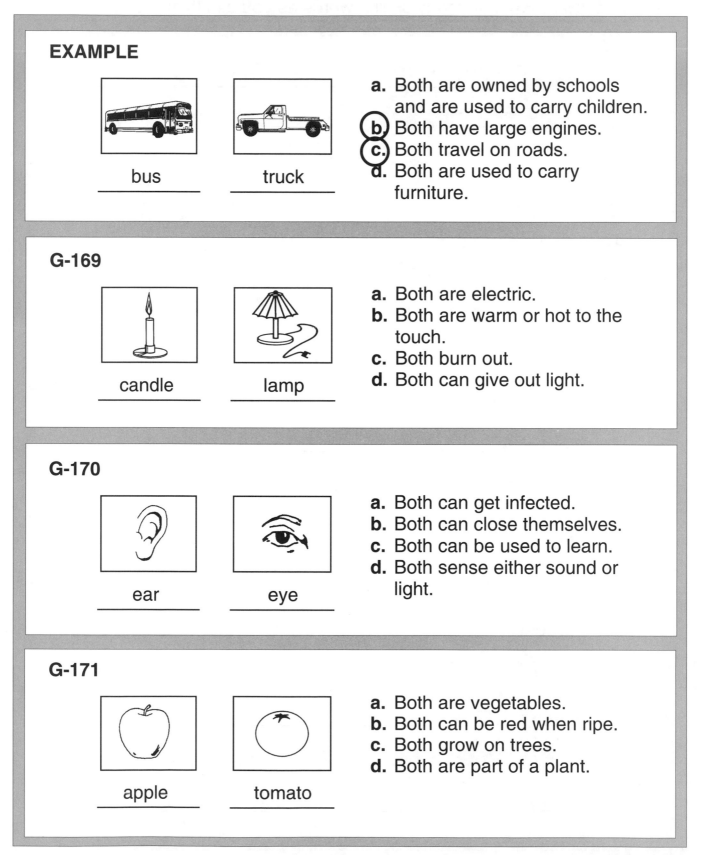

EXAMPLE

bus   truck

a. Both are owned by schools and are used to carry children.
b. Both have large engines.
c. Both travel on roads.
d. Both are used to carry furniture.

G-169

candle   lamp

a. Both are electric.
b. Both are warm or hot to the touch.
c. Both burn out.
d. Both can give out light.

G-170

ear   eye

a. Both can get infected.
b. Both can close themselves.
c. Both can be used to learn.
d. Both sense either sound or light.

G-171

apple   tomato

a. Both are vegetables.
b. Both can be red when ripe.
c. Both grow on trees.
d. Both are part of a plant.

HOW ALIKE?—SELECT

DIRECTIONS: Each activity contains two pictures. Think about the ways these two things are alike. Circle the letters of the sentences that are true of both items.

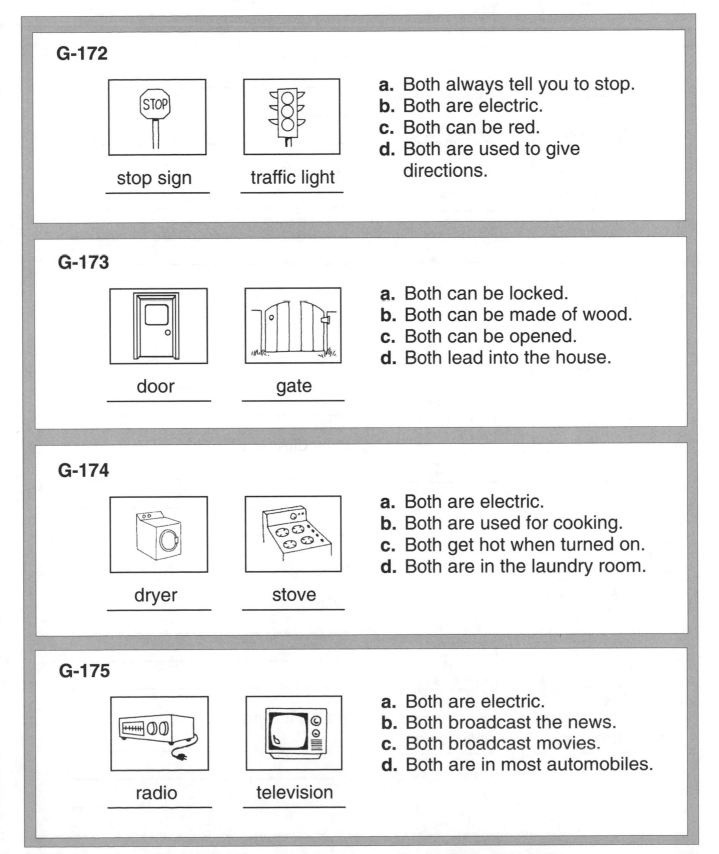

G-172

stop sign   traffic light

a. Both always tell you to stop.
b. Both are electric.
c. Both can be red.
d. Both are used to give directions.

G-173

door   gate

a. Both can be locked.
b. Both can be made of wood.
c. Both can be opened.
d. Both lead into the house.

G-174

dryer   stove

a. Both are electric.
b. Both are used for cooking.
c. Both get hot when turned on.
d. Both are in the laundry room.

G-175

radio   television

a. Both are electric.
b. Both broadcast the news.
c. Both broadcast movies.
d. Both are in most automobiles.

HOW ALIKE AND HOW DIFFERENT?

DIRECTIONS: Each activity contains two pictures. Think about the ways these two things are alike and different. Tell how they are alike and how they are different, and give your reasons why.

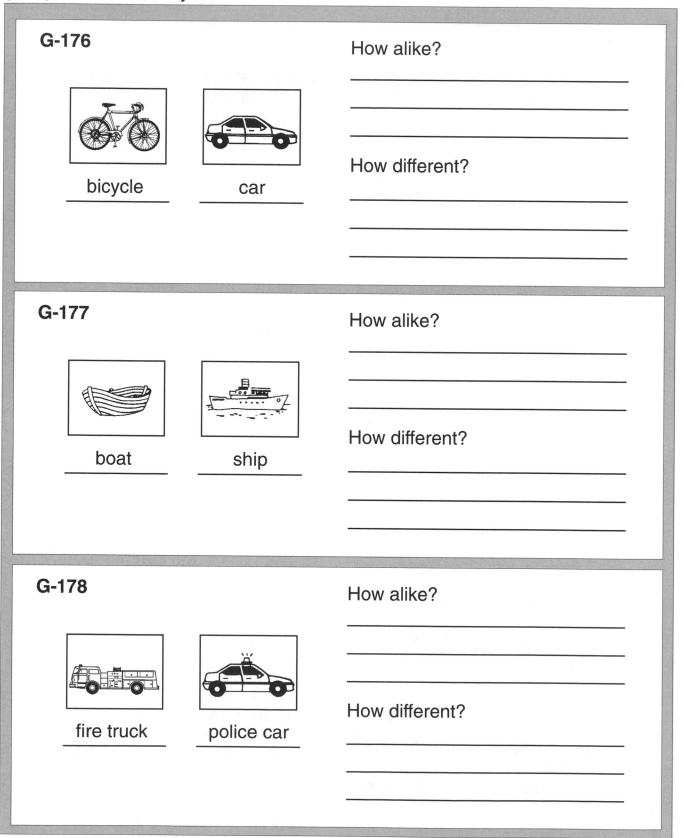

G-176

bicycle

car

How alike?

How different?

G-177

boat

ship

How alike?

How different?

G-178

fire truck

police car

How alike?

How different?

HOW ALIKE AND HOW DIFFERENT?

DIRECTIONS: Each activity contains two pictures. Think about the ways these two things are alike and different. Tell how they are alike and how they are different, and give your reasons why.

G-179

book   television

How alike?

_____

_____

_____

How different?

_____

_____

_____

G-180

baseball   football

How alike?

_____

_____

_____

How different?

_____

_____

_____

G-181

mother   teacher

How alike?

_____

_____

_____

How different?

_____

_____

_____

HOW ALIKE AND HOW DIFFERENT?

DIRECTIONS: Each activity contains two pictures. Think about the ways these two things are alike and different. Tell how they are alike and how they are different, and give your reasons why.

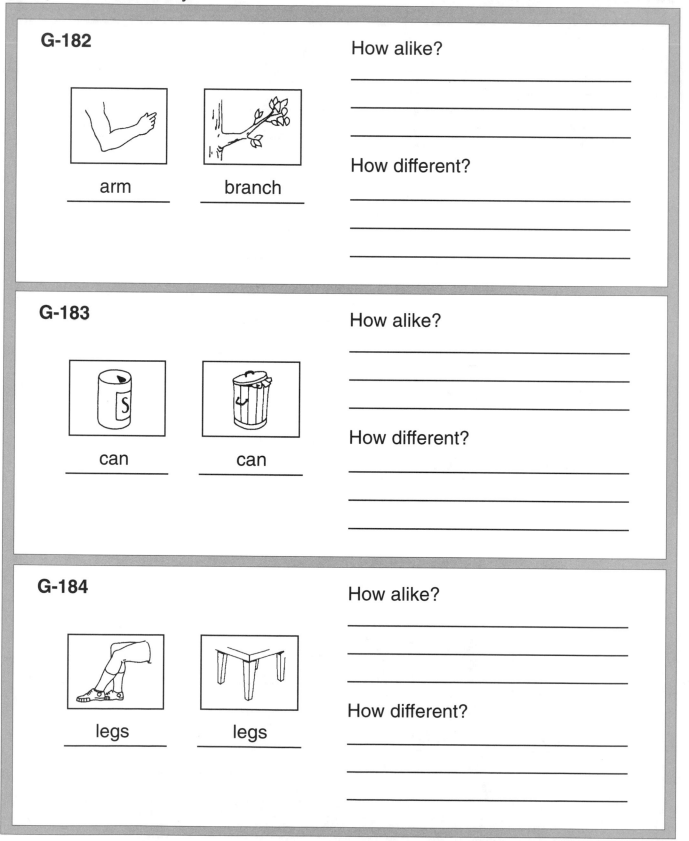

G-182

arm   branch

How alike?

_____

_____

_____

How different?

_____

_____

_____

G-183

can   can

How alike?

_____

_____

_____

How different?

_____

_____

_____

G-184

legs   legs

How alike?

_____

_____

_____

How different?

_____

_____

_____

HOW ALIKE AND HOW DIFFERENT?

DIRECTIONS: Each activity contains two pictures. Think about the ways these two things are alike and different. Tell how they are alike and how they are different, and give your reasons why.

G-185

snake   lizard

How alike?

_____

_____

_____

How different?

_____

_____

_____

G-186

deer   horse

How alike?

_____

_____

_____

How different?

_____

_____

_____

G-187

shark   whale

How alike?

_____

_____

_____

How different?

_____

_____

_____

COMPARE AND CONTRAST—GRAPHIC ORGANIZER

DIRECTIONS: Read the passage carefully to decide how nouns and verbs are alike and different. Record the information on the diagram.

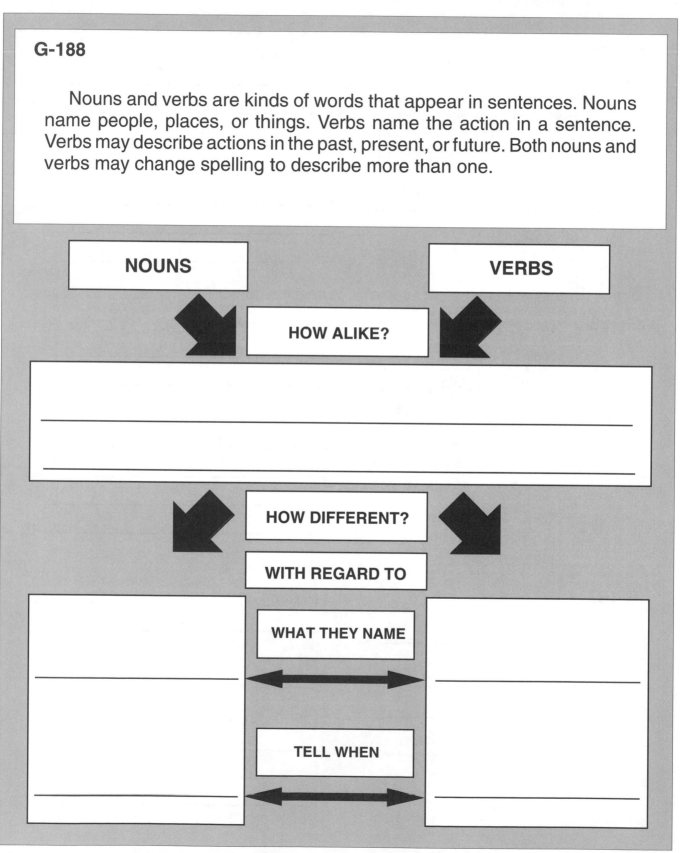

G-188

Nouns and verbs are kinds of words that appear in sentences. Nouns name people, places, or things. Verbs name the action in a sentence. Verbs may describe actions in the past, present, or future. Both nouns and verbs may change spelling to describe more than one.

NOUNS

VERBS

HOW ALIKE?

HOW DIFFERENT?

WITH REGARD TO

WHAT THEY NAME

TELL WHEN

COMPARE AND CONTRAST—GRAPHIC ORGANIZER

DIRECTIONS: Use the diagram to show how statements and questions are alike and how they are different.

G-189

Statements and questions are kinds of sentences and tell whole thoughts. Both contain a subject and a verb and end with a punctuation mark. Both are used to give or get information. Paragraphs can have both statements and questions.

Statements give information about people, places, things, or ideas. They usually end with a period. The whole verb usually follows the subject; for example, "The motor <u>is running</u>."

Questions ask for information about people, places, things, or ideas. They always end with a question mark. The subject usually comes between parts of the verb; for example, "Is the <u>motor</u> running?"

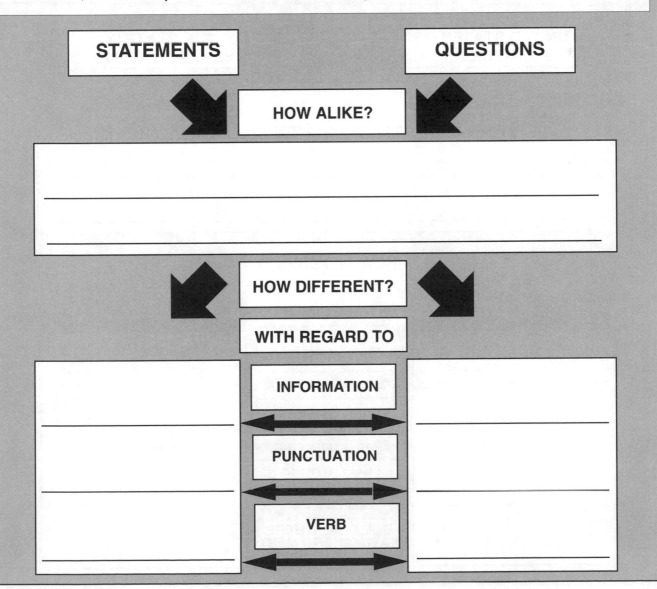

COMPARE AND CONTRAST—GRAPHIC ORGANIZER

DIRECTIONS: Locate your state on a map of the United States of America. Read the passage carefully to see how the United States of America and your state are alike and how they are different. Record the information on the diagram.

G-190

   The United States government and your state government each have a chief official, meet in a particular city, and have a special building. The governor is the chief official of a state. The governor sees that the laws made by the state legislature are carried out. The state government is located in the state capital. The state legislature meets in the state capitol building.

   The chief official of the national government is the president of the United States, who carries out laws passed by the Congress. Congress meets in the Capitol building in Washington, D.C.

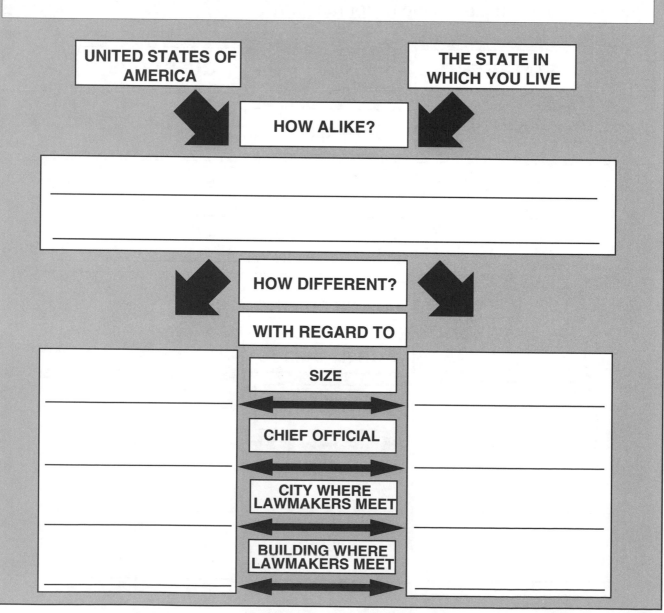

© 1997 CRITICAL THINKING BOOKS & SOFTWARE, P. O. BOX 448, PACIFIC GROVE, CA 93950 • 800-458-4849

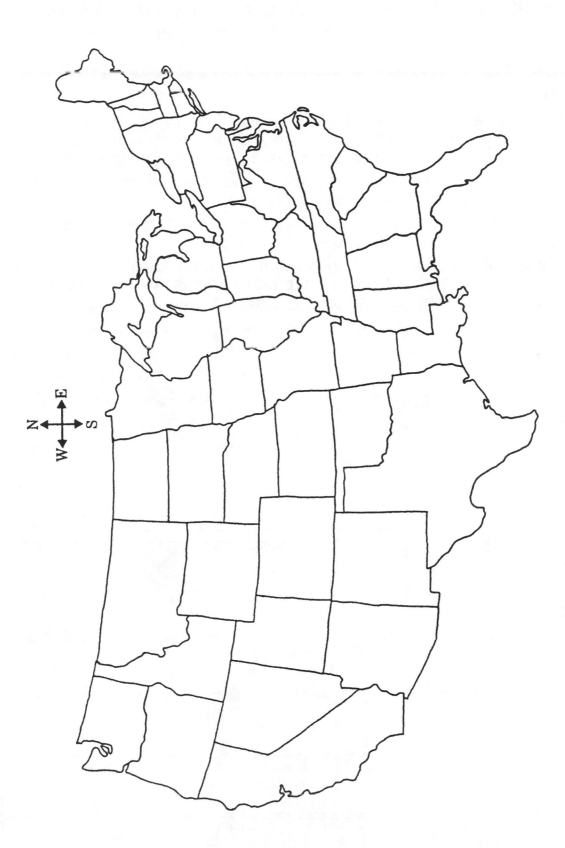

COMPARING LIVING AND NONLIVING THINGS

DIRECTIONS: Read the passage carefully, then use the diagram below to record how living and nonliving things are alike and how they are different.

G-191

All things have weight and take up space. Both living and nonliving things come in many sizes and shapes. There are tiny plants, tiny animals, and tiny grains of sand as well as large plants, large animals, and large mountains.

Most animals can move themselves around. Plants must be moved by wind or animals. No nonliving thing can move by itself.

All living things breathe, but plants breathe differently from animals. Nonliving things do not breathe. Breathing is called respiration.

Nonliving things do not eat and do not give birth. Giving birth is known as reproduction. All plants and animals reproduce themselves. Plants and animals need nourishment but get their food in different ways.

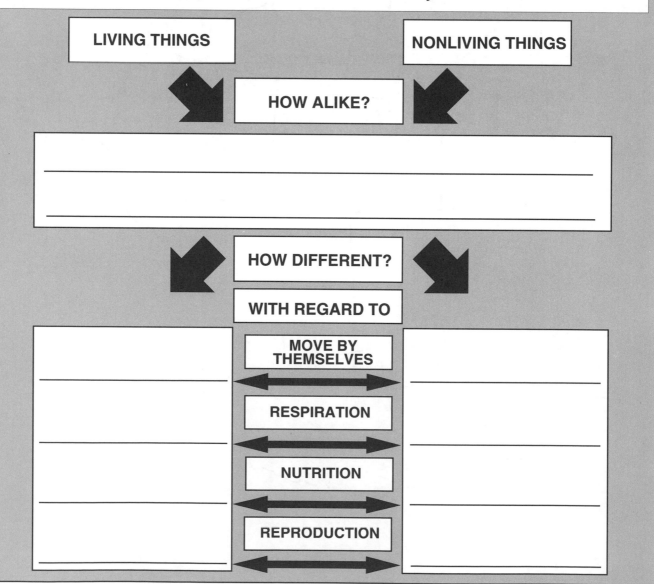

CHAPTER EIGHT

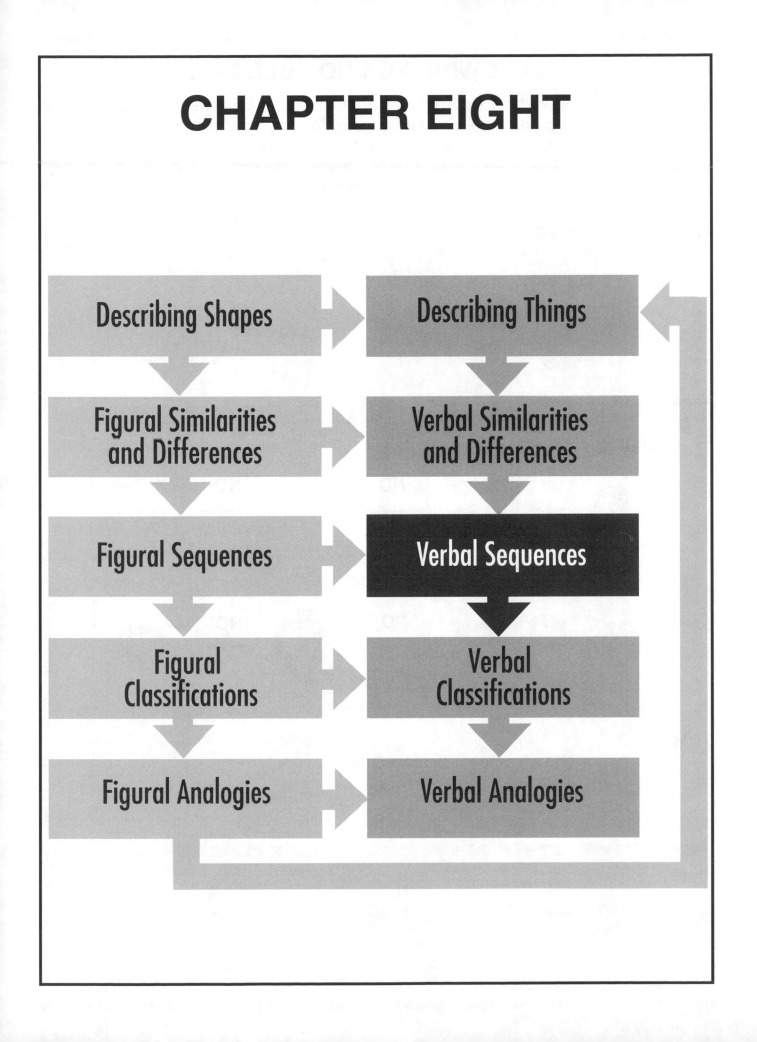

FOLLOWING YES-NO RULES—A

DIRECTIONS: You will be following rules about circles. **YES** is used to show that the two circles are the same size, and **NO** is used to show that the circles are not the same size. Draw circles of the right size to follow the yes-or-no rule.

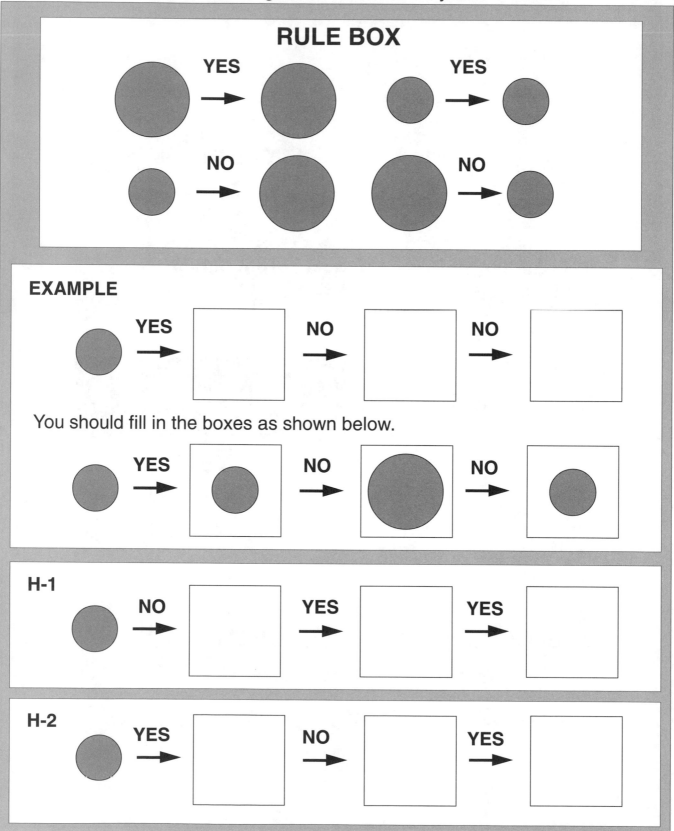

FOLLOWING YES-NO RULES—A

DIRECTIONS: In the blank boxes, draw dark or white circles to correctly illustrate the yes-or-no rules.

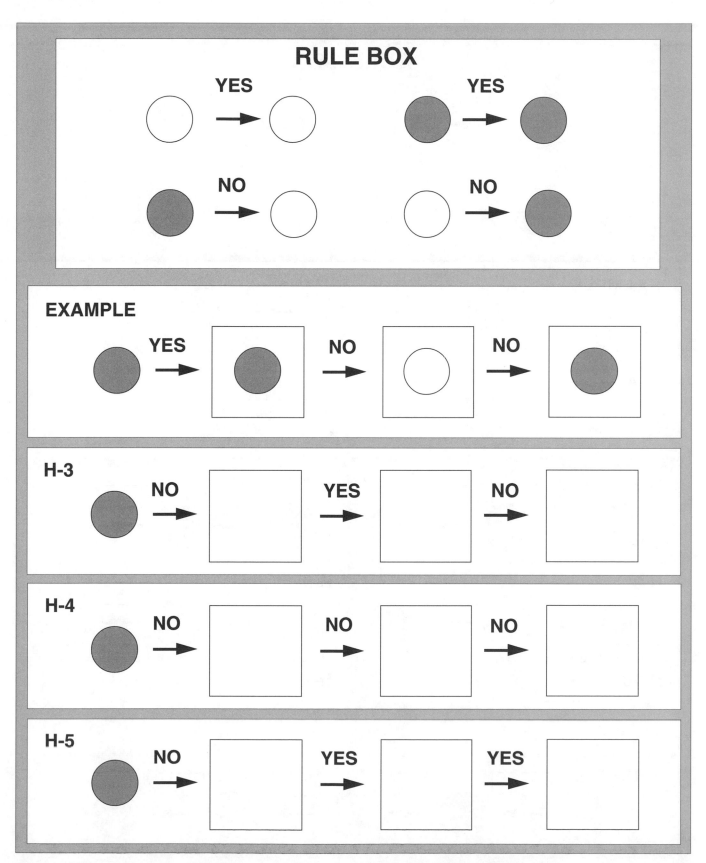

WRITING YES-NO RULES

DIRECTIONS: In the boxes above the arrows, write yes or no to correctly label the illustrated rules.

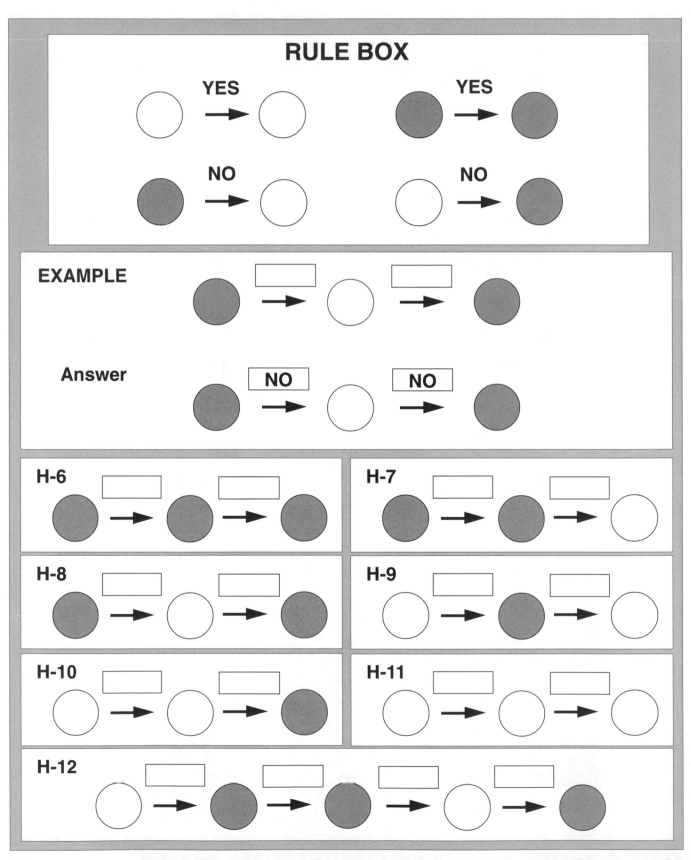

WRITING YES-NO RULES

DIRECTIONS: In the blank boxes, write yes or no to correctly label the yes-or-no rules.

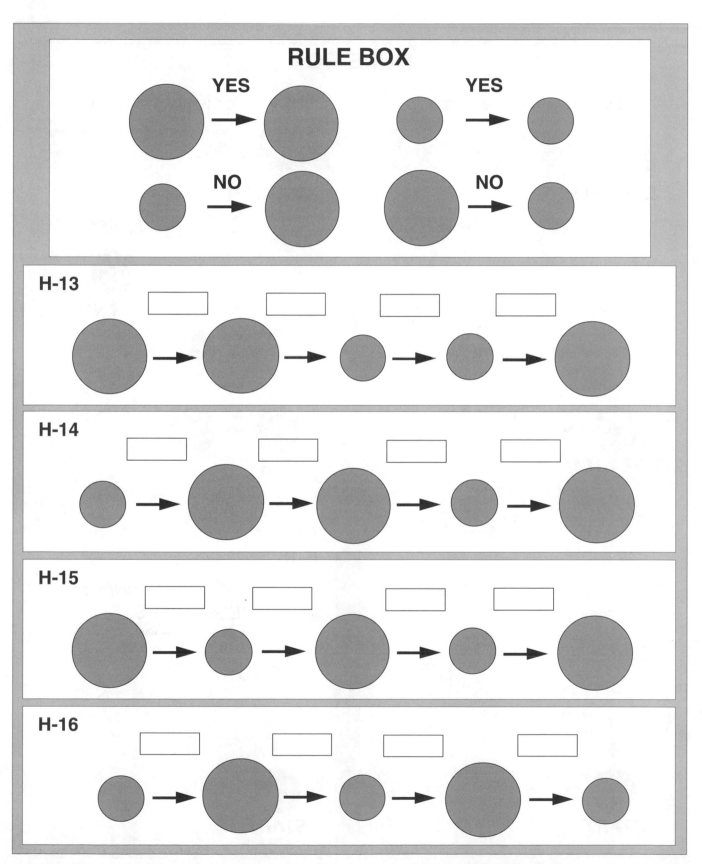

FOLLOWING YES-NO RULES—B

DIRECTIONS: Following the yes-or-no rule, darken the correct circles along the path from start to finish.

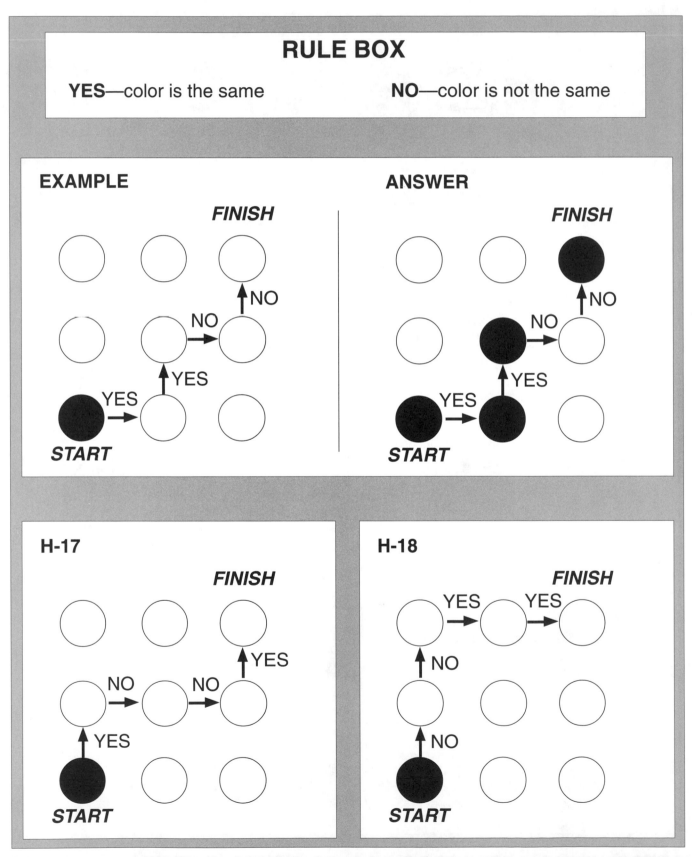

FOLLOWING YES-NO RULES—B

DIRECTIONS: Following the yes-or-no rule, darken the correct circles along the path from start to finish.

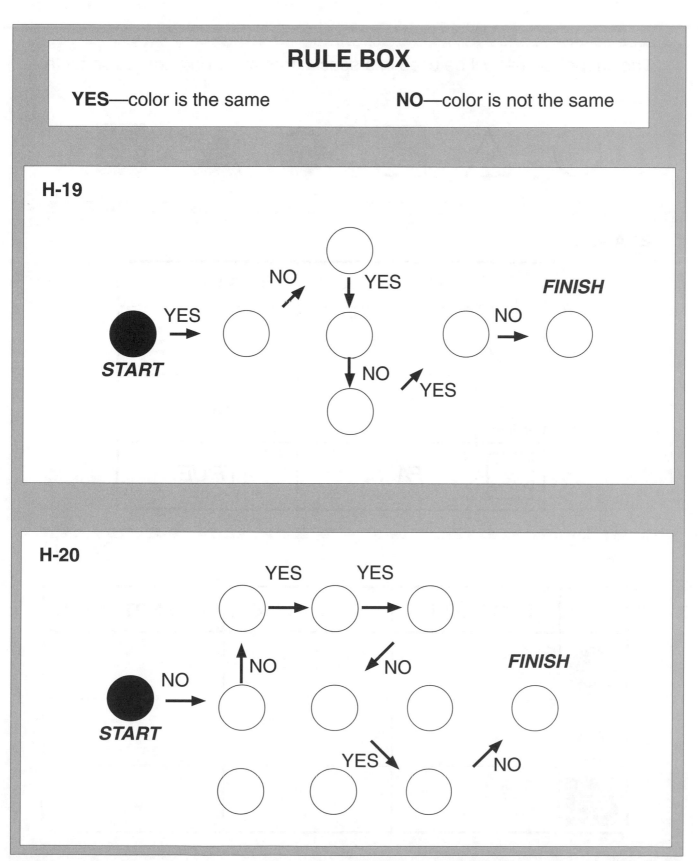

RULE BOX

YES—color is the same   **NO**—color is not the same

H-19

H-20

COMPLETING TRUE-FALSE TABLES

DIRECTIONS: Study the given true-false table and then complete the blank table.

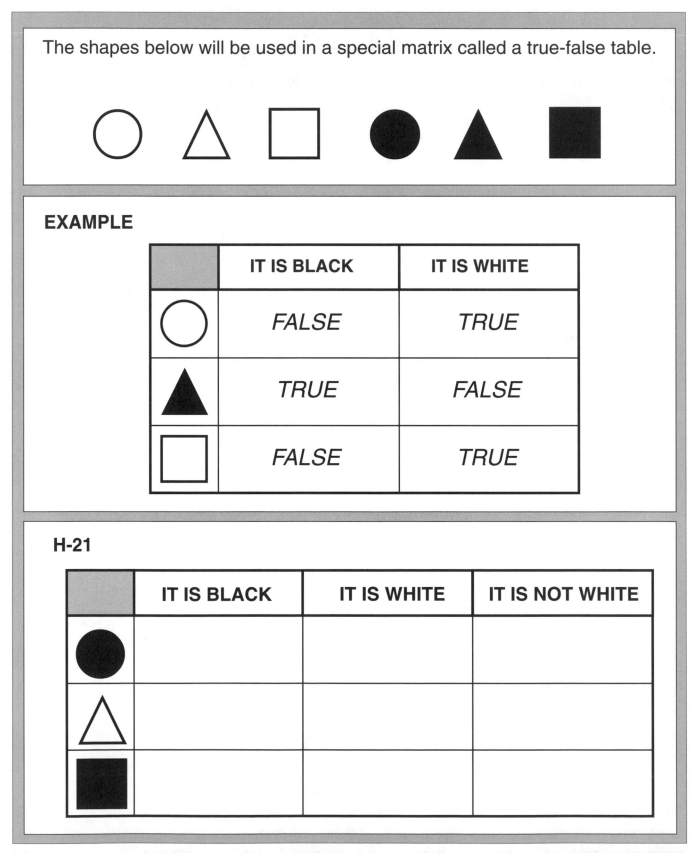

The shapes below will be used in a special matrix called a true-false table.

EXAMPLE

	IT IS BLACK	IT IS WHITE
○	*FALSE*	*TRUE*
▲	*TRUE*	*FALSE*
□	*FALSE*	*TRUE*

H-21

	IT IS BLACK	IT IS WHITE	IT IS NOT WHITE
●			
△			
■			

COMPLETING TRUE-FALSE TABLES

DIRECTIONS: Complete the blank true-false tables.

H-22

	IT IS WHITE	IT IS BLACK	IT IS NOT BLACK
 ▲			
 ○			
□			

H-23

	IT IS A SQUARE	IT IS A CIRCLE	IT IS NOT A CIRCLE
■			
 ○			
●			

COMPLETING TRUE-FALSE TABLES

DIRECTIONS: Complete the blank true-false tables.

H-24

	IT IS ALL BLACK	IT IS ALL WHITE	IT IS NOT ALL WHITE
■			
 ○			
 ◐			

H-25

	IT IS HALF BLACK	IT IS HALF WHITE	IT IS NOT A CIRCLE
●			
▮			
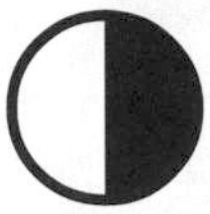 ◐			

FINDING LOCATIONS ON MAPS

DIRECTIONS: Using the map, follow the directions or answer the question in each exercise.

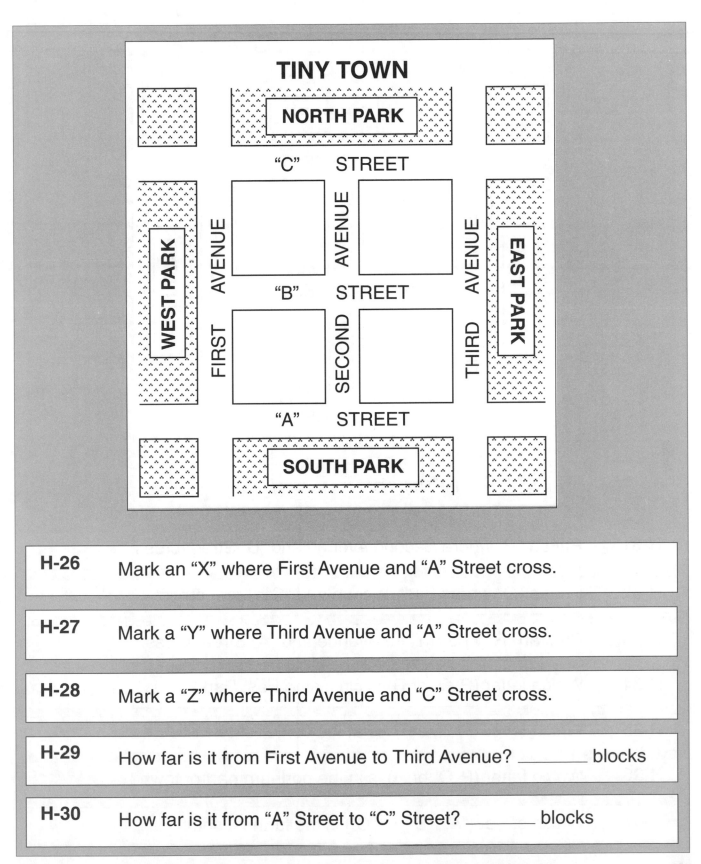

H-26	Mark an "X" where First Avenue and "A" Street cross.

H-27	Mark a "Y" where Third Avenue and "A" Street cross.

H-28	Mark a "Z" where Third Avenue and "C" Street cross.

H-29	How far is it from First Avenue to Third Avenue? _____ blocks

H-30	How far is it from "A" Street to "C" Street? _____ blocks

FINDING LOCATIONS ON MAPS

DIRECTIONS: Using the map, follow the directions or answer the question in each exercise.

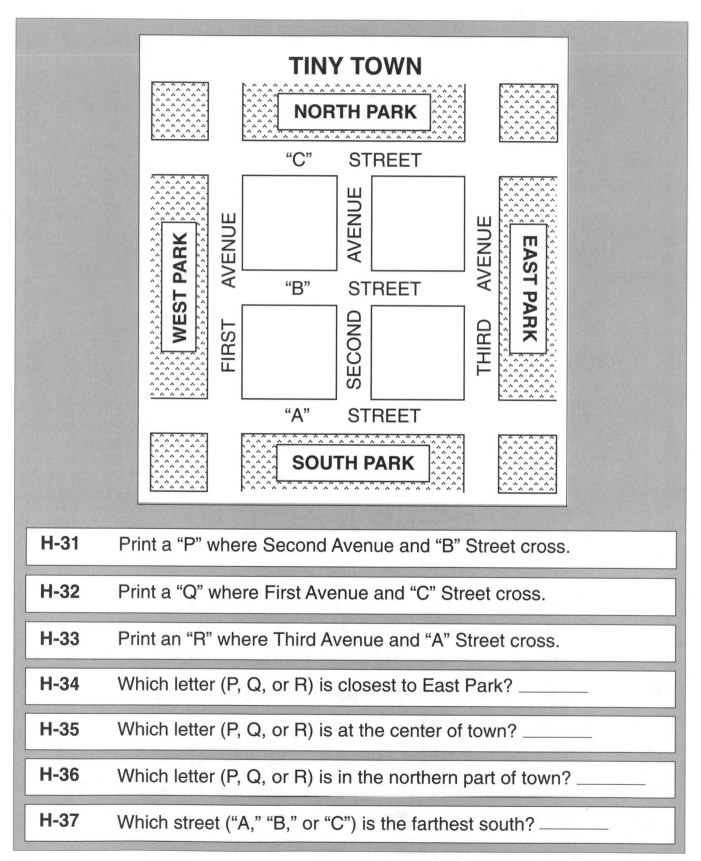

H-31	Print a "P" where Second Avenue and "B" Street cross.
H-32	Print a "Q" where First Avenue and "C" Street cross.
H-33	Print an "R" where Third Avenue and "A" Street cross.
H-34	Which letter (P, Q, or R) is closest to East Park? _____
H-35	Which letter (P, Q, or R) is at the center of town? _____
H-36	Which letter (P, Q, or R) is in the northern part of town? _____
H-37	Which street ("A," "B," or "C") is the farthest south? _____

DESCRIBING LOCATIONS—A

DIRECTIONS: Look at the map and pretend you are standing at Second Avenue and "C" Street facing North Park. Based on that information, answer the questions below.

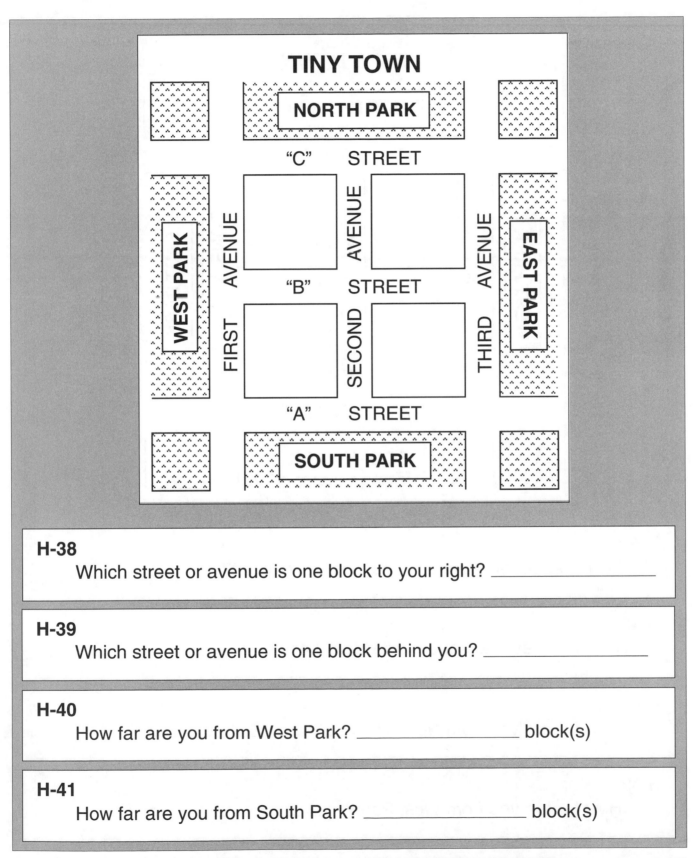

TINY TOWN

NORTH PARK

"C" STREET

WEST PARK

FIRST AVENUE

AVENUE

"B" STREET

SECOND

THIRD AVENUE

EAST PARK

"A" STREET

SOUTH PARK

H-38

Which street or avenue is one block to your right? _____

H-39

Which street or avenue is one block behind you? _____

H-40

How far are you from West Park? _____ block(s)

H-41

How far are you from South Park? _____ block(s)

DESCRIBING LOCATIONS—A

DIRECTIONS: Look at the map and pretend you are standing at Third Avenue and "B" Street facing East Park. Based on that information, answer the questions below.

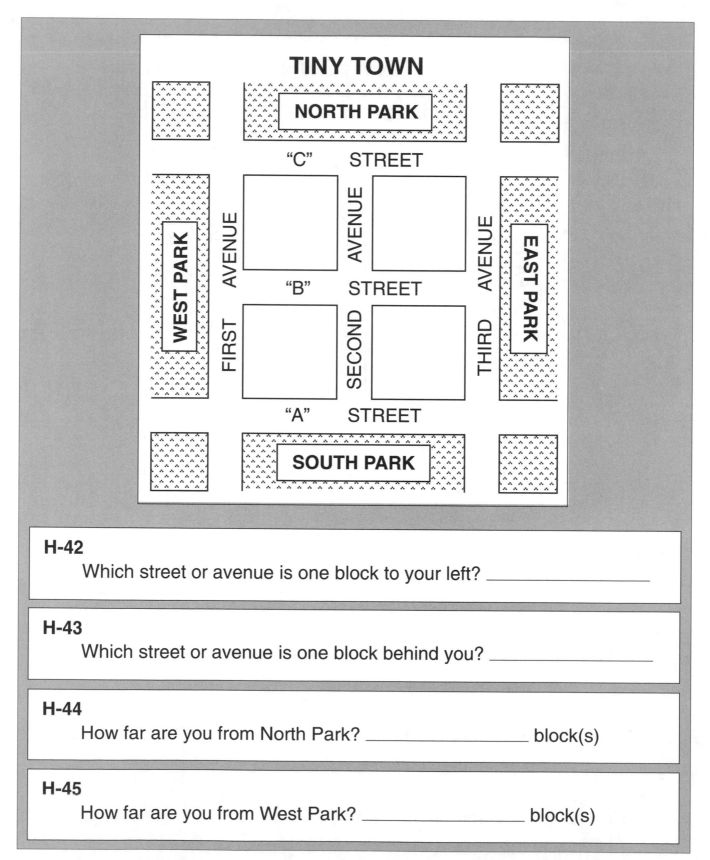

H-42

Which street or avenue is one block to your left? _____

H-43

Which street or avenue is one block behind you? _____

H-44

How far are you from North Park? _____ block(s)

H-45

How far are you from West Park? _____ block(s)

DESCRIBING DIRECTIONS—A

DIRECTIONS: Look at the path along the arrows from "P" to "Q" to "R." Answer the following questions about parts of the path.

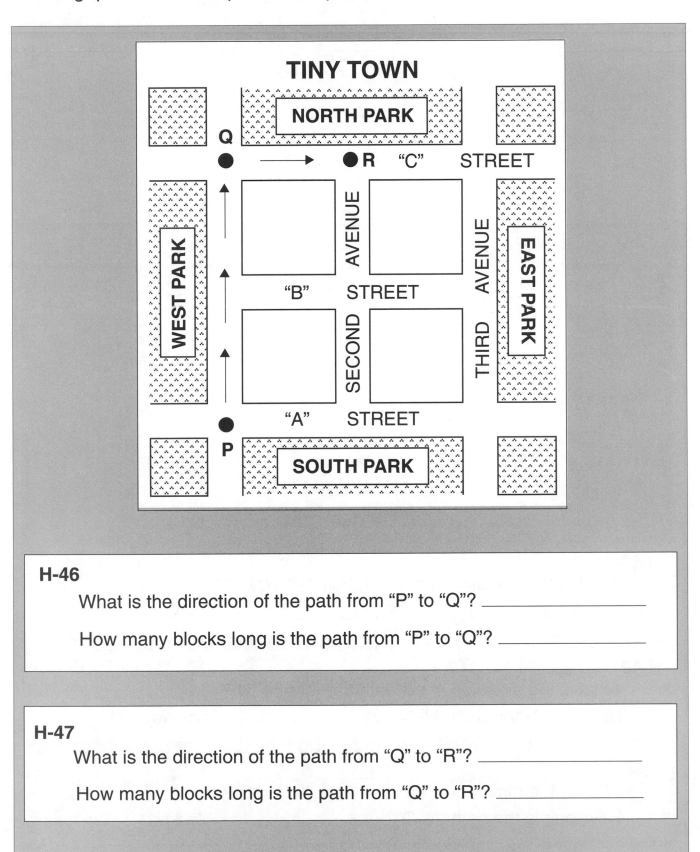

H-46

What is the direction of the path from "P" to "Q"? _____

How many blocks long is the path from "P" to "Q"? _____

H-47

What is the direction of the path from "Q" to "R"? _____

How many blocks long is the path from "Q" to "R"? _____

DESCRIBING DIRECTIONS—A

DIRECTIONS: Look at the path along the arrows from "L" to "M" to "N" to "O." Answer the following questions about parts of the path.

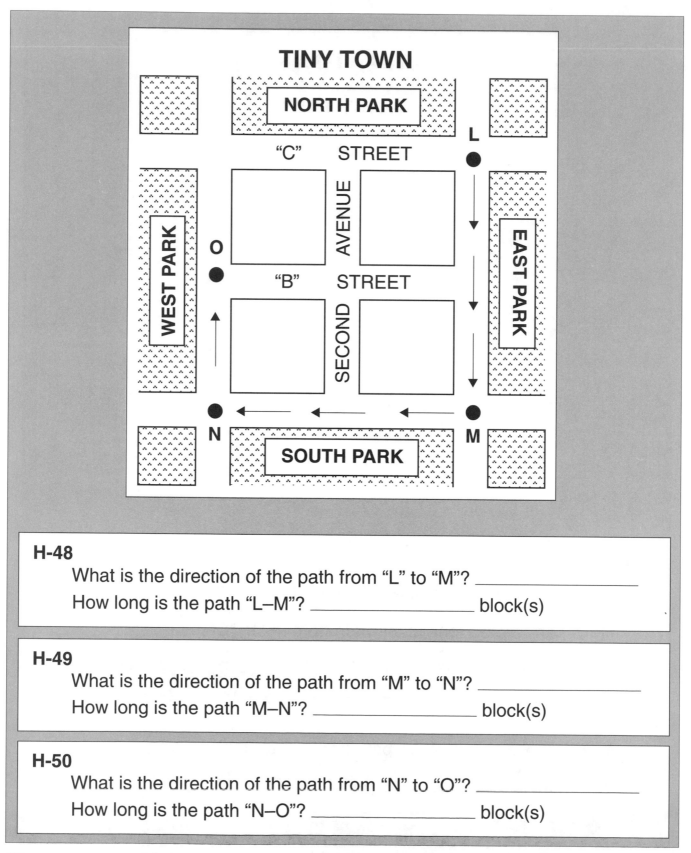

H-48

What is the direction of the path from "L" to "M"? _____

How long is the path "L–M"? _____ block(s)

H-49

What is the direction of the path from "M" to "N"? _____

How long is the path "M–N"? _____ block(s)

H-50

What is the direction of the path from "N" to "O"? _____

How long is the path "N–O"? _____ block(s)

DESCRIBING LOCATIONS—B

DIRECTIONS: Use the map to answer the questions below.

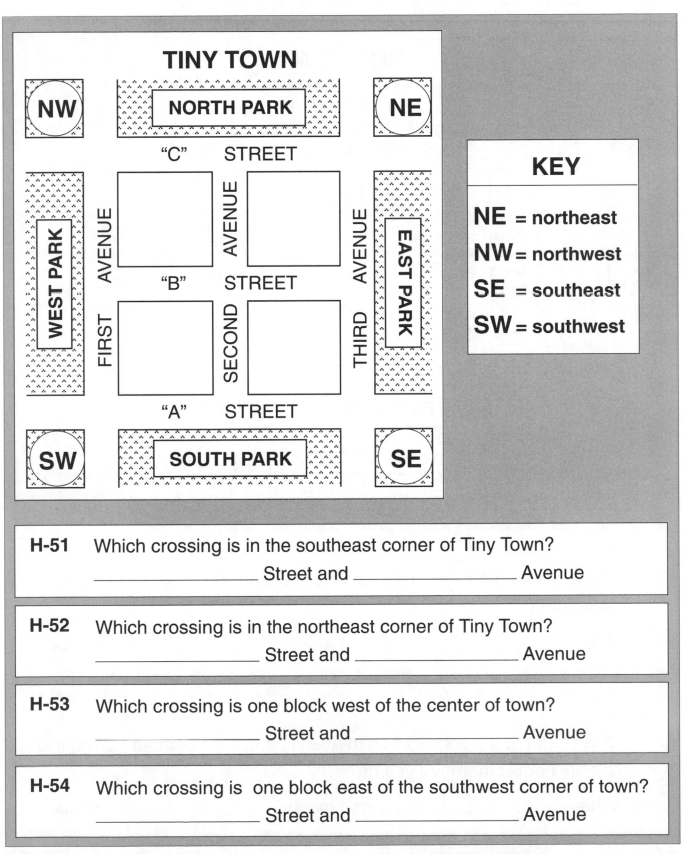

TINY TOWN

NW   NORTH PARK   NE

"C"   STREET

FIRST AVENUE   SECOND AVENUE   THIRD AVENUE

WEST PARK   EAST PARK

"B"   STREET

"A"   STREET

SW   SOUTH PARK   SE

KEY

NE = northeast
NW = northwest
SE = southeast
SW = southwest

H-51 Which crossing is in the southeast corner of Tiny Town?

_____ Street and _____ Avenue

H-52 Which crossing is in the northeast corner of Tiny Town?

_____ Street and _____ Avenue

H-53 Which crossing is one block west of the center of town?

_____ Street and _____ Avenue

H-54 Which crossing is one block east of the southwest corner of town?

_____ Street and _____ Avenue

DESCRIBING DIRECTIONS—B

DIRECTIONS: If you start at Second Avenue and "C" Street and travel two blocks south, you will be on the corner of Second Avenue and "A" Street (follow the arrow from *START* to *FINISH*). Answer the questions below.

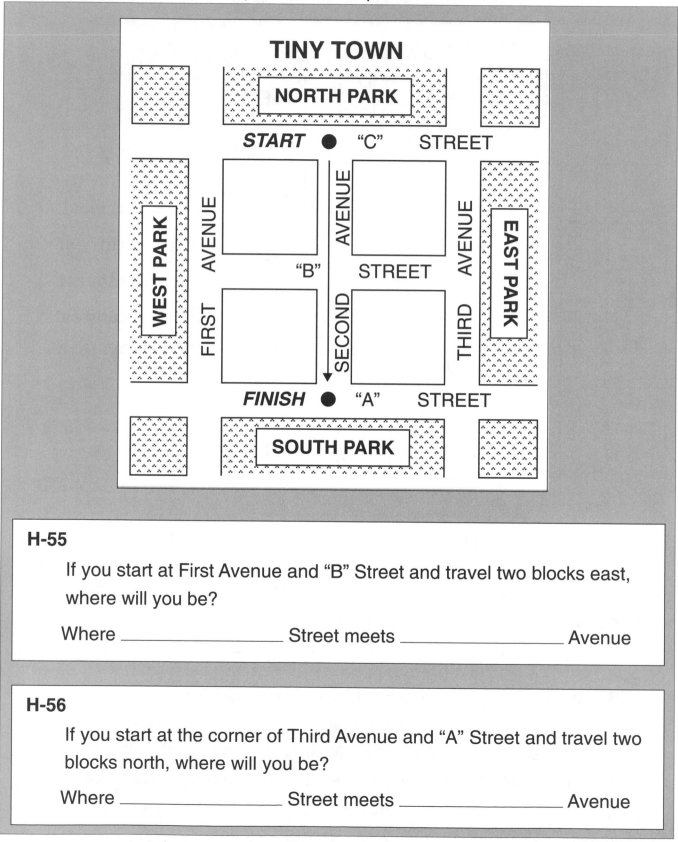

H-55

If you start at First Avenue and "B" Street and travel two blocks east, where will you be?

Where _____ Street meets _____ Avenue

H-56

If you start at the corner of Third Avenue and "A" Street and travel two blocks north, where will you be?

Where _____ Street meets _____ Avenue

DESCRIBING DIRECTIONS—B

DIRECTIONS: Use the map to answer the questions below.

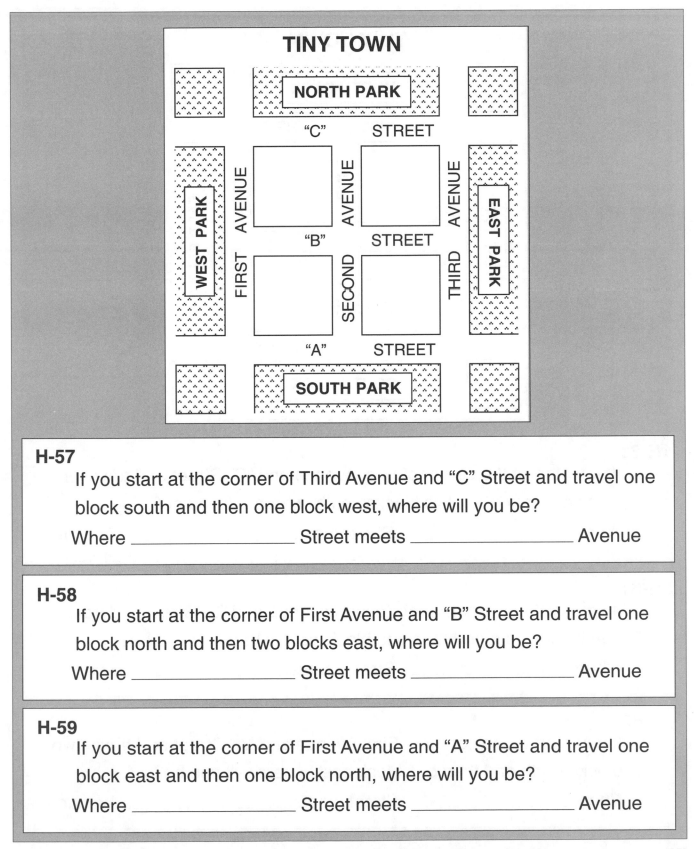

H-57

If you start at the corner of Third Avenue and "C" Street and travel one block south and then one block west, where will you be?

Where _____ Street meets _____ Avenue

H-58

If you start at the corner of First Avenue and "B" Street and travel one block north and then two blocks east, where will you be?

Where _____ Street meets _____ Avenue

H-59

If you start at the corner of First Avenue and "A" Street and travel one block east and then one block north, where will you be?

Where _____ Street meets _____ Avenue

DESCRIBING DIRECTIONS—B

DIRECTIONS: Use the map to answer the questions below.

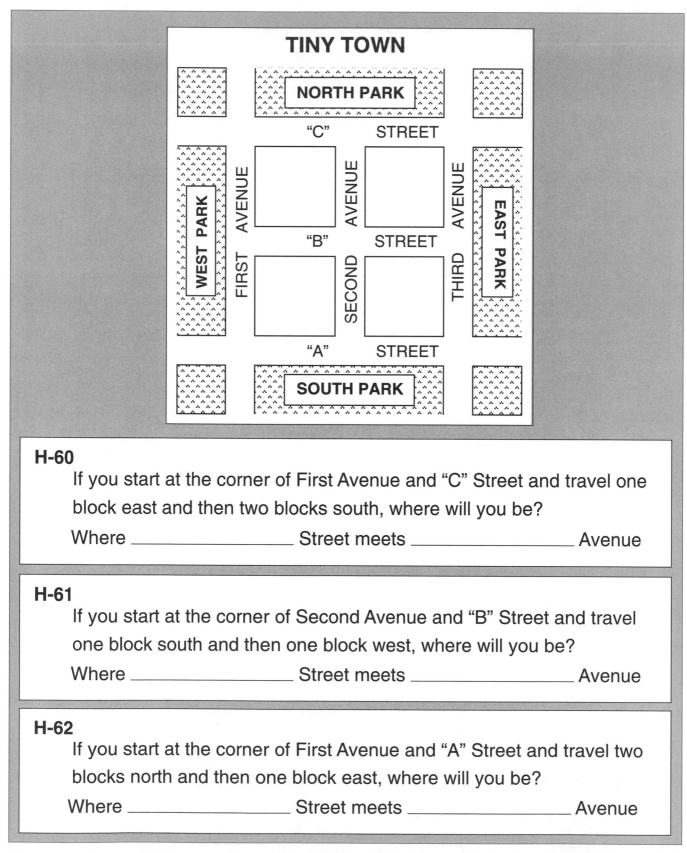

TINY TOWN

NORTH PARK

"C" STREET

WEST PARK

FIRST AVENUE

SECOND AVENUE

THIRD AVENUE

EAST PARK

"B" STREET

"A" STREET

SOUTH PARK

H-60

If you start at the corner of First Avenue and "C" Street and travel one block east and then two blocks south, where will you be?

Where _____ Street meets _____ Avenue

H-61

If you start at the corner of Second Avenue and "B" Street and travel one block south and then one block west, where will you be?

Where _____ Street meets _____ Avenue

H-62

If you start at the corner of First Avenue and "A" Street and travel two blocks north and then one block east, where will you be?

Where _____ Street meets _____ Avenue

SELECT THE WORD THAT CONTINUES THE SEQUENCE

DIRECTIONS: The first two words in each group suggest a time sequence. From the box, choose the word that should come next in the sequence. Write the word in the blank.

H-63

before, during, _____

> after
> beside
> whole

H-64

Monday, Tuesday, _____

> Saturday
> Sunday
> Wednesday

H-65

day, month, _____

> hour
> week
> year

H-66

first, second, _____

> beginning
> last
> third

H-67

Halloween, Thanksgiving, _____

> April Fool's Day
> Christmas
> Labor Day

SELECT THE WORD THAT CONTINUES THE SEQUENCE

DIRECTIONS: The first two words in each group suggest a sequence of amount. From the box, choose the word that should come next in the sequence. Write the word in the blank.

H-68

pint, quart, _____

| cup |
| gallon |
| teaspoon |

H-69

more, same, _____

| equal |
| less |
| most |

H-70

small, medium, _____

| large |
| regular |
| tiny |

H-71

some, more, _____

| few |
| many |
| most |

H-72

inch, foot, _____

| minute |
| pound |
| yard |

SELECT THE WORD THAT CONTINUES THE SEQUENCE

DIRECTIONS: The first two words in each group suggest a sequence of rank, degree, size, or order. From the box, choose the word that should come next in the sequence. Write the word in the blank.

H-73

above, beside, _____

below
between
over

H-74

bad, worse, _____

better
less
worst

H-75

boy, teen, _____

baby
child
man

H-76

enter, stay, _____

arrive
leave
remain

H-77

good, better, _____

best
well
worst

RANKING

DIRECTIONS: On the line under each group of words, rewrite the group in order from lowest or smallest to highest or largest in size, degree, rank, or order.

EXAMPLE

all, none, some

none, some, all

H-78

afternoon, morning, night

H-79

always, never, sometimes

H-80

giant, large, regular

H-81

many, more, most

H-82

first, last, middle

RANKING

DIRECTIONS: On the line under each group of words, rewrite the group in order from lowest or smallest to highest or largest in size, degree, rank, or order.

H-83

dime, dollar, quarter

_____

H-84

highway, sidewalk, street

_____

H-85

lake, ocean, pond

_____

H-86

city, nation, state

_____

H-87

century, month, year

_____

H-88

dime, nickel, penny

_____

RANKING

DIRECTIONS: On the line under each group of words, rewrite the group in order from lowest or smallest to highest or largest in size, degree, rank, or order.

H-89

body, head, tail

_____

H-90

rope, string, thread

_____

H-91

game, inning, out

_____

H-92

continue, finish, start

_____

H-93

book, page, word

_____

H-94

baseball, basketball, Ping-Pong ball

_____

SUPPLY A WORD THAT CONTINUES A SEQUENCE

DIRECTIONS: The first two words in each sequence suggest a degree, rank, size, or order. Think of a word that will continue the sequence and write it on the line. You may use a dictionary to get help.

H-95

second, minute, _____

H-96

ready, set, _____

H-97

March, April, _____

H-98

breakfast, lunch, _____

H-99

inch, foot, _____

H-100

small, medium, _____

H-101

beginning, middle, _____

H-102

spring, summer, _____

H-103

penny, nickel, _____

SUPPLY A WORD THAT CONTINUES A SEQUENCE

DIRECTIONS: The first two words in each sequence suggest a degree, rank, size, or order. Think of a word that will continue the sequence and write it on the line. You may use a dictionary to get help.

H-104

ten, twenty, _____

H-105

yesterday, today, _____

H-106

second, third, _____

H-107

baby, girl, _____

H-108

ounce, pound, _____

H-109

go, going, _____

H-110

white, gray, _____

H-111

cook, serve, _____

H-112

one, three, _____

WARM-UP DEDUCTIVE REASONING

DIRECTIONS: The example below shows how to complete the exercises on the following pages, in which people are being compared. Given the clues in the sentences, you can determine who is the fastest swimmer (see the directions below).

EXAMPLE

Maria swims faster than Fred. Kim swims faster than Maria.

Who swims the fastest? _____

HOW TO FIGURE IT OUT

STEP 1: Read the first clue and write the names, with the faster swimmer on top, in the space below.

Maria swims faster than Fred. Kim swims faster than Maria.

Maria

Fred

STEP 2: Read the second clue and decide how Kim compares to the other two. Since Kim is faster than Maria, her name should be on top.

Maria swims faster than Fred. **Kim swims faster than Maria.**

Kim

Maria

Fred

Now you can answer that Kim swims the fastest (see below).

EXAMPLE

Maria swims faster than Fred. Kim swims faster than Maria.

Who swims the fastest? _____ Kim _____

Kim

Maria

Fred

WARM-UP DEDUCTIVE REASONING

DIRECTIONS: In the sentences below, people are being compared according to some characteristic (weight, age, height, score, etc.). Read the sentences; in the space below the sentences, write the names in order, then answer the question.

H-113

Charlie is heavier than Bill. Bill is heavier than Albert.

Who is the heaviest? _____

H-114

James is younger than Alice. Betty is younger than James.

Who is the youngest? _____

H-115

Sally has more cats than Clare. Irene has more cats than Sally.

Who has the most cats? _____

WARM-UP DEDUCTIVE REASONING

DIRECTIONS: In the sentences below, people are being compared according to some characteristic (weight, age, height, score, etc.). Read the sentences and fill in the blanks.

H-116

Doug runs faster than Ivan. Ivan runs faster than Lee.

List the runners in order from fastest to slowest.

_____   _____   _____

List the runners in order from slowest to fastest.

_____   _____   _____

H-117

John is older than Sam but younger than Lois.

List the people in order from oldest to youngest.

_____   _____   _____

List the people in order from youngest to oldest.

_____   _____   _____

H-118

David is taller than Fred. Fred is taller than George. George is taller than Harold.

Who is the tallest? _____

WARM-UP DEDUCTIVE REASONING

DIRECTIONS: In the sentences below, people are being compared according to some characteristic (weight, age, height, score, etc.). Read the sentences and fill in the blanks.

H-119

Delores is shorter than Mary. June is shorter than Delores. Mary is shorter than Nancy.

Who is the shortest? _____

Who is the tallest? _____

H-120

Gina caught fewer fish than Spiro. Nick caught fewer fish than Gina.

List the people in order from the one who caught the most fish to the one who caught the fewest fish.

_____   _____   _____

List the people in order from the one who caught the fewest fish to the one who caught the most fish.

_____   _____   _____

H-121

Pedro is older than Jose but younger than Manuel.

List the people in order from youngest to oldest.

_____   _____   _____

WARM-UP DEDUCTIVE REASONING

DIRECTIONS: In the sentences below, people are being compared according to some characteristic (weight, age, height, score, etc.). Read the sentences and fill in the blanks.

H-122

Emil made more points in a basketball game than Carlos. Emil did not make as many points as Larry.

List the boys in order from high scorer to low scorer.

_____   _____   _____

List the boys in order from low scorer to high scorer.

_____   _____   _____

H-123

Pedro got more hits than Sol but fewer than Nina.

List the players in order from the one who made the most hits to the one who made the fewest hits.

_____   _____   _____

List the players in order from the one who made the fewest hits to the one who made the most hits.

_____   _____   _____

H-124

John is taller than Marna but shorter than Larry.

List the people in order from tallest to shortest.

_____   _____   _____

List the people in order from shortest to tallest.

_____   _____   _____

DEDUCTIVE REASONING

DIRECTIONS: The example below shows how to solve a Mind Benders® problem. Study it before going on to the next pages.

A Mind Benders® problem asks you to match items with their characteristics. Making a matrix helps you work the problem. The easiest Mind Bender® is one involving two things.

Here is an example.

Spot and Prince are two pets. One pet is a dog and the other a horse. Spot is not the dog. Find the names of the pets.

Step 1   On the chart,

"S" stands for Spot
"P" stands for Prince
"D" stands for dog and
"H" stands for horse

From the clue "Spot is not the dog," we can put NO in the dog column in the Spot row.

Step 2   Look down the "D" for dog column on the chart. There is only one blank place. Remember the clue, "One pet is a dog and the other a horse"? Since Spot is not the dog, Prince must be the dog. Put YES in the blank.

Step 3   Look across the row having a YES. YES is in the "P" for Prince row. Since Prince is a dog, you can write NO in the "H" for horse list.

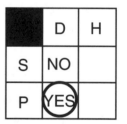

Step 4   The only choice left is to put YES in the last open space.

Now the Mind Bender® is complete. Spot is the horse, and Prince is the dog.

DEDUCTIVE REASONING

DIRECTIONS: Using the method given in the previous example, complete each of the following Mind Benders® problems. Figure out who was first, second, and third in each contest.

H-125

Hernando, Isaac, and Juanita are in a spelling contest.

1. Isaac spells three words correctly.

2. Juanita spells correctly one more word than Isaac.

3. The winner spells five words correctly.

	1st	2nd	3rd
H			
I			
J			

Hernando was _____.

Isaac was _____.

Juanita was _____.

H-126

Donna, Ernie, and Frank run a race.

1. Ernie drops out on the first lap.

2. Frank finishes behind Donna.

	1st	2nd	3rd
D			
E			
F			

Donna was _____.

Ernie was _____.

Frank was _____.

DEDUCTIVE REASONING

DIRECTIONS: Complete each of the following Mind Benders® problems.

H-127

Juan, Kyle, and Lori own bikes. The bikes are a one-speed, a three-speed, and a ten-speed.

1. Juan and Lori have bikes with more than one gear speed.

2. Lori's bike has the most gear speeds.

Find out the owners of the three kinds of bikes.

	1	3	10
J			
K			
L			

The one-speed is owned by _____.

The three-speed is owned by _____.

The ten-speed is owned by _____.

H-128

Three students—Green, Jones, and Perez—ride to school together. The students are in the second, third, and fourth grades.

1. Jones is in an odd-numbered grade.

2. Green is in a higher grade than Jones.

Find out which student is in each grade.

	G	J	P
2			
3			
4			

Green is in the _____ grade.

Jones is in the _____ grade.

Perez is in the _____ grade.

DEDUCTIVE REASONING

DIRECTIONS: Complete each of the following Mind Benders® problems.

H-129

Mrs. Grant is giving her grandchildren presents from her bicycle store. Her grandchildren are 3, 6, and 12 years old.

1. Mrs. Grant gave her grandson a tricycle.

2. The oldest received a 10-speed bicycle, but her sister was unhappy because she got a bicycle with training wheels.

Find out which of the children are boys and which are girls.

	B	G
3	Y	N
6	N	Y
12	N	Y

The 3 year old is a _____.

The 6 year old is a _____.

The 12 year old is a _____.

H-130

Amanda, Desiree, and Jose listed their favorite foods. One liked beef burgers, one liked chicken, and one liked salads.

Amanda does not eat meat, and Jose does not eat beef.

Find out the favorite food of each person.

	B	C	S
A	N	N	Y
D	Y	N	N
J	N	Y	N

Amanda likes _____.

Desiree likes _____.

Jose likes _____.

DEDUCTIVE REASONING

DIRECTIONS: Complete the following Mind Benders® problem.

H-131

Three boys named Nick, Pablo, and Tim own athletic shoes. One boy has basketball shoes, another has running shoes, and another has sneakers.

1. The basketball shoes are the largest.
2. Tim has the smallest feet.
3. Nick wears a larger shoe than Pablo, who owns the sneakers.

Find out the owners of each shoe style.

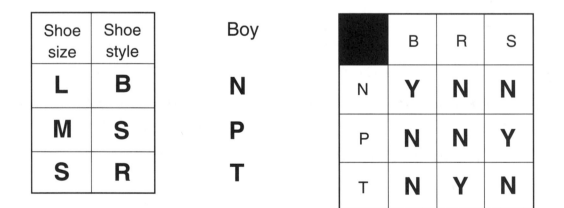

Shoe size	Shoe style
L	B
M	S
S	R

Boy

N

P

T

	B	R	S
N	Y	N	N
P	N	N	Y
T	N	Y	N

The basketball shoes are owned by _____.

The running shoes are owned by _____.

The sneakers are owned by _____.

RANKING TIME MEASURES

DIRECTIONS: Use the chart below to list time measures in order from shortest to longest. Remember that 1 day equals 24 hours, 1 month equals 30 or 31 days, and 1 year equals 12 months or 365 days.

H-132

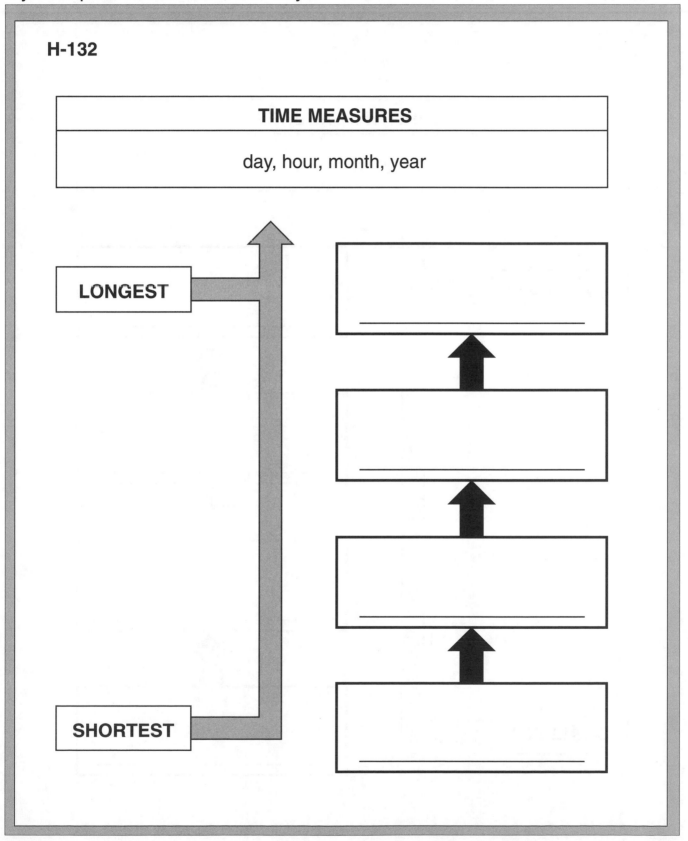

TIME MEASURES

day, hour, month, year

LONGEST

SHORTEST

RANKING LENGTH MEASURES

DIRECTIONS: Use the chart below to list length measures in order from smallest to largest. Remember that 1 foot equals 12 inches, 1 yard equals 3 feet, 3 feet equals 36 inches, and 1 mile equals 5280 feet.

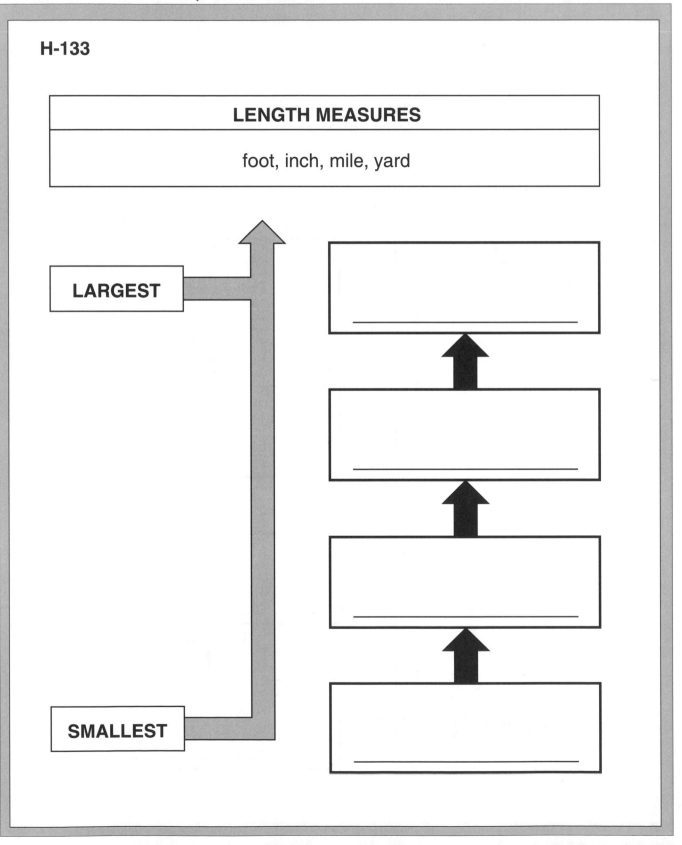

H-133

LENGTH MEASURES

foot, inch, mile, yard

LARGEST

SMALLEST

RANKING IN GEOGRAPHY

DIRECTIONS: Use the chart below to list the geographic regions in order from smallest to largest.

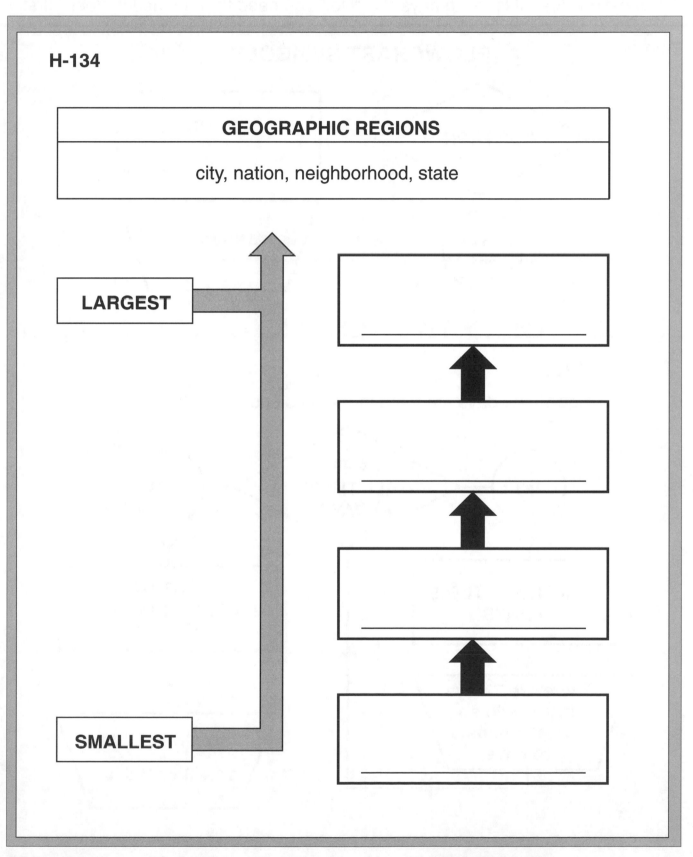

H-134

GEOGRAPHIC REGIONS

city, nation, neighborhood, state

LARGEST

SMALLEST

FLOWCHART—EXAMPLE

DIRECTIONS: Look at the "flowchart symbols." Next, read the example question and follow the flowchart to see how the problem is solved. Since the answer to the question "Are all times in days?" is "No," you need to read the left "loop" first.

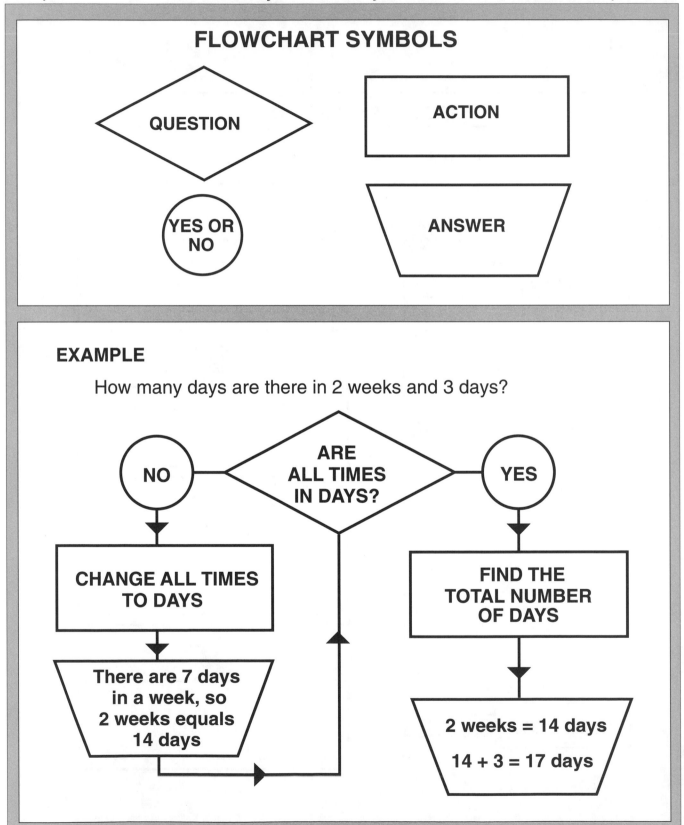

FLOWCHART SYMBOLS

QUESTION

YES OR NO

ACTION

ANSWER

EXAMPLE

How many days are there in 2 weeks and 3 days?

ARE ALL TIMES IN DAYS?

NO

YES

CHANGE ALL TIMES TO DAYS

There are 7 days in a week, so 2 weeks equals 14 days

FIND THE TOTAL NUMBER OF DAYS

2 weeks = 14 days

14 + 3 = 17 days

FLOWCHART—ARITHMETIC

DIRECTIONS: A flowchart can show a sequence of steps to be followed. Use the flowchart below to help you solve arithmetic problems.

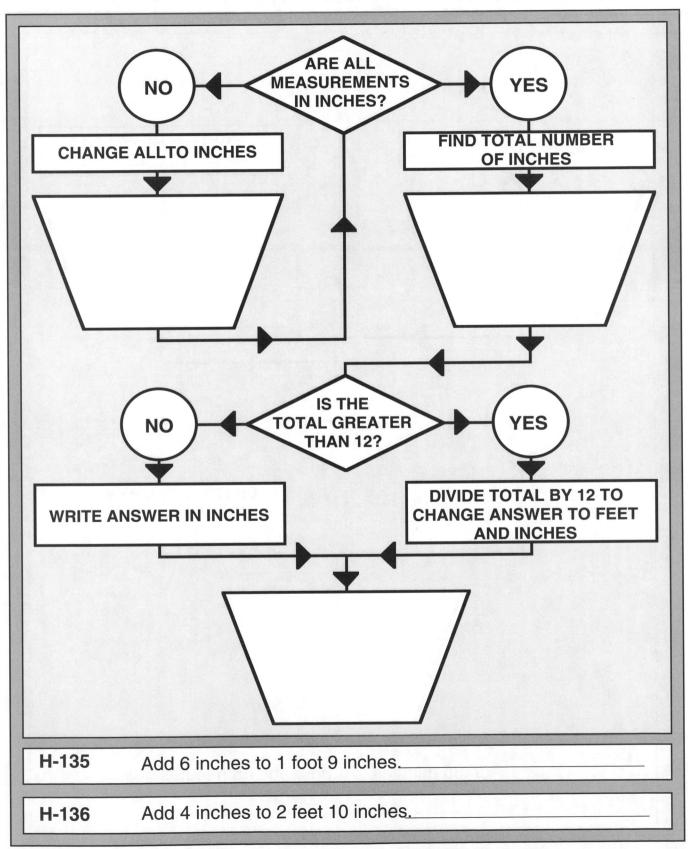

H-135	Add 6 inches to 1 foot 9 inches._____
H-136	Add 4 inches to 2 feet 10 inches._____

FLOWCHART—ARITHMETIC

DIRECTIONS: A flowchart can show a sequence of steps to be followed. Think about how to add hours and minutes. Fill in the blanks on the decision diamond and the action rectangles, and complete the flowchart to solve the problem below.

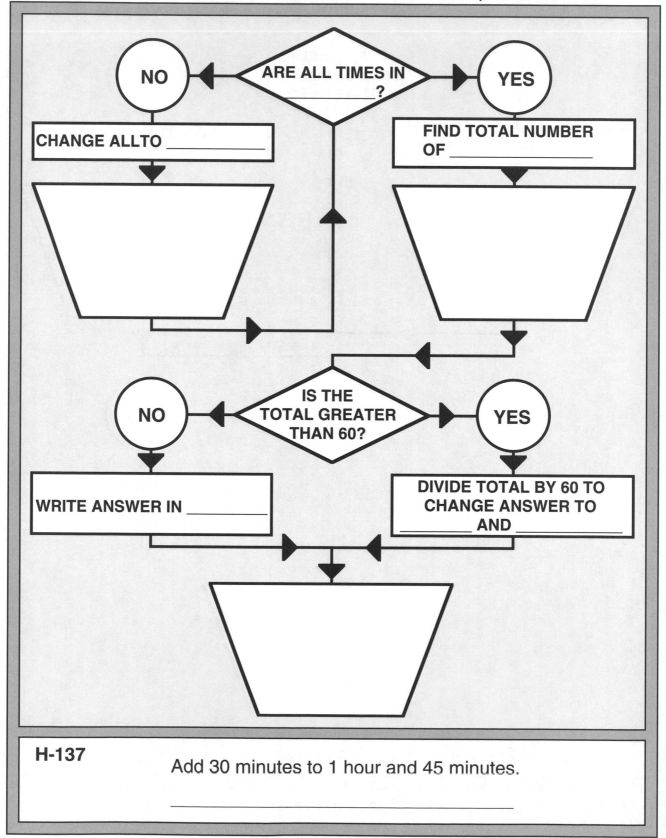

ARE ALL TIMES IN _____ ?

NO

YES

CHANGE ALLTO _____

FIND TOTAL NUMBER OF _____

IS THE TOTAL GREATER THAN 60?

NO

YES

WRITE ANSWER IN _____

DIVIDE TOTAL BY 60 TO CHANGE ANSWER TO _____ AND _____

H-137

Add 30 minutes to 1 hour and 45 minutes.

_____

CHAPTER NINE

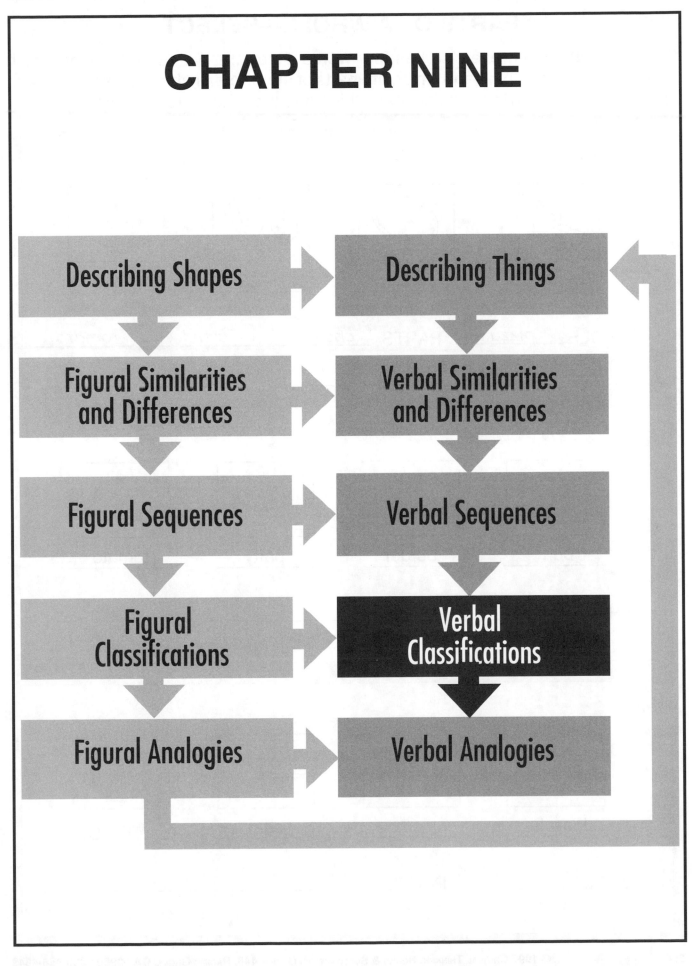

PARTS OF A WHOLE—SELECT

DIRECTIONS: Each exercise has four words. Read the words and decide which represents a whole thing and which are parts of the whole. In the blanks below each group, write the word that is the whole thing and then the words that are the parts.

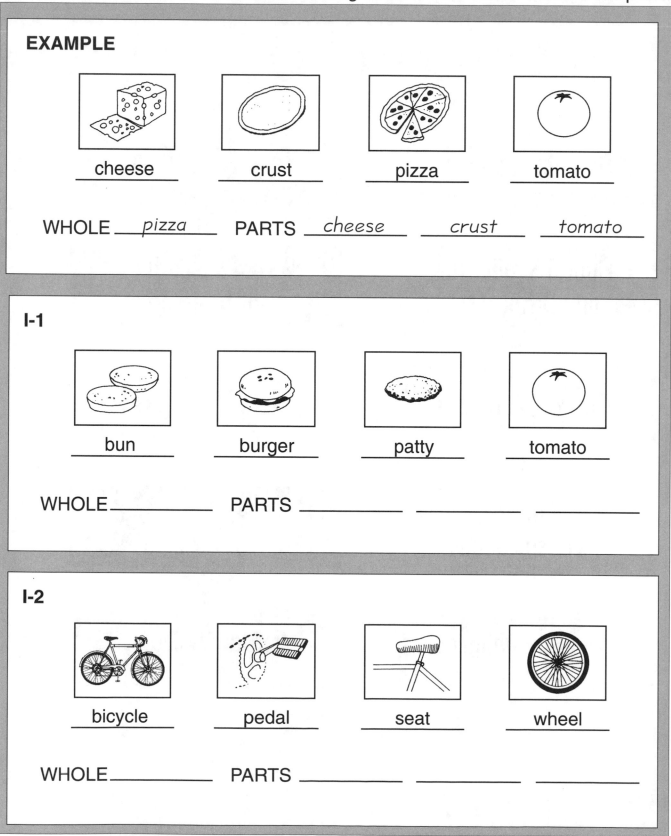

EXAMPLE

cheese   crust   pizza   tomato

WHOLE _pizza_   PARTS _cheese_   _crust_   _tomato_

I-1

bun   burger   patty   tomato

WHOLE_____   PARTS _____   _____   _____

I-2

bicycle   pedal   seat   wheel

WHOLE_____   PARTS _____   _____   _____

PARTS OF A WHOLE—SELECT

DIRECTIONS: Each exercise has four words. Read the words and decide which represents a whole thing and which are parts of the whole. In the blanks below each group, write the word that is the whole thing and then the words that are the parts.

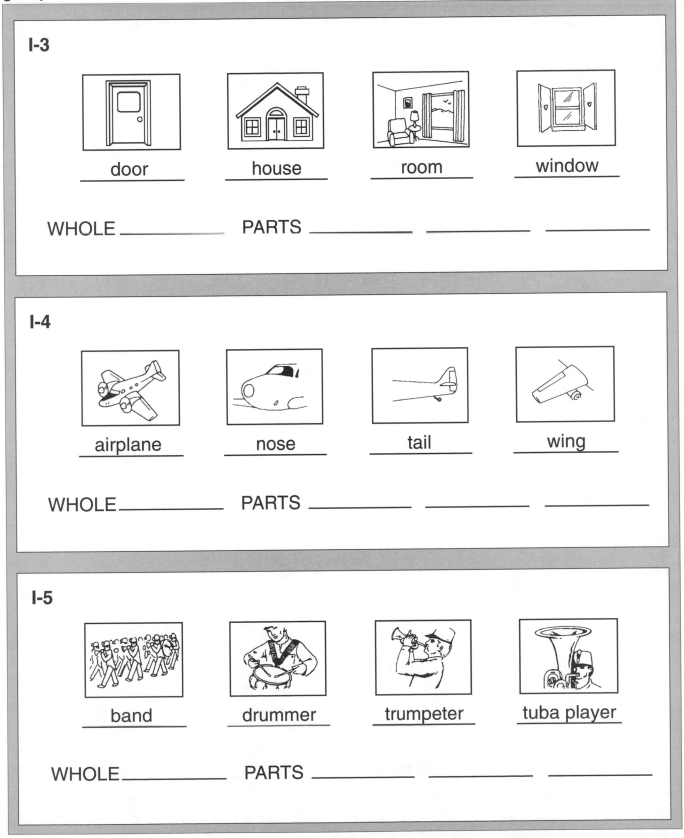

I-3

door   house   room   window

WHOLE _____ PARTS _____ _____ _____

I-4

airplane   nose   tail   wing

WHOLE _____ PARTS _____ _____ _____

I-5

band   drummer   trumpeter   tuba player

WHOLE _____ PARTS _____ _____ _____

PARTS OF A WHOLE—SELECT

DIRECTIONS: Each exercise has four words. Read the words and decide which represents a whole thing and which are parts of the whole. In the blanks below each group, write the word that is the whole thing and then the words that are the parts.

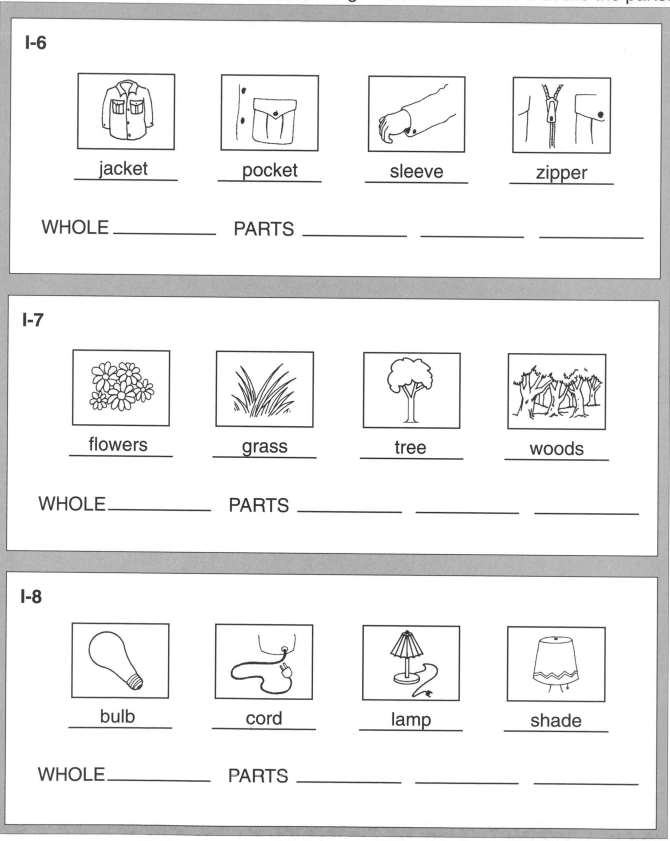

I-6

jacket   pocket   sleeve   zipper

WHOLE _____   PARTS _____   _____   _____

I-7

flowers   grass   tree   woods

WHOLE _____   PARTS _____   _____   _____

I-8

bulb   cord   lamp   shade

WHOLE _____   PARTS _____   _____   _____

PARTS OF A WHOLE—SELECT

DIRECTIONS: Each exercise has four words. Read the words and decide which represents a whole thing and which are parts of the whole. In the blanks below each group, write the word that is the whole thing and then the words that are the parts.

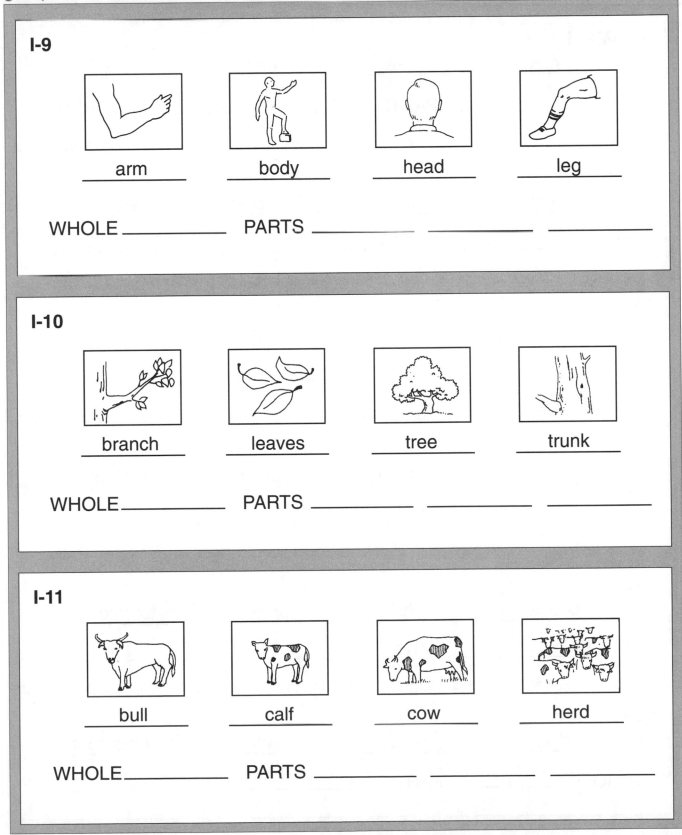

I-9

arm   body   head   leg

WHOLE _____   PARTS _____   _____   _____

I-10

branch   leaves   tree   trunk

WHOLE _____   PARTS _____   _____   _____

I-11

bull   calf   cow   herd

WHOLE _____   PARTS _____   _____   _____

PARTS OF A WHOLE—SELECT

DIRECTIONS: Each exercise has four words. Read the words and decide which represents a whole thing and which are parts of the whole. In the blanks below each group, write the word that is the whole thing and then the words that are the parts.

EXAMPLE

___drink___   ___meal___   ___meat___   ___salad___

WHOLE ___meal___   PARTS ___drink___   ___meat___   ___salad___

I-12

___body___   ___car___   ___engine___   ___wheel___

WHOLE _____   PARTS _____   _____   _____

I-13

___army___   ___trucks___   ___soldiers___   ___tanks___

WHOLE _____   PARTS _____   _____   _____

I-14

___cashier___   ___market___   ___meat___   ___vegetables___

WHOLE _____   PARTS _____   _____   _____

I-15

___beans___   ___chili___   ___onions___   ___tomatoes___

WHOLE _____   PARTS _____   _____   _____

I-16

___dial___   ___radio___   ___switch___   ___volume control___

WHOLE _____   PARTS _____   _____   _____

PARTS OF A WHOLE—SELECT

DIRECTIONS: Each exercise has four words. Read the words and decide which represents a whole thing and which are parts of the whole. In the blanks below each group, write the word that is the whole thing and then the words that are the parts.

I-17

    antenna   channel selector   picture tube   television

WHOLE _____   PARTS _____ _____ _____

I-18

    dressing   lettuce   salad   tomato

WHOLE _____   PARTS _____ _____ _____

I-19

    blade   engine   handle   lawnmower

WHOLE _____   PARTS _____ _____ _____

I-20

    cap   ink   pen   point

WHOLE _____   PARTS _____ _____ _____

I-21

    acrobats   animals   clowns   circus

WHOLE _____   PARTS _____ _____ _____

I-22

    principal   school   students   teachers

WHOLE _____   PARTS _____ _____ _____

PARTS OF A WHOLE—SELECT

DIRECTIONS: Each exercise has four words. Read the words and decide which represents a whole thing and which are parts of the whole. In the blanks below each group, write the word that is the whole thing and then the words that are the parts.

I-23

addition   arithmetic   numbers   subtraction

WHOLE _____ PARTS _____ _____ _____

I-24

adjectives   language   nouns   verbs

WHOLE _____ PARTS _____ _____ _____

I-25

government   judge   president   senator

WHOLE _____ PARTS _____ _____ _____

I-26

book   cover   pages   words

WHOLE _____ PARTS _____ _____ _____

I-27

city   houses   stores   schools

WHOLE _____ PARTS _____ _____ _____

I-28

key   map   mountains   rivers

WHOLE _____ PARTS _____ _____ _____

PARTS OF A WHOLE—GRAPHIC ORGANIZER

DIRECTIONS: The words in the choice box represent the parts of a nation. Fill in the blank boxes of the diagram to show how these parts are related. Write a statement about their relationships, starting with the smallest part of the whole.

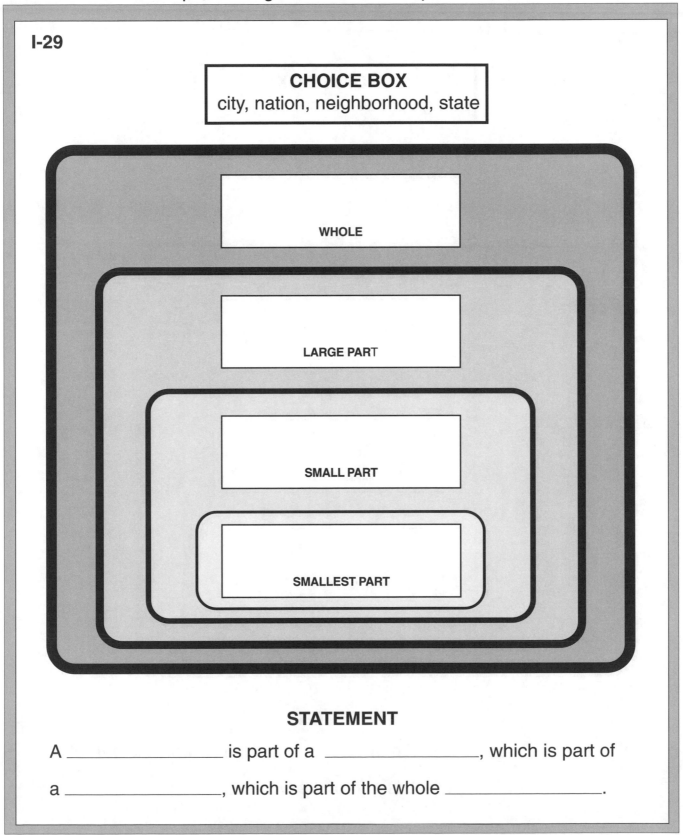

I-29

CHOICE BOX
city, nation, neighborhood, state

WHOLE

LARGE PART

SMALL PART

SMALLEST PART

STATEMENT

A _____ is part of a _____, which is part of

a _____, which is part of the whole _____.

PARTS OF A WHOLE—GRAPHIC ORGANIZER

DIRECTIONS: Decide how the words in the choice box are related, and fill in the blank boxes of the diagram. Write a statement about their relationships, starting with the smallest part of the whole.

I-30

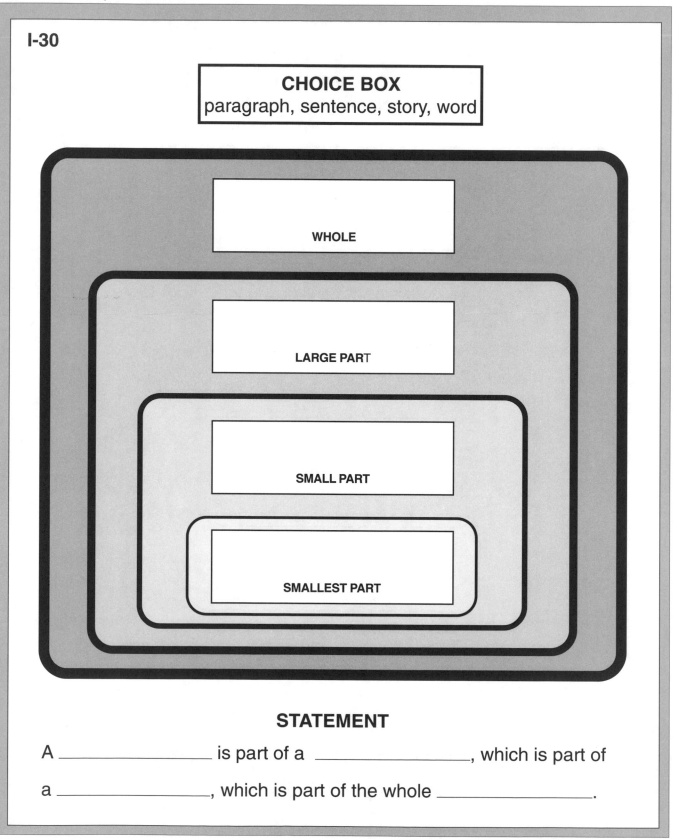

CHOICE BOX
paragraph, sentence, story, word

WHOLE

LARGE PART

SMALL PART

SMALLEST PART

STATEMENT

A _____ is part of a _____, which is part of

a _____, which is part of the whole _____.

CLASS AND MEMBERS—SELECT

DIRECTIONS: In each exercise are four words. Read the words and decide which represents a class to which the others belong. In the blanks below each group, write the word that represents the class and then the words that are its members.

EXAMPLE

| coin | dime | nickel | penny |

CLASS _coin_   MEMBERS _dime_   _nickel_   _penny_

I-31

| clothing | coat | hat | pants |

CLASS _____   MEMBERS _____ _____ _____

I-32

| baseball | basketball | football | sport |

CLASS _____   MEMBERS _____ _____ _____

I-33

| blue | color | green | red |

CLASS _____   MEMBERS _____ _____ _____

I-34

| hammer | saw | screwdriver | tool |

CLASS _____   MEMBERS _____ _____ _____

I-35

| arithmetic | reading | school subject | writing |

CLASS _____   MEMBERS _____ _____ _____

CLASS AND MEMBERS—SELECT

DIRECTIONS: Each exercise has four words. Read the words and decide which represents a class to which the others belong. In the blanks below each group, write the word that represents the class and then the words that are its members.

I-36

English   French   language   Spanish

CLASS _____ MEMBERS _____ _____ _____

I-37

corn   grain   oats   wheat

CLASS _____ MEMBERS _____ _____ _____

I-38

bass   fish   salmon   tuna

CLASS _____ MEMBERS _____ _____ _____

I-39

fruit   grain   plant   vegetable

CLASS _____ MEMBERS _____ _____ _____

I-40

animal   bird   fish   reptile

CLASS _____ MEMBERS _____ _____ _____

I-41

oak   palm   pine   tree

CLASS _____ MEMBERS _____ _____ _____

WHAT IS TRUE OF BOTH WORDS?—SELECT

DIRECTIONS: Decide what the following pairs of words have in common. Circle the letters of the characteristics that are true of both items.

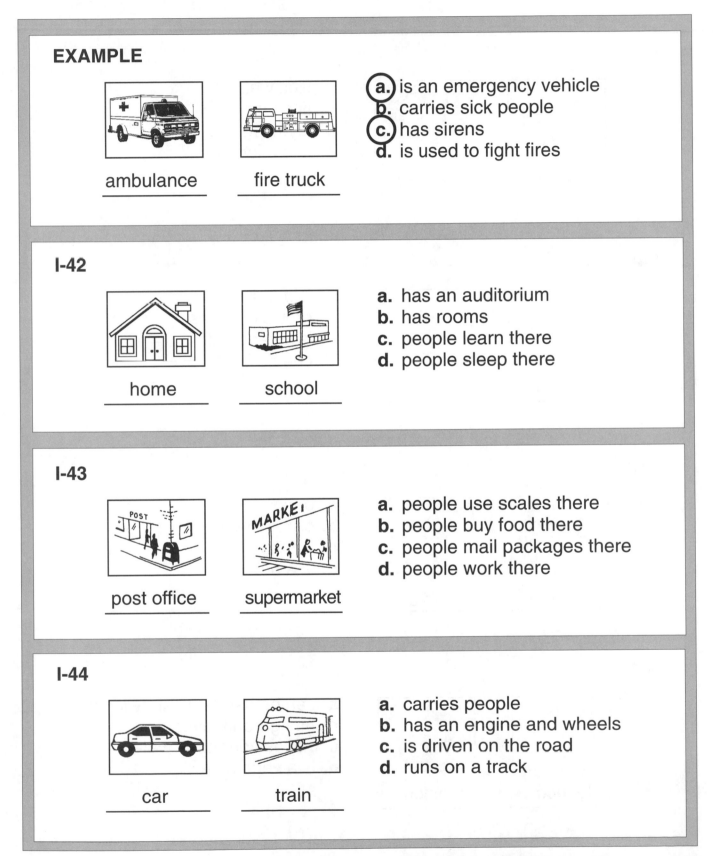

EXAMPLE

ambulance   fire truck

(a.) is an emergency vehicle
b. carries sick people
(c.) has sirens
d. is used to fight fires

I-42

home   school

a. has an auditorium
b. has rooms
c. people learn there
d. people sleep there

I-43

post office   supermarket

a. people use scales there
b. people buy food there
c. people mail packages there
d. people work there

I-44

car   train

a. carries people
b. has an engine and wheels
c. is driven on the road
d. runs on a track

WHAT IS TRUE OF BOTH WORDS?—SELECT

DIRECTIONS: Decide what the following pairs of words have in common. Circle the letters of the characteristics that are true of both items.

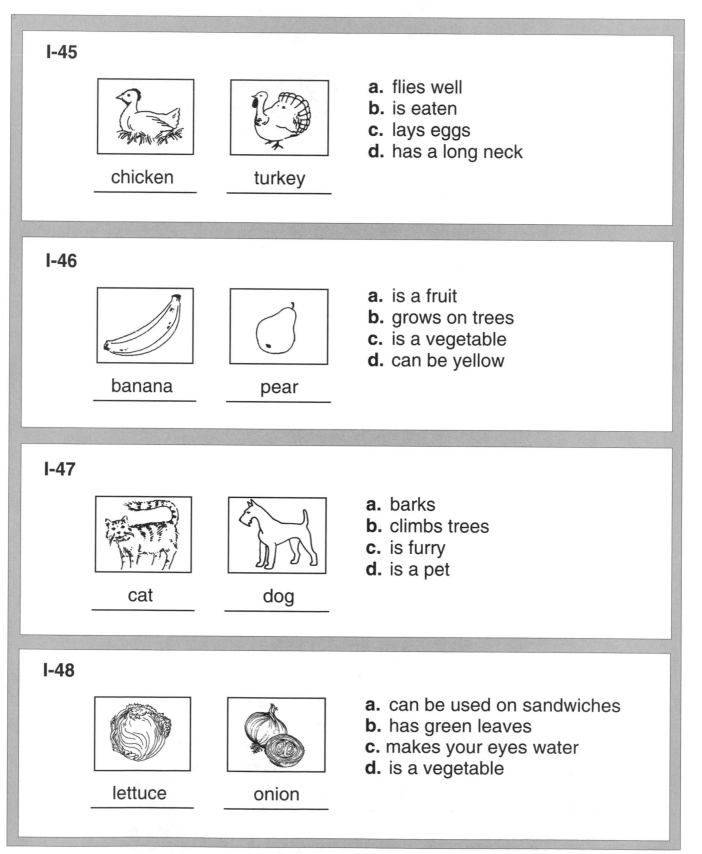

I-45

chicken   turkey

a. flies well
b. is eaten
c. lays eggs
d. has a long neck

I-46

banana   pear

a. is a fruit
b. grows on trees
c. is a vegetable
d. can be yellow

I-47

cat   dog

a. barks
b. climbs trees
c. is furry
d. is a pet

I-48

lettuce   onion

a. can be used on sandwiches
b. has green leaves
c. makes your eyes water
d. is a vegetable

WHAT IS TRUE OF BOTH WORDS?—SELECT

DIRECTIONS: Decide what the following pairs of words have in common. Circle the letters of the characteristics that are true of both items.

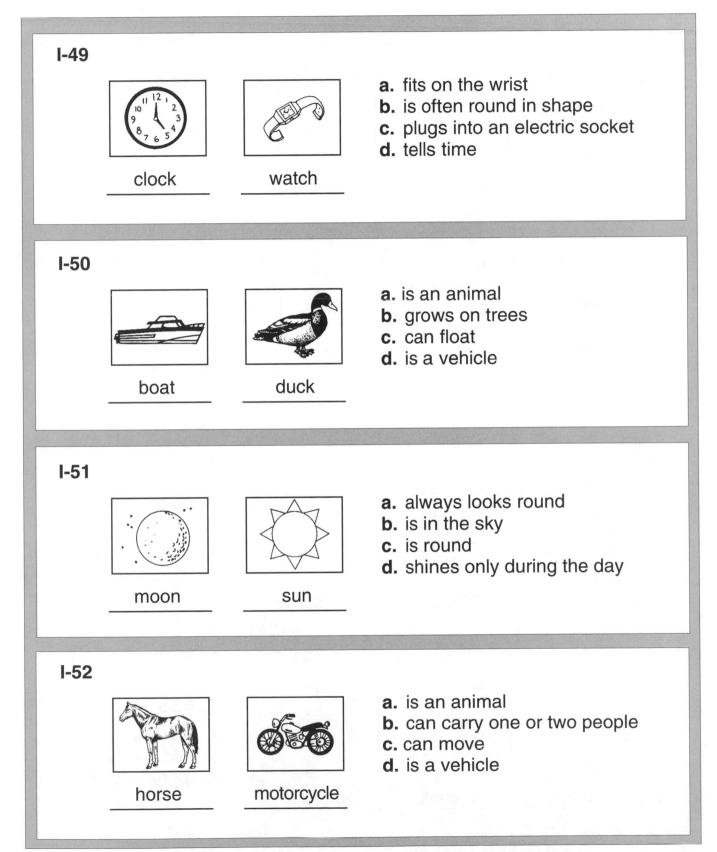

I-49

clock   watch

a. fits on the wrist
b. is often round in shape
c. plugs into an electric socket
d. tells time

I-50

boat   duck

a. is an animal
b. grows on trees
c. can float
d. is a vehicle

I-51

moon   sun

a. always looks round
b. is in the sky
c. is round
d. shines only during the day

I-52

horse   motorcycle

a. is an animal
b. can carry one or two people
c. can move
d. is a vehicle

HOW ARE THESE WORDS ALIKE?—SELECT

DIRECTIONS: Decide what the words in each group have in common. Circle the letter of the one answer that best describes the class of the words.

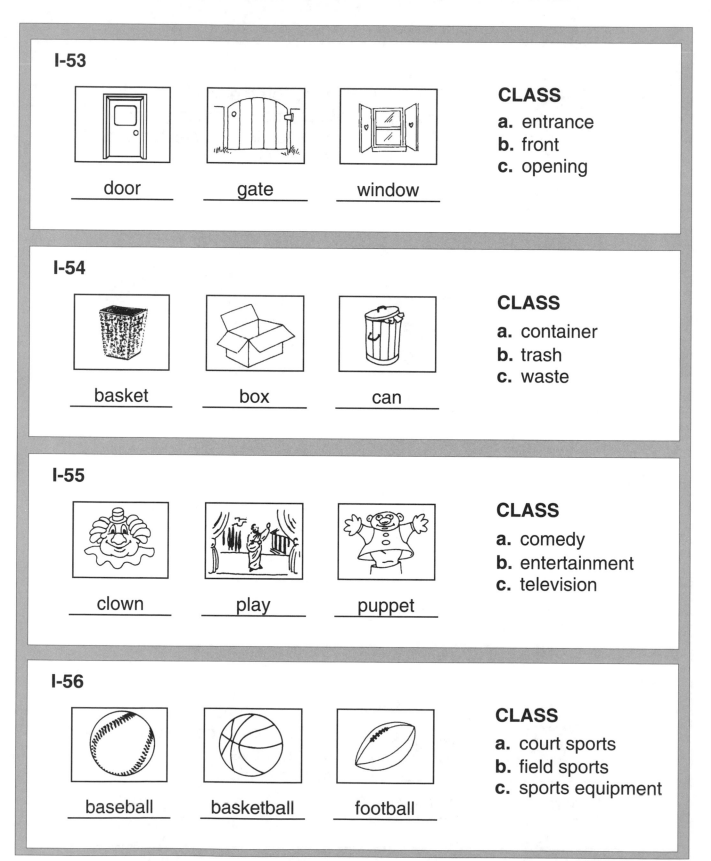

I-53

door   gate   window

CLASS
a. entrance
b. front
c. opening

I-54

basket   box   can

CLASS
a. container
b. trash
c. waste

I-55

clown   play   puppet

CLASS
a. comedy
b. entertainment
c. television

I-56

baseball   basketball   football

CLASS
a. court sports
b. field sports
c. sports equipment

HOW ARE THESE WORDS ALIKE?—SELECT

DIRECTIONS: Decide what the words in each group have in common. Circle the letter of the one answer that best describes the class of the words.

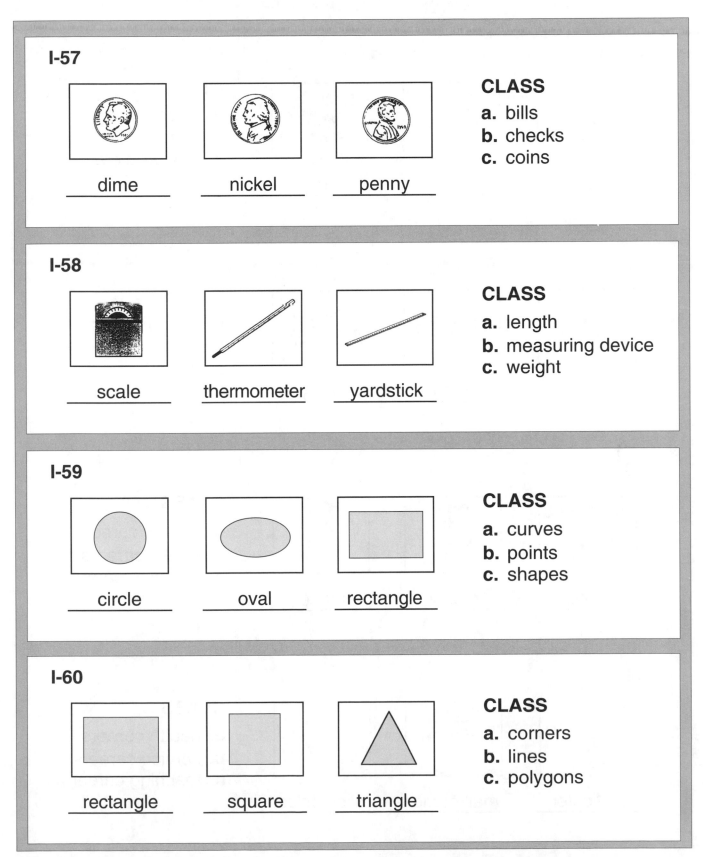

I-57

dime   nickel   penny

CLASS

a. bills
b. checks
c. coins

I-58

scale   thermometer   yardstick

CLASS

a. length
b. measuring device
c. weight

I-59

circle   oval   rectangle

CLASS

a. curves
b. points
c. shapes

I-60

rectangle   square   triangle

CLASS

a. corners
b. lines
c. polygons

HOW ARE THESE WORDS ALIKE?—SELECT

DIRECTIONS: Decide what the words in each group have in common. Circle the letter of the one answer that best describes the class of the words.

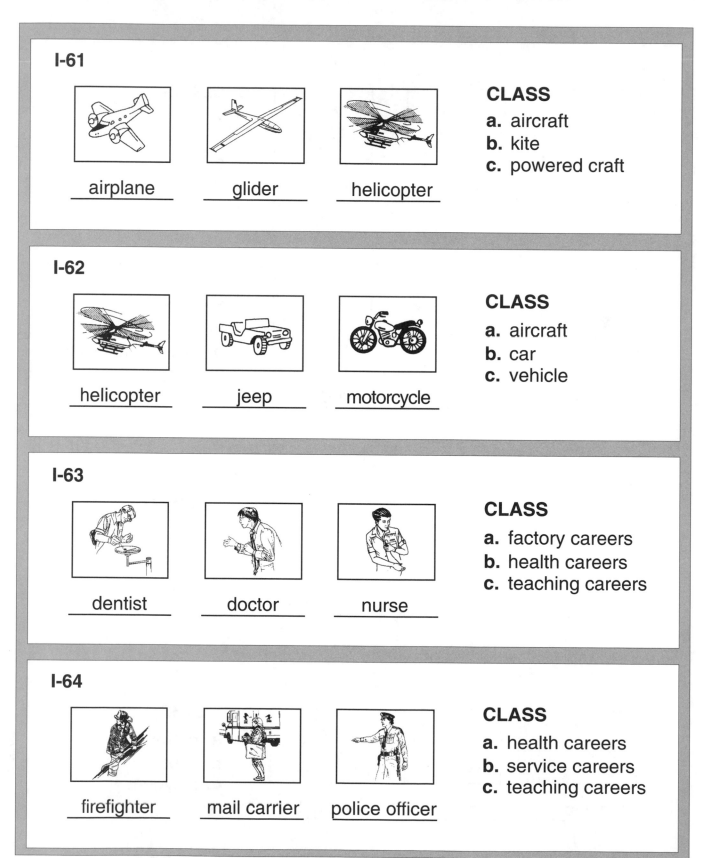

I-61

airplane   glider   helicopter

CLASS
a. aircraft
b. kite
c. powered craft

I-62

helicopter   jeep   motorcycle

CLASS
a. aircraft
b. car
c. vehicle

I-63

dentist   doctor   nurse

CLASS
a. factory careers
b. health careers
c. teaching careers

I-64

firefighter   mail carrier   police officer

CLASS
a. health careers
b. service careers
c. teaching careers

HOW ARE THESE WORDS ALIKE?—SELECT

DIRECTIONS: Decide what the words in each group have in common. Circle the letter of the one answer that best describes the class of the words.

EXAMPLE

_____cake_____   _____cookie_____   _____pie_____

CLASS
(a.) dessert
b. dinner
c. fruit

Dinner is not the best answer; these foods are usually eaten after dinner. Fruit is not the answer, even though these foods can be made of fruit. Dessert is the best answer because it is a term which describes all three foods.

I-65

_____boxer_____   _____poodle_____   _____shepherd_____

CLASS
a. clothing
b. dog
c. job

I-66

_____button_____   _____snap_____   _____zipper_____

CLASS
a. fastener
b. hardware
c. tool

I-67

_____bed_____   _____desk_____   _____table_____

CLASS
a. chair
b. furniture
c. kitchen

I-68

_____curtains_____   _____drapes_____   _____shades_____

CLASS
a. floor covering
b. furniture covering
c. window covering

HOW ARE THESE WORDS ALIKE?—SELECT

DIRECTIONS: Decide what the words in each group have in common. Circle the letter of the one answer that best describes the class of the words.

I-69

letter   poem   song

CLASS
a. things people sing
b. things people speak
c. things people write

I-70

grow   increase   swell

CLASS
a. become higher
b. become larger
c. become lighter

I-71

baby   boy   girl

CLASS
a. children
b. mother
c. student

I-72

bush   flower   tree

CLASS
a. blossom
b. plant
c. wood

I-73

blue   rose   violet

CLASS
a. bird
b. color
c. flower

I-74

decrease   reduce   shrink

CLASS
a. become colder
b. become larger
c. become smaller

HOW ARE THESE WORDS ALIKE?—EXPLAIN

DIRECTIONS: Decide what the words in each group have in common. On the line below the group, explain how the words in the class are alike.

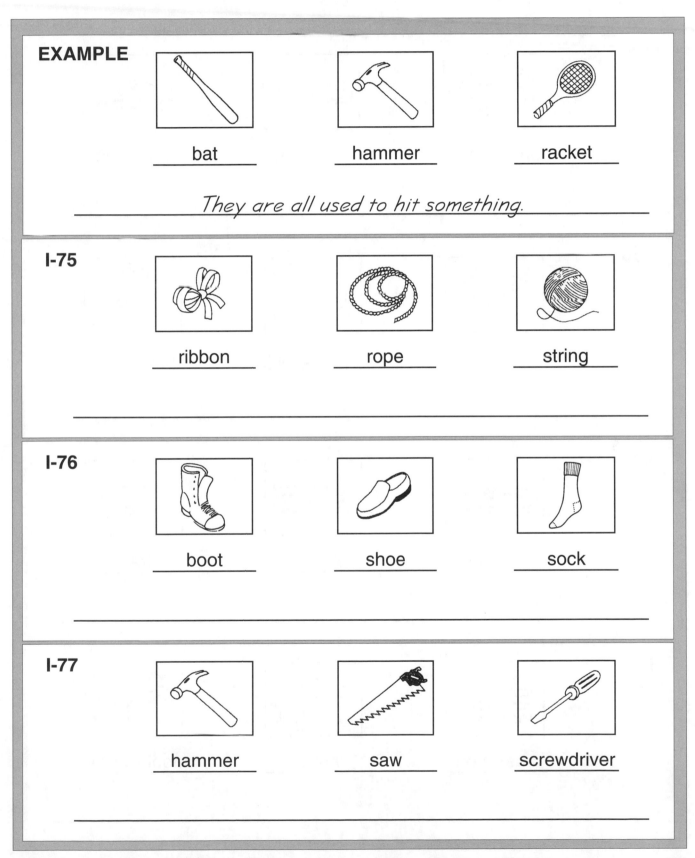

EXAMPLE

bat   hammer   racket

They are all used to hit something.

I-75

ribbon   rope   string

_____

I-76

boot   shoe   sock

_____

I-77

hammer   saw   screwdriver

_____

HOW ARE THESE WORDS ALIKE?—EXPLAIN

DIRECTIONS: Decide what the words in each group have in common. On the line below the group, explain how the words in the class are alike.

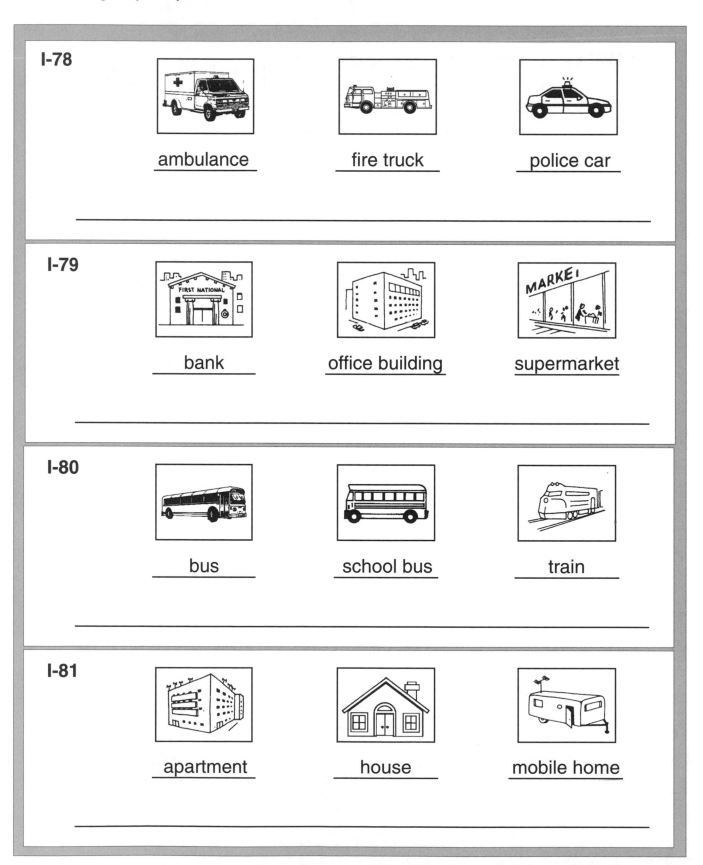

I-78

ambulance

fire truck

police car

_____

I-79

bank

office building

supermarket

_____

I-80

bus

school bus

train

_____

I-81

apartment

house

mobile home

_____

HOW ARE THESE WORDS ALIKE?—EXPLAIN

DIRECTIONS: Decide what the words in each group have in common. On the line below the group, explain how the words in the class are alike.

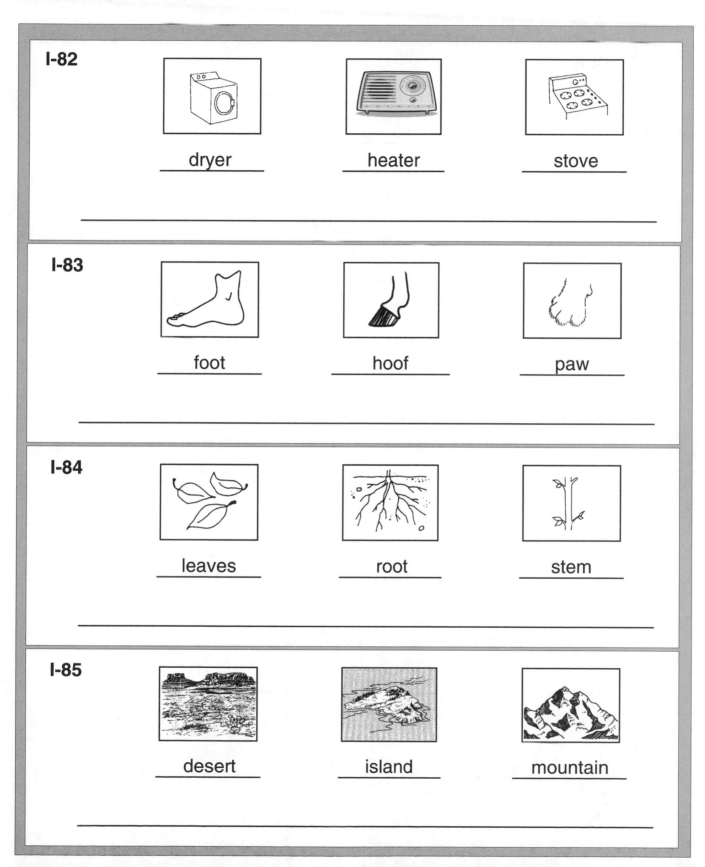

I-82

dryer   heater   stove

_____

I-83

foot   hoof   paw

_____

I-84

leaves   root   stem

_____

I-85

desert   island   mountain

_____

HOW ARE THESE WORDS ALIKE?—EXPLAIN

DIRECTIONS: Decide what the words in each group have in common. On the line below the group, explain how the words in the class are alike.

EXAMPLE

diamond   square   triangle

These words name different shapes.

I-86

cap   cork   lid

_____

I-87

drip   leak   spill

_____

I-88

glue   paste   tape

_____

I-89

float   sail   swim

_____

I-90

bang   boom   pop

_____

HOW ARE THESE WORDS ALIKE?—EXPLAIN

DIRECTIONS: Decide what the words in each group have in common. On the line below the group, explain how the words in the class are alike.

I-91

iron   stove   toaster

_____

I-92

grapefruit   lemon   orange

_____

I-93

eye   ear   nose

_____

I-94

blade   leaf   needle

_____

I-95

clouds   ice   rain

_____

I-96

leopard   lion   tiger

_____

EXPLAIN THE EXCEPTION

DIRECTIONS: Each group of words contains one member that is an exception to the class. On the lines under the group, explain how the similar words are alike and how the exception is different.

EXAMPLE

stove   lamp   iron   dryer

Lamp is the exception because its purpose is to produce light. The other devices are used to produce heat.

I-97

screwdriver   pliers   nails   hammer

_____

_____

I-98

whistle   tuba   guitar   bugle

_____

_____

EXPLAIN THE EXCEPTION

DIRECTIONS: Each group of words contains one member that is an exception to the class. On the lines under the group, explain how the similar words are alike and how the exception is different.

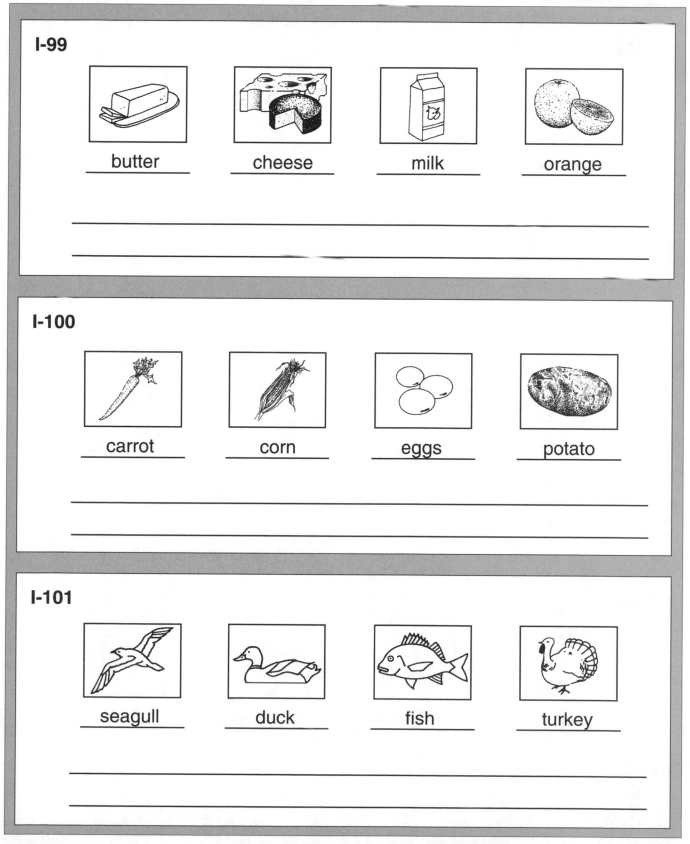

I-99

butter   cheese   milk   orange

_____

_____

I-100

carrot   corn   eggs   potato

_____

_____

I-101

seagull   duck   fish   turkey

_____

_____

EXPLAIN THE EXCEPTION

DIRECTIONS: Each group of words contains one member that is an exception to the class. On the lines under the group, explain how the similar words are alike and how the exception is different.

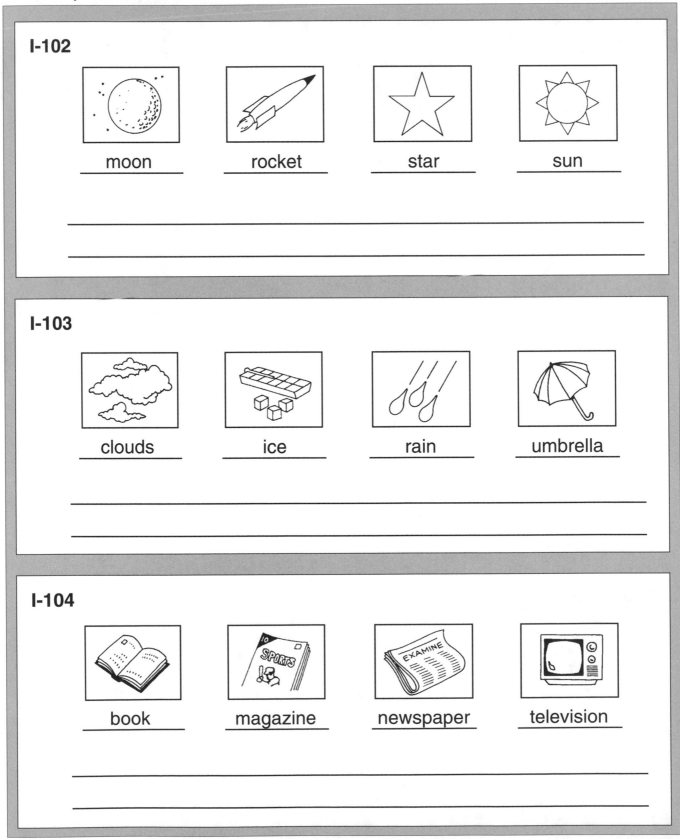

I-102

moon   rocket   star   sun

_____

_____

I-103

clouds   ice   rain   umbrella

_____

_____

I-104

book   magazine   newspaper   television

_____

_____

EXPLAIN THE EXCEPTION

DIRECTIONS: Each group of words contains one member that is an exception to the class. On the lines under the group, explain how the similar words are alike and how the exception is different.

EXAMPLE

| explain | listen | talk | tell |

Listen is the exception because listening involves hearing. The other words represent forms of speaking.

I-105

| jog | run | sleep | walk |

I-106

| chalk | crayons | pencil | ruler |

I-107

| fork | knife | scissors | spoon |

I-108

| reading | recess | spelling | writing |

EXPLAIN THE EXCEPTION

DIRECTIONS: Each group of words contains one member that is an exception to the class. On the lines under the group, explain how the similar words are alike and how the exception is different.

I-109

color   draw   paint   write

_____

_____

I-110

few   many   none   some

_____

_____

I-111

banana   grapefruit   lemon   orange

_____

_____

I-112

bicycle   helicopter   jeep   motorcycle

_____

_____

I-113

chew   cook   drink   eat

_____

 © 1997 Critical Thinking Books & Software, P. O. Box 448, Pacific Grove, CA 93950 • 800-458-4849

PICTURE DICTIONARY—SORTING INTO CLASSES

DIRECTIONS: Each picture is labeled with a place name. Sort the names into three groups by writing each place name in the appropriate column on the chart.

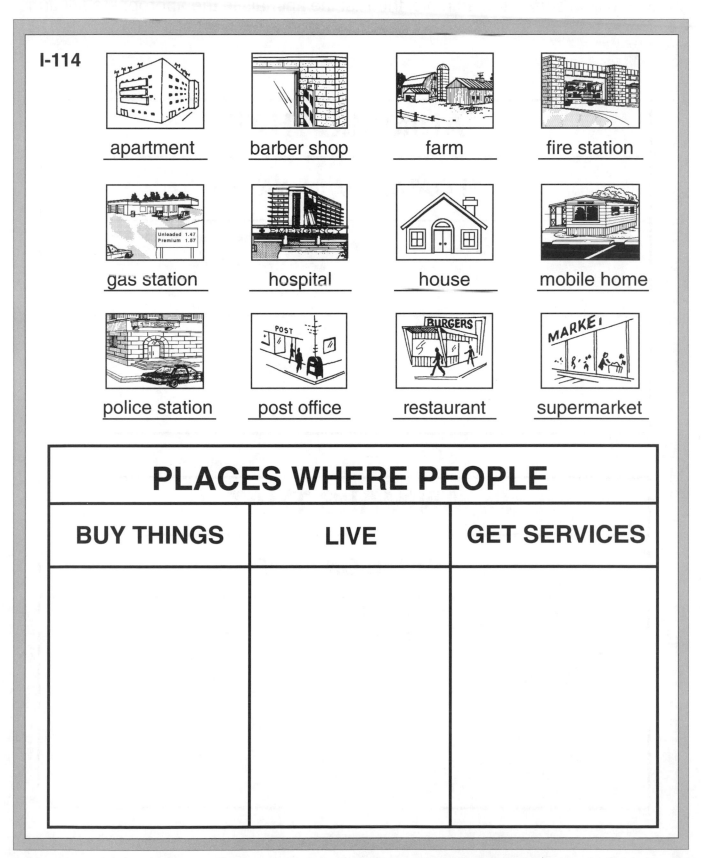

I-114

apartment	barber shop	farm	fire station
gas station	hospital	house	mobile home
police station	post office	restaurant	supermarket

PLACES WHERE PEOPLE		
BUY THINGS	**LIVE**	**GET SERVICES**

PICTURE DICTIONARY—SORTING INTO CLASSES

DIRECTIONS: Using the picture dictionary on the next two pages, sort the animals in a different way on each chart below. Divide and label the following diagrams to show how you sorted the animals, then list the animals in the appropriate sections.

I-115

ANIMALS THAT

FLOAT/SWIM IN WATER

frog
jellyfish
snake (some)

shark
whale

ANIMALS THAT

MOVE ON LAND

deer
duck
frog
kangaroo
lion

lizard
monkey
mouse
ostrich

snail
snake
spider
squirrel

PICTURE DICTIONARY—SORTING INTO CLASSES

DIRECTIONS: Use the words from the picture dictionary to fill in the charts on page 284.

PICTURE DICTIONARY—SORTING INTO CLASSES

DIRECTIONS: Use the words from the picture dictionary to fill in the charts on page 284.

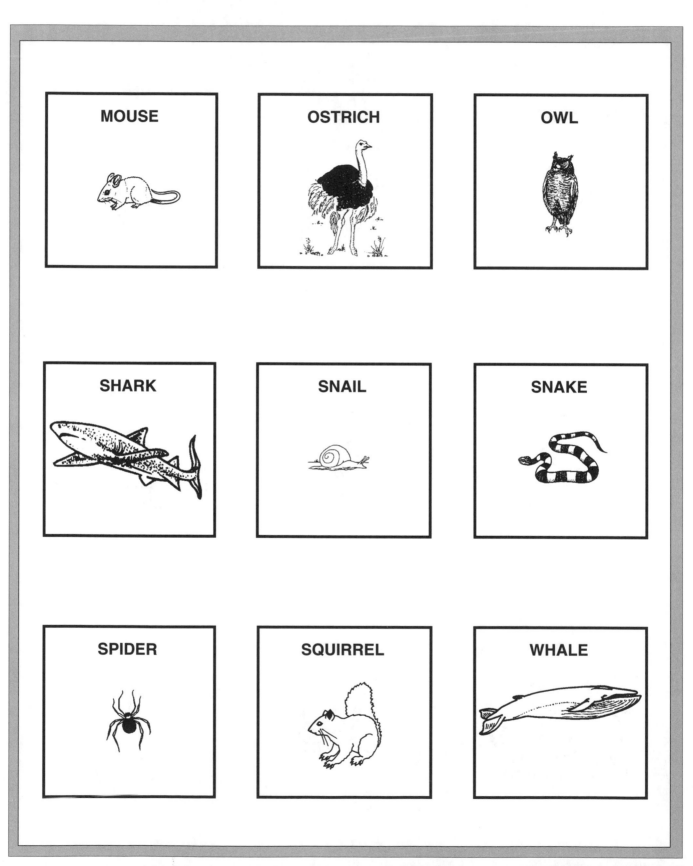

SORTING INTO CLASSES

DIRECTIONS: Sort the words in the choice box into "happy" words and "sad" words.

I-116

CHOICE BOX

bright, cheerful, crying, glad, gloomy, grumpy, jolly, joyous, merry, upset

HAPPY WORDS	SAD WORDS

SORTING INTO CLASSES

DIRECTIONS: Sort the words in the choice box into "when" words and "where" words.

I-117

CHOICE BOX

above, across, already, always, behind, below, between, never, often, seldom

WHEN	WHERE

PICTURE DICTIONARY—SORTING INTO CLASSES

DIRECTIONS: Use the words in the picture dictionary on page 290. Some words may be used more than once. Sort the words into the following four classes or groups.

I-118

THINGS THAT			
MAKE MUSIC	**ARE USED FOR INFORMATION**	**ARE USED FOR ENTERTAINMENT**	**WE RIDE ON**

PICTURE DICTIONARY—SORTING INTO CLASSES

DIRECTIONS: Use the words from the picture dictionary to fill in the chart on page 289.

airplane

baseball

bike

boat

bus

circus

drum

helicopter

horn

horse

jeep

letter

motorcycle

newspaper

piano

play

puppet

radio

ship

sled

swing

telephone

television

train

SORTING INTO CLASSES

DIRECTIONS: Sort the words in the choice box according to how they are used with the concepts of "open" and "closed."

I-119

CHOICE BOX

clear, end, entrance, fence, finish, free, indoors, locked, lower, off, on, outdoors, raise, shut, start, stop, wall, wide

OPEN	CLOSED

WORD CLASSES—SELECT

DIRECTIONS: Select a word from the choice box and write it on the line below the picture to which the word belongs. You may need to use some of the words more than once in order to fill in all the blanks.

I-120

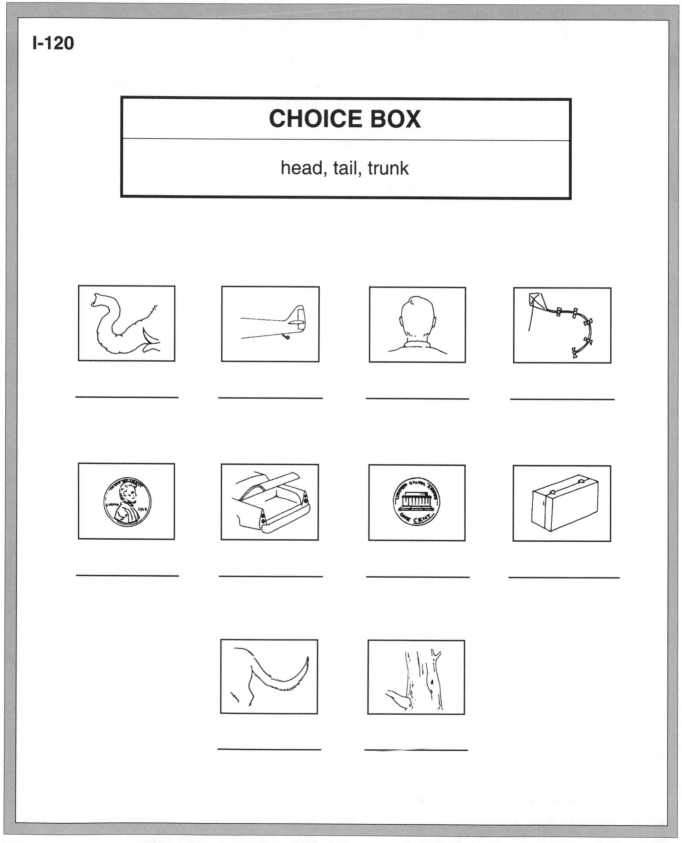

CHOICE BOX

head, tail, trunk

WORD CLASSES—SELECT

DIRECTIONS: Select a word from the choice box and write it on the line below the picture to which the word belongs. You may need to use some of the words more than once in order to fill in all the blanks.

I-121

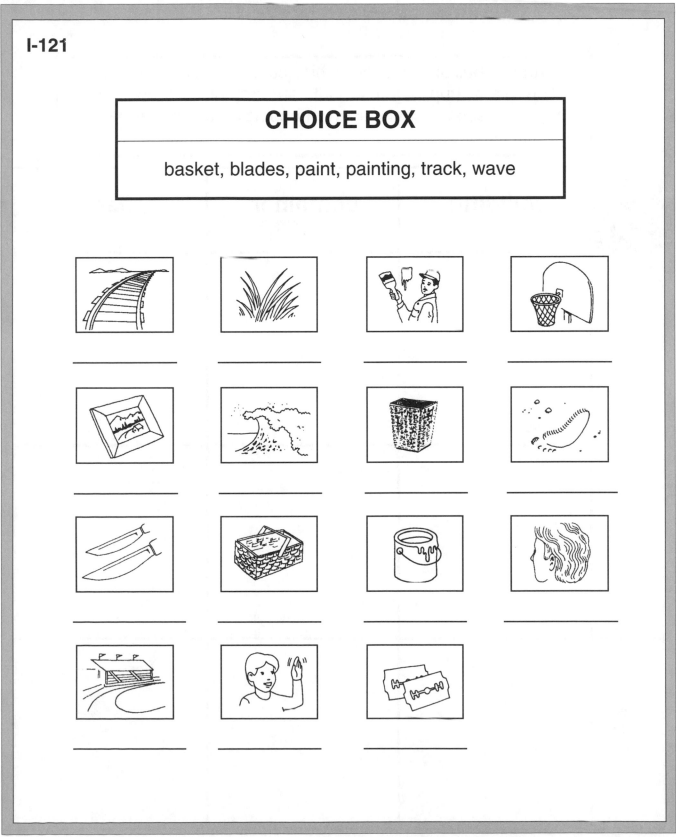

CHOICE BOX

basket, blades, paint, painting, track, wave

SORTING BY CLASS AND SIZE

DIRECTIONS: The words in the box at the top of the page are taken from the picture dictionary on the next two pages. In the chart below, write each word in the box that best describes it.

I-122

apartment building, barrel, cabin, cup, fast food restaurant, gallon, glass, guppy, house, hut, laundromat, minnow, perch, pint, quart, school, shark, shed, shopping center, supermarket, trout, tuna

	building	**container**	**fish**
small			
medium			
large			

PICTURE DICTIONARY

DIRECTIONS: Use the words from the picture dictionary to fill in the chart on page 294.

PICTURE DICTIONARY

DIRECTIONS: Use the words from the picture dictionary to fill in the chart on page 294.

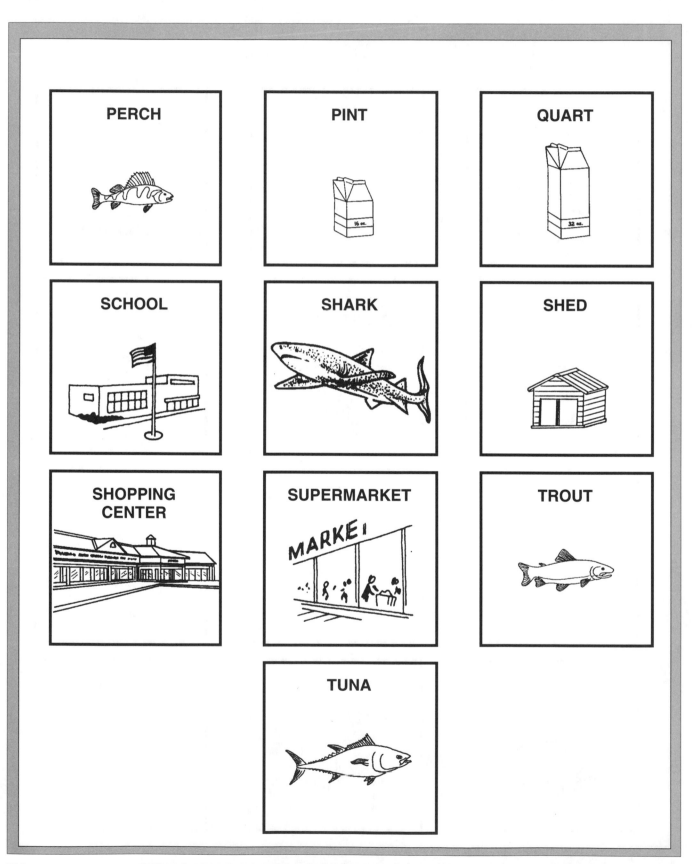

© 1997 CRITICAL THINKING BOOKS & SOFTWARE, P. O. BOX 448, PACIFIC GROVE, CA 93950 • 800-458-4849

RECOGNIZING CLASSES—GRAPHIC ORGANIZER

DIRECTIONS: Fill in the diagram to show how the words in the choice box are related. The most general class belongs in the large rounded box. The most specialized class belongs in the small rounded box.

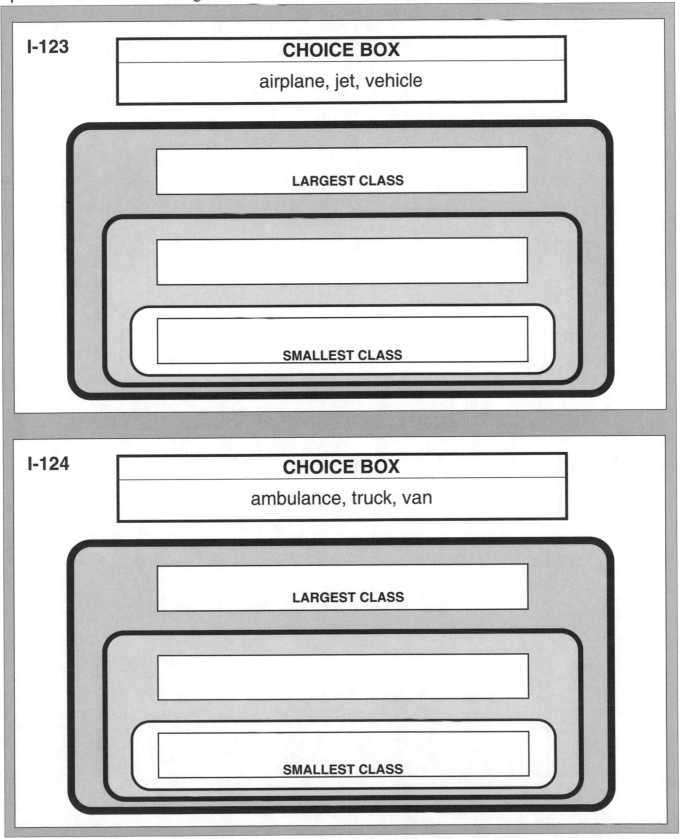

I-123

CHOICE BOX

airplane, jet, vehicle

LARGEST CLASS

SMALLEST CLASS

I-124

CHOICE BOX

ambulance, truck, van

LARGEST CLASS

SMALLEST CLASS

RECOGNIZING CLASSES—GRAPHIC ORGANIZER

DIRECTIONS: Fill in the diagram to show how the words in the choice box are related. The most general class belongs in the large rounded box. The most specialized class belongs in the small rounded box.

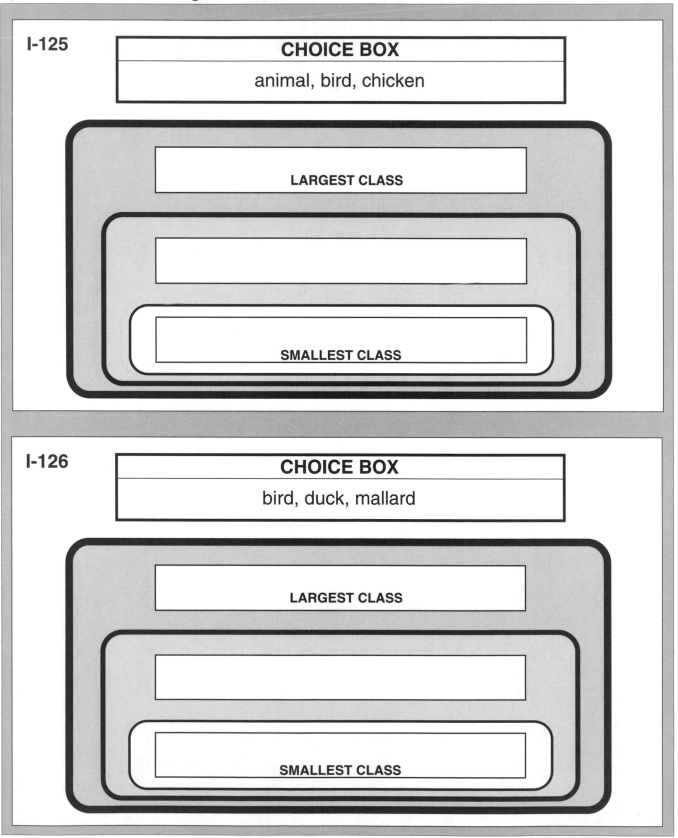

I-125

CHOICE BOX

animal, bird, chicken

LARGEST CLASS

SMALLEST CLASS

I-126

CHOICE BOX

bird, duck, mallard

LARGEST CLASS

SMALLEST CLASS

RECOGNIZING CLASSES—GRAPHIC ORGANIZER

DIRECTIONS: Read the passage carefully to decide how special four-sided closed figures are related. Record the information on the diagram. In each box, draw an example of the shape.

I-127

If the opposite sides of a four-sided figure are parallel, the figure is a parallelogram. A rectangle is a special parallelogram that has four right angles (square corners). A square is a special rectangle that has four equal sides.

MOST GENERAL CLASS

MOST SPECIALIZED CLASS

CHAPTER TEN

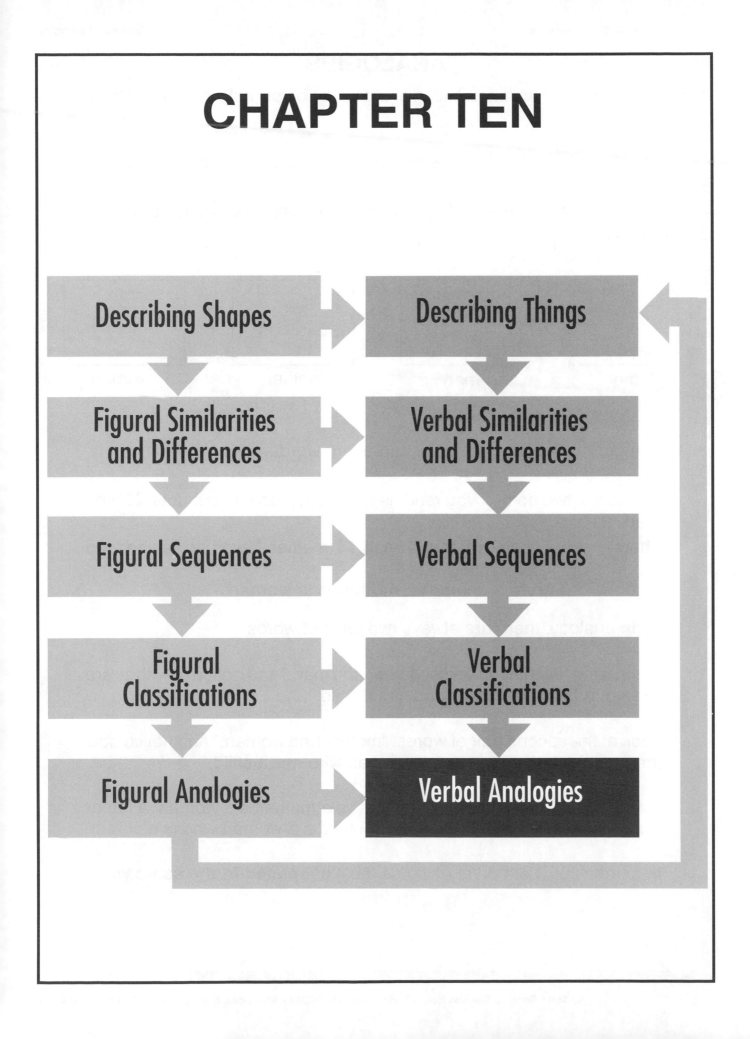

Describing Shapes → Describing Things

Figural Similarities and Differences → Verbal Similarities and Differences

Figural Sequences → Verbal Sequences

Figural Classifications → Verbal Classifications

Figural Analogies → Verbal Analogies

ANALOGIES

DIRECTIONS: Read the explanation of analogies below before going on to the next page.

The relationship between the following two pairs of words is called an **analogy.**

| father | man | mother | woman |

The groups of dots **:** and **::** represent words.

In place of two dots **:** you read "is to" and in place of four dots **::** you read "as."

Therefore, the analogy father **:** man **::** mother **:** woman can be read

father is to **man** as **mother** is to **woman**

In an analogy, there are always two pairs of words.

Look at the first pair of words, "father and man," and notice how they are related: A father is a man who has a child.

Look at the second pair of words, "mother and woman," and notice how they are related: A mother is a woman who has a child.

In this analogy, a father is a man just as a mother is a woman. A father is a man who is a parent just as a mother is a woman who is a parent.

In an analogy, both pairs of words must be **related in the same way.**

PICTURE ANALOGIES—SELECT

DIRECTIONS: Look at the first two words and think about how they are related. Next, look at the third word and decide which word in the choice box is related to the third word in the same way the first two words are related. Write it in the blank.

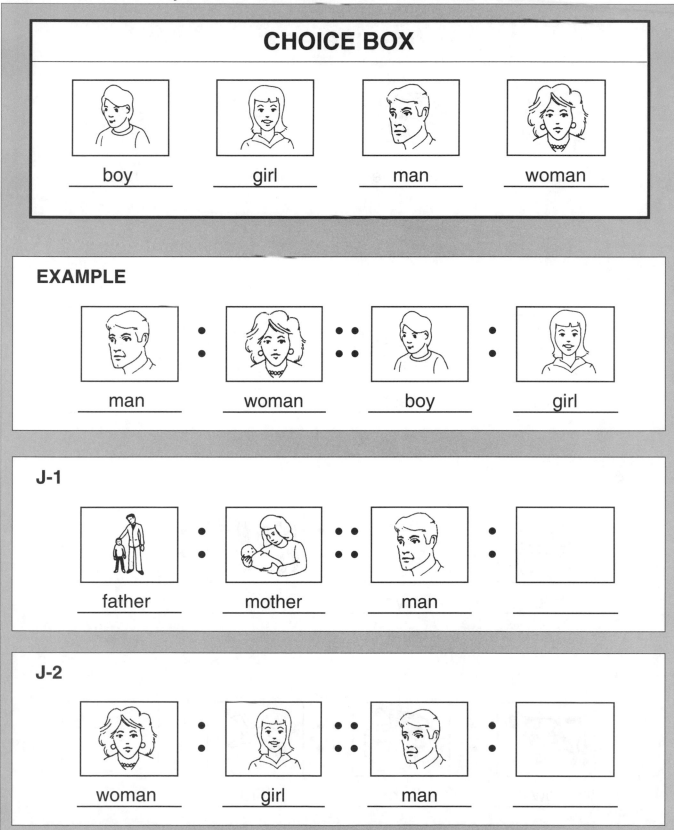

CHOICE BOX

boy   girl   man   woman

EXAMPLE

man   :   woman   ::   boy   :   girl

J-1

father   :   mother   ::   man   :   _____

J-2

woman   :   girl   ::   man   :   _____

PICTURE ANALOGIES—SELECT

DIRECTIONS: Look at the first two words and think about how they are related. Next, look at the third word and decide which word in the choice box is related to the third word in the same way the first two words are related. Write it in the blank.

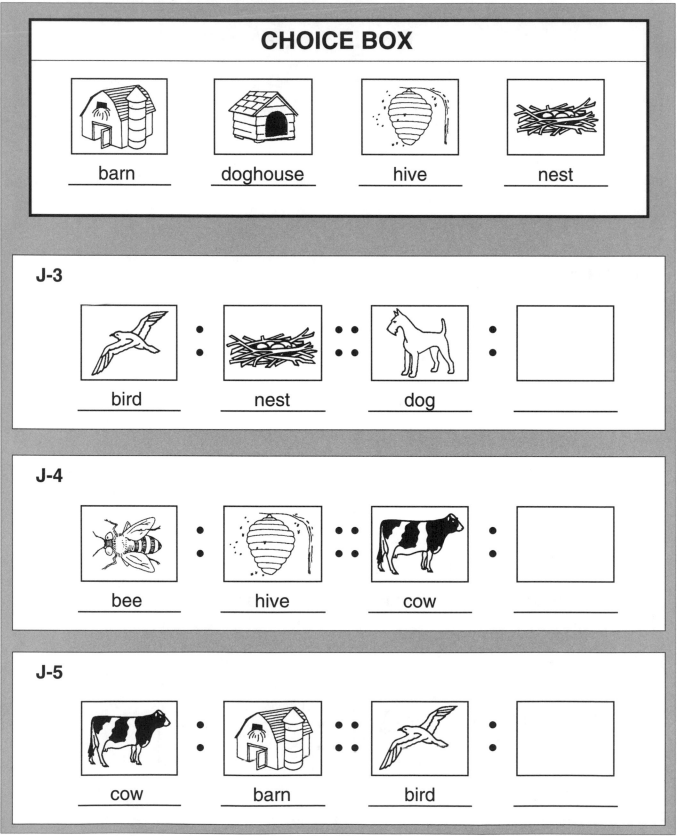

CHOICE BOX

barn   doghouse   hive   nest

J-3

bird : nest :: dog :

J-4

bee : hive :: cow :

J-5

cow : barn :: bird :

PICTURE ANALOGIES—SELECT

DIRECTIONS: Look at the first two words and think about how they are related. Next, look at the third word and decide which word in the choice box is related to the third word in the same way the first two words are related. Write it in the blank.

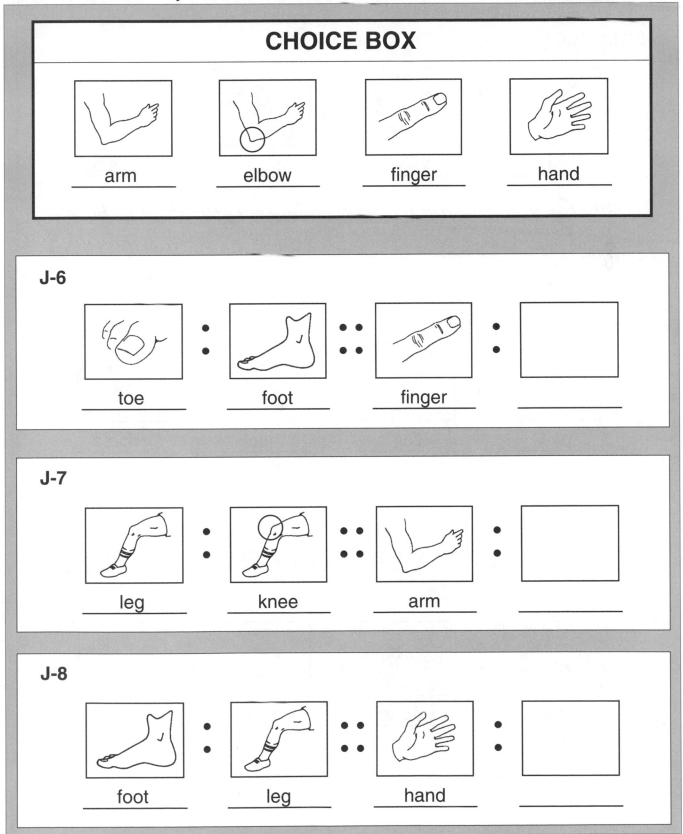

CHOICE BOX

| arm | elbow | finger | hand |

J-6

toe : foot :: finger :

J-7

leg : knee :: arm :

J-8

foot : leg :: hand :

PICTURE ANALOGIES—NAME THE RELATIONSHIP

DIRECTIONS: Read the analogies and decide how the words in each pair are related. On the lines below each analogy, explain how the words are related.

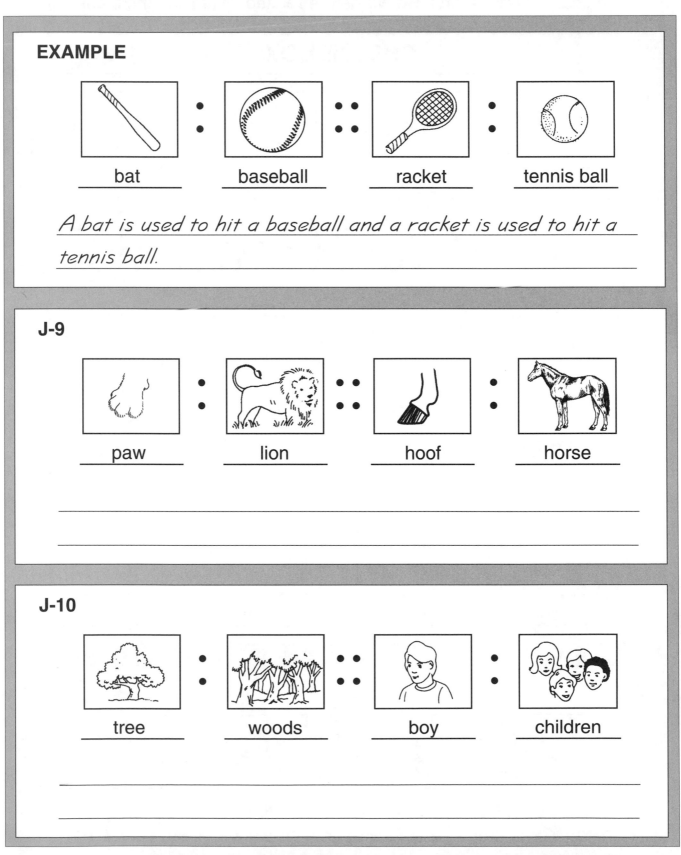

EXAMPLE

bat : baseball :: racket : tennis ball

A bat is used to hit a baseball and a racket is used to hit a tennis ball.

J-9

paw : lion :: hoof : horse

_____

_____

J-10

tree : woods :: boy : children

_____

_____

PICTURE ANALOGIES—NAME THE RELATIONSHIP

DIRECTIONS: Read the analogies and decide how the words in each pair are related. On the lines below each analogy, explain how the words are related.

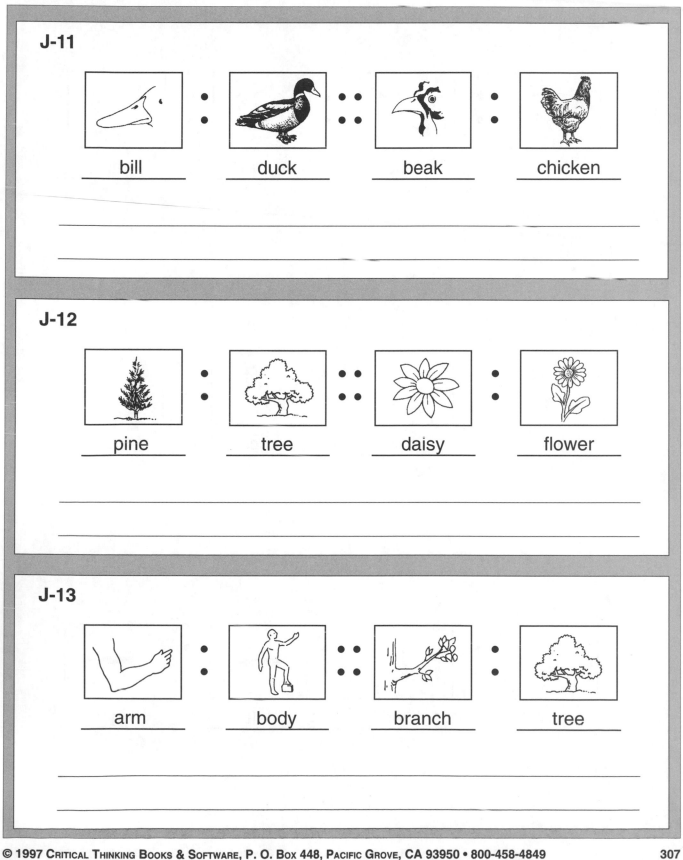

J-11

bill : duck :: beak : chicken

J-12

pine : tree :: daisy : flower

J-13

arm : body :: branch : tree

PICTURE ANALOGIES—NAME THE RELATIONSHIP

DIRECTIONS: Read the analogies and decide how the words in each pair are related. On the lines below each analogy, explain how the words are related.

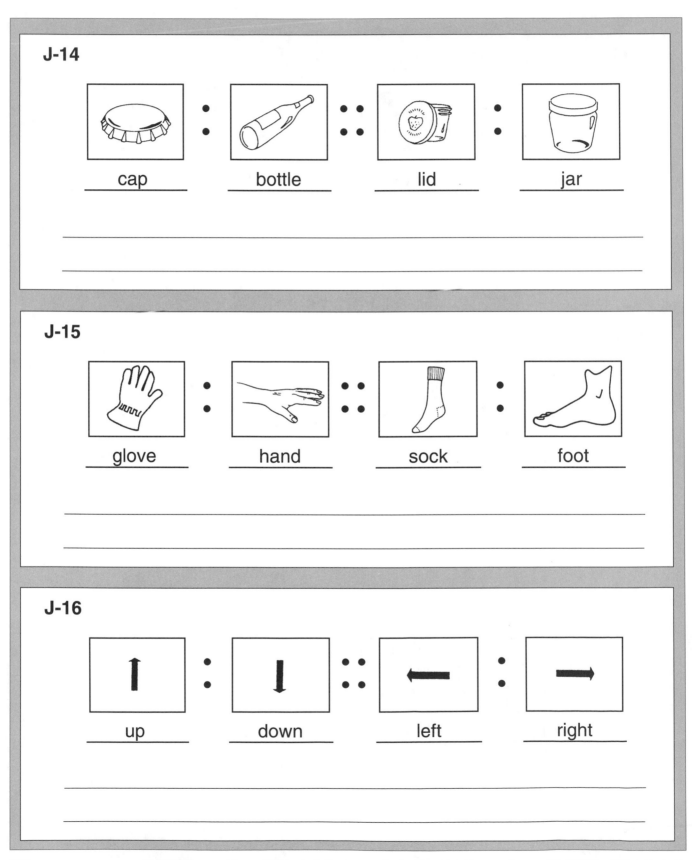

J-14

cap : bottle :: lid : jar

_____

_____

J-15

glove : hand :: sock : foot

_____

_____

J-16

up : down :: left : right

_____

_____

ANALOGIES—SELECT

DIRECTIONS: In each exercise, decide how the first two words are related. Next, look at the third word and find a word in the choice box that will complete a similar relationship. Some words may be used more than once; not all words must be used.

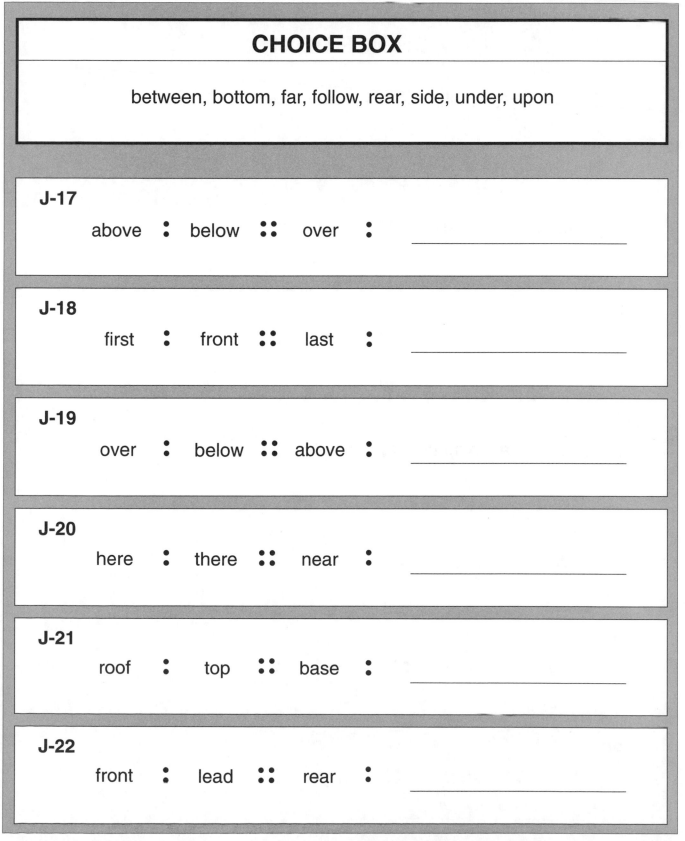

CHOICE BOX

between, bottom, far, follow, rear, side, under, upon

J-17

above : below :: over : _____

J-18

first : front :: last : _____

J-19

over : below :: above : _____

J-20

here : there :: near : _____

J-21

roof : top :: base : _____

J-22

front : lead :: rear : _____

ANALOGIES—SELECT

DIRECTIONS: In each exercise, decide how the first two words are related. Next, look at the third word and find a word in the choice box that will complete a similar relationship. Some words may be used more than once; not all words must be used.

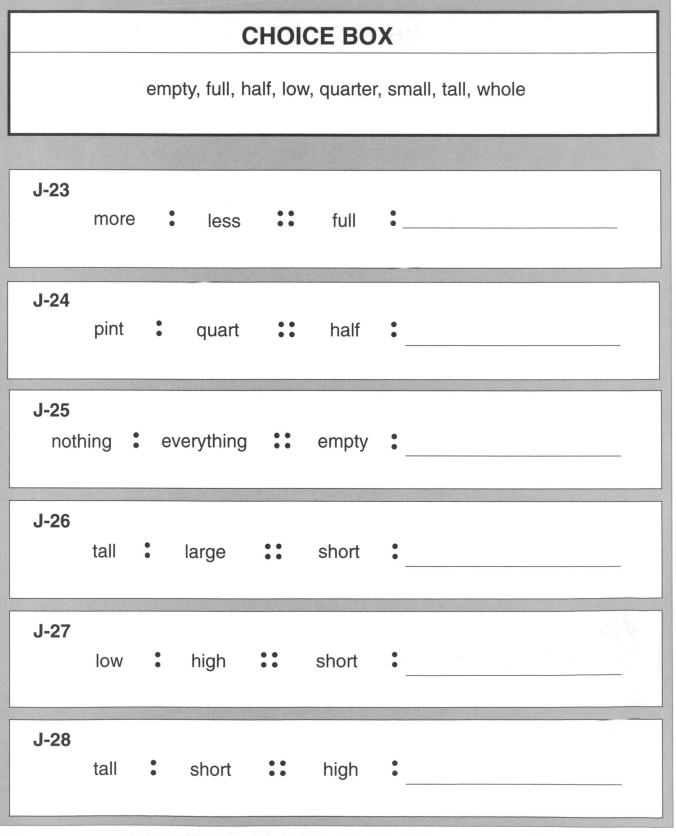

CHOICE BOX

empty, full, half, low, quarter, small, tall, whole

J-23

more **:** less **::** full **:** _____

J-24

pint **:** quart **::** half **:** _____

J-25

nothing **:** everything **::** empty **:** _____

J-26

tall **:** large **::** short **:** _____

J-27

low **:** high **::** short **:** _____

J-28

tall **:** short **::** high **:** _____

ANALOGIES—SELECT

DIRECTIONS: In each exercise, decide how the first two words are related. Next, look at the third word and find a word in the choice box that will complete a similar relationship. Some words may be used more than once; not all words must be used.

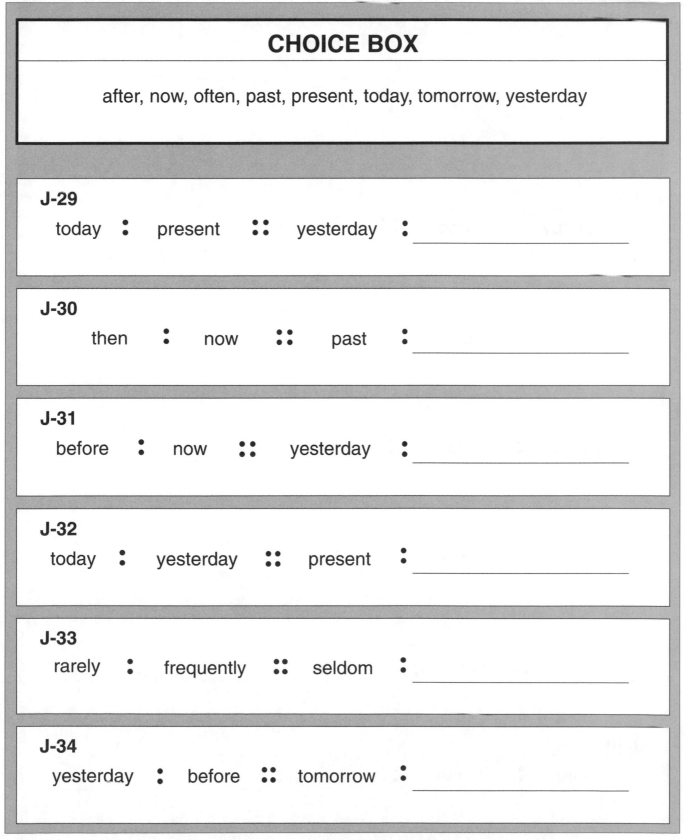

CHOICE BOX

after, now, often, past, present, today, tomorrow, yesterday

J-29

today **:** present **::** yesterday **:** _____

J-30

then **:** now **::** past **:** _____

J-31

before **:** now **::** yesterday **:** _____

J-32

today **:** yesterday **::** present **:** _____

J-33

rarely **:** frequently **::** seldom **:** _____

J-34

yesterday **:** before **::** tomorrow **:** _____

ANALOGIES—SELECT

DIRECTIONS: In each exercise, decide how the first two words are related. Next, look at the third word and find a word in the choice box that will complete a similar relationship. Some words may be used more than once; not all words must be used.

CHOICE BOX

bird, cat, cow, deer, fish, horse, lion

J-35

puppy **:** dog **::** colt **:** _____

J-36

antlers **:** deer **::** mane **:** _____

J-37

meow **:** cat **::** roar **:** _____

J-38

swim **:** fish **::** fly **:** _____

J-39

fur **:** cat **::** scales **:** _____

J-40

mare **:** horse **::** doe **:** _____

ANALOGIES—SELECT

DIRECTIONS: In each exercise, decide how the first two words are related. Next, look at the third word and find a word in the choice box that will complete a similar relationship. Some words may be used more than once; not all words must be used.

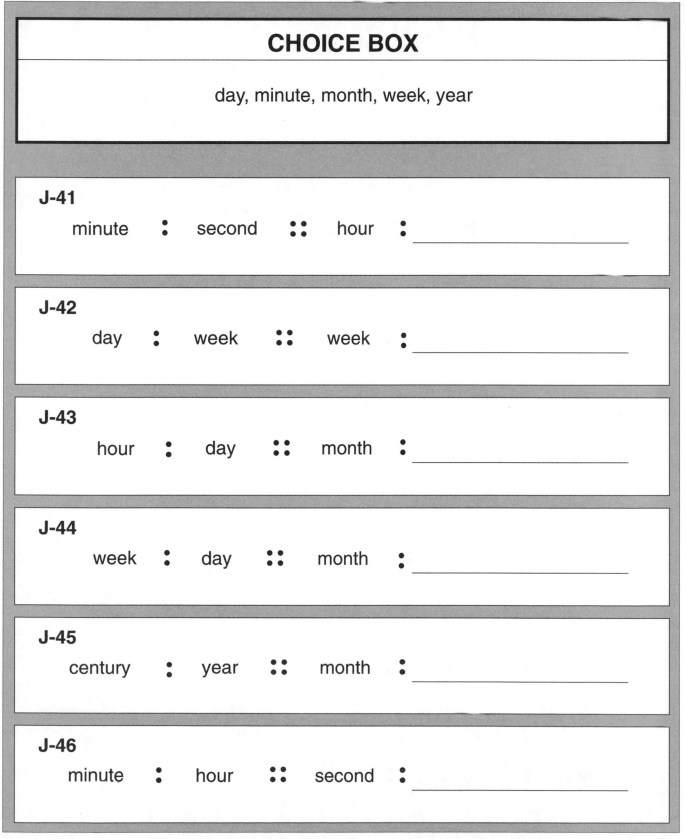

CHOICE BOX

day, minute, month, week, year

J-41

     minute **:** second **::** hour **:** _____

J-42

     day **:** week **::** week **:** _____

J-43

     hour **:** day **::** month **:** _____

J-44

     week **:** day **::** month **:** _____

J-45

     century **:** year **::** month **:** _____

J-46

     minute **:** hour **::** second **:** _____

ANALOGIES—SELECT

DIRECTIONS: In each exercise, decide how the first two words are related. Next, look at the third word and find a word in the choice box that will complete a similar relationship. Some words may be used more than once; not all words must be used.

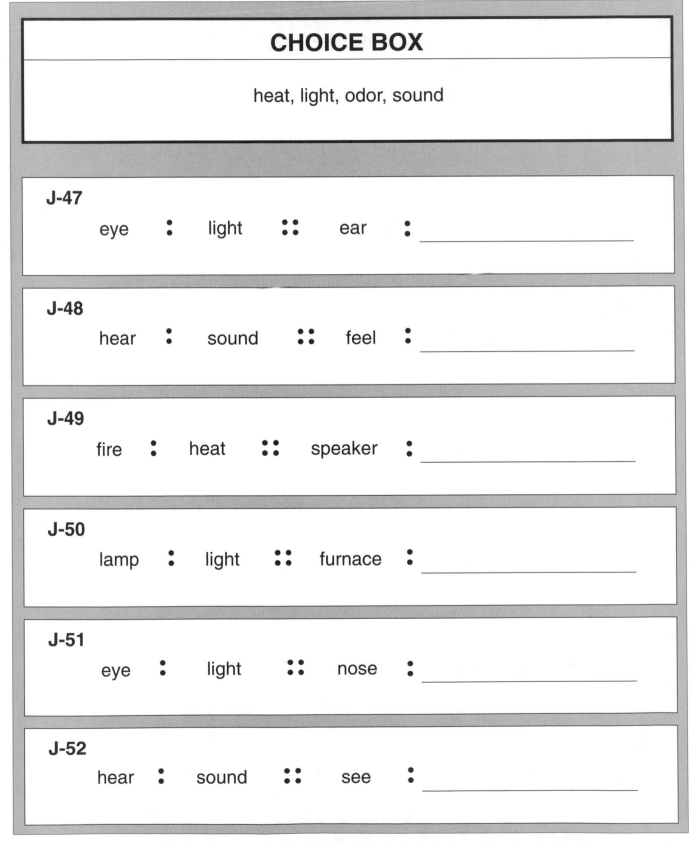

CHOICE BOX

heat, light, odor, sound

J-47

eye : light :: ear : _____

J-48

hear : sound :: feel : _____

J-49

fire : heat :: speaker : _____

J-50

lamp : light :: furnace : _____

J-51

eye : light :: nose : _____

J-52

hear : sound :: see : _____

ANALOGIES—SELECT

DIRECTIONS: In each exercise, decide how the first two words are related. Next, look at the third word and find a word in the choice box that will complete a similar relationship. Some words may be used more than once; not all words must be used.

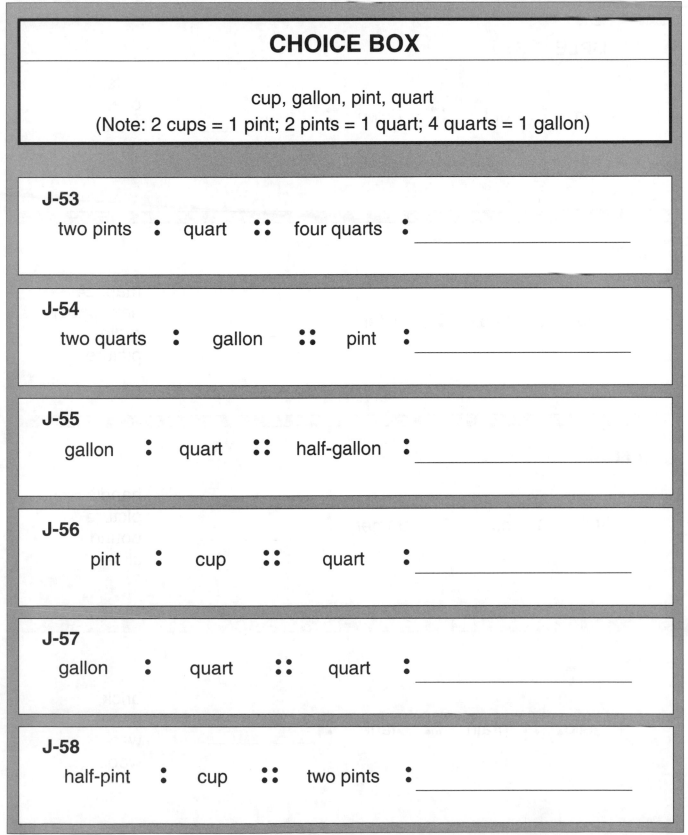

CHOICE BOX

cup, gallon, pint, quart
(Note: 2 cups = 1 pint; 2 pints = 1 quart; 4 quarts = 1 gallon)

J-53

two pints : quart :: four quarts : _____

J-54

two quarts : gallon :: pint : _____

J-55

gallon : quart :: half-gallon : _____

J-56

pint : cup :: quart : _____

J-57

gallon : quart :: quart : _____

J-58

half-pint : cup :: two pints : _____

ANALOGIES—SELECT

DIRECTIONS: In each exercise, decide how the first two words are related. Next, look at the third word and find a word in the list at right that will complete a similar relationship.

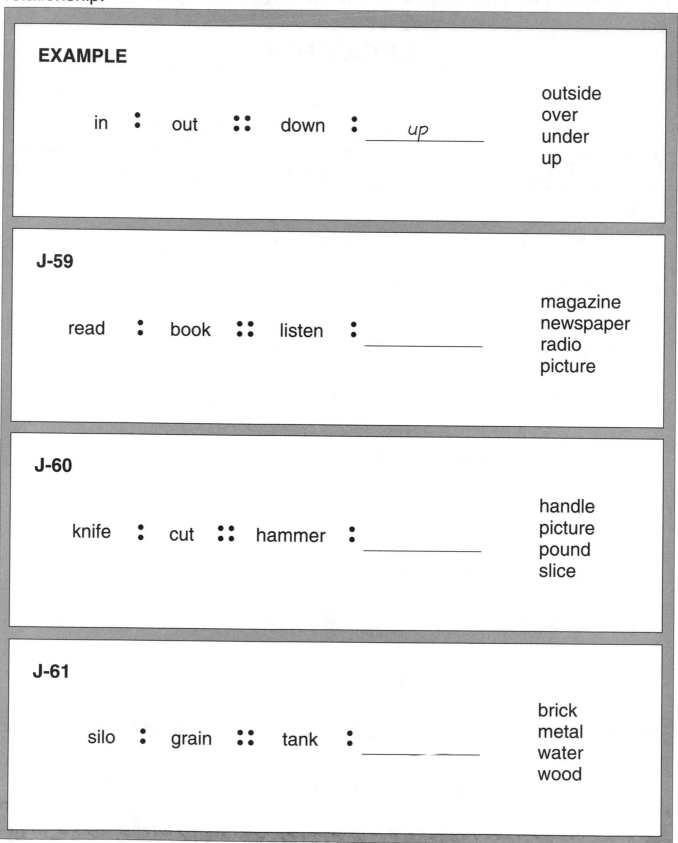

EXAMPLE

in : out :: down : *up*

outside
over
under
up

J-59

read : book :: listen : _____

magazine
newspaper
radio
picture

J-60

knife : cut :: hammer : _____

handle
picture
pound
slice

J-61

silo : grain :: tank : _____

brick
metal
water
wood

ANALOGIES—SELECT

DIRECTIONS: In each exercise, decide how the first two words are related. Next, look at the third word and find a word in the list at right that will complete a similar relationship.

J-62

this **:** that **::** these **:** _____

here
them
those
there

J-63

hot dog **:** sausage **::** orange **:** _____

blossom
cherry
fruit
sandwich

J-64

read **:** poem **::** sing **:** _____

song
talk
whisper
word

J-65

swim **:** water **::** fly **:** _____

air
land
ocean
sea

ANALOGIES—SELECT

DIRECTIONS: In each exercise, decide how the first two words are related. Next, look at the third word and find a word in the list at right that will complete a similar relationship.

J-66

buy : sell :: take : _____

bought
give
have
save

J-67

here : there :: this : _____

that
them
these
those

J-68

come : go :: enter : _____

bring
give
have
leave

J-69

car : garage :: tractor : _____

barn
cow
field
plow

ANALOGIES—SELECT

DIRECTIONS: In each exercise, decide how the first two words are related. Next, look at the third word and find a word in the list at right that will complete a similar relationship.

J-70

nose **:** smell **::** tongue **:** _____

feel
see
taste
touch

J-71

mower **:** lawn **::** saw **:** _____

blade
handle
nail
wood

J-72

overpass **:** highway **::** bridge **:** _____

cards
rail
river
train

J-73

breakfast **:** lunch **::** lunch **:** _____

eating
food
supper
vegetables

ANALOGIES—SUPPLY

DIRECTIONS: In each exercise, decide how the first two words are related. Next, look at the third word and pick a word from your memory that belongs in the blank. In this exercise, all the words have to do with things you wear.

J-74

shoe **:** sock **::** jacket **:** _____

J-75

button **:** shirt **::** lace or string **:** _____

J-76

bracelet **:** arm **::** ring **:** _____

J-77

shoe **:** foot **::** glove **:** _____

J-78

scarf **:** neck **::** hat **:** _____

J-79

pants **:** legs **::** sweater **:** _____

ANALOGIES—SUPPLY

DIRECTIONS: In each exercise, decide how the first two words are related. Next, look at the third word and pick a word from your memory that belongs in the blank.

J-80

above **:** below **::** ceiling **:** _____

J-81

outside **:** inside **::** porch **:** _____

J-82

door **:** wood **::** window **:** _____

J-83

above **:** ceiling **::** side **:** _____

J-84

shingles **:** roof **::** rug **:** _____

J-85

chimney **:** roof **::** window **:** _____

© 1997 CRITICAL THINKING BOOKS & SOFTWARE, P. O. BOX 448, PACIFIC GROVE, CA 93950 • 800-458-4849

ANALOGIES—SUPPLY

DIRECTIONS: In each exercise, decide how the first two words are related. Next, look at the third word and pick a word from your memory that belongs in the blank.

J-86

cool : cold :: warm : _____

J-87

iron : heavy :: feathers : _____

J-88

penny : coin :: dollar : _____

J-89

rabbit : fast :: turtle : _____

J-90

lid : eye :: shade : _____

J-91

soldier : army :: sailor : _____

ANALOGIES—SUPPLY

DIRECTIONS: In each exercise, decide how the first two words are related. Next, look at the third word and pick a word from your memory that belongs in the blank.

J-92

tan **:** brown **::** pink **:** _____

J-93

handle bar **:** bicycle **::** steering wheel **:** _____

J-94

over **:** above **::** under **:** _____

J-95

front **:** first **::** rear **:** _____

J-96

sky **:** air **::** lake **:** _____

J-97

knife **:** slice **::** scissors **:** _____

ANALOGIES—SUPPLY

DIRECTIONS: In each exercise, decide how the first two words are related. Next, look at the third word and pick a word from your memory that belongs in the blank.

J-98

red : stop :: green : _____

J-99

fast : slow :: run : _____

J-100

side : wall :: bottom : _____

J-101

enter : come :: leave : _____

J-102

cotton : soft :: steel : _____

J-103

bottle : cap :: pan : _____

ANALOGIES—SUPPLY

DIRECTIONS: In each exercise, decide how the first two words are related. Next, look at the third word and pick a word from your memory that belongs in the blank.

J-104

late **:** last **::** early **:** _____

J-105

last **:** first **::** least **:** _____

J-106

rain **:** spring **::** snow **:** _____

J-107

book **:** read **::** pencil **:** _____

J-108

freeze **:** refrigerator **::** boil **:** _____

J-109

boil **:** pot **::** fry **:** _____

ANALOGIES—SELECT THE RIGHT PAIR

DIRECTIONS: In each exercise, decide how the first two words are related. Next, look at the pairs of words in the list at right; find the pair with a similar relationship. Fill in the blanks to complete the analogy.

J-110

below **:** under **::**

_____ **:** _____

above **:** behind

above **:** over

between **:** over

beneath **:** over

J-111

dog **:** puppy **::**

_____ **:** _____

calf **:** cow

cat **:** kitten

child **:** adult

colt **:** horse

J-112

now **:** then **::**

_____ **:** _____

give **:** take

here **:** there

present **:** past

this **:** that

J-113

true **:** false **::**

_____ **:** _____

lie **:** wrong

love **:** promise

right **:** answer

right **:** wrong

ANALOGIES—SELECT THE RIGHT PAIR

DIRECTIONS: In each exercise, decide how the first two words are related. Next, look at the pairs of words in the list at right; find the pair with a similar relationship. Fill in the blanks to complete the analogy.

J-114

up : down ::

_____ : _____

below : under

beneath : under

over : under

over : upper

J-115

more : less ::

_____ : _____

always : often

much : more

now : then

plus : minus

J-116

mother : child ::

_____ : _____

brother : sister

girl : boy

parent : baby

son : mother

J-117

slow : fast ::

_____ : _____

always : often

minus : less

much : more

seldom : often